THE CONE SISTERS OF BALTIMORE

The Cone Sisters of Baltimore

COLLECTING AT FULL TILT

Ellen B. Hirschland

Nancy Hirschland Ramage

NORTHWESTERN UNIVERSITY PRESS   EVANSTON, ILLINOIS

Northwestern University Press
www.nupress.northwestern.edu

Copyright © 2008 by Northwestern University Press. Published 2008.
All rights reserved.

Printed in China

10 9 8 7 6 5 4 3 2 1

Library of Congress Cataloging-in-Publication Data

Hirschland, Ellen B.
    The Cone sisters of Baltimore : collecting at full tilt / Ellen B. Hirschland,
  Nancy Hirschland Ramage.
        p. cm.
    Includes bibliographical references and index.
    ISBN-13: 978-0-8101-2481-3 (trade cloth : alk. paper)
    ISBN-10: 0-8101-2481-5 (trade cloth : alk. paper)
    1. Cone, Etta—Art collections. 2. Cone, Claribel—Art collections. 3.
Women art collectors—Maryland—Baltimore—Biography. 4. Art, Modern—
20th century—Private collections—Maryland—Baltimore. I. Ramage, Nancy H.,
1942– II. Title.
    N5220.C75H57 2008
    709.22—dc22
                                                                2007049754

For Edward C. Hirschland and Roger B. Hirschland

CONTENTS

ILLUSTRATIONS

ACKNOWLEDGMENTS

On behalf of both Ellen B. Hirschland and myself, I gratefully acknowledge the support from many colleagues, friends, and family members in the preparation of this book. Although a number of people are no longer living, we would like to record our appreciation to them as well. For help in one way or another, we thank Vivian Endicott Barnett, Stephanie Barron, Robert L. Berney, Victor Carlson, Alan W. Cone, Edward T. Cone, Laura Cone, Sydney M. Cone Jr., Holland Cotter, Cornelia Dean, Barbara Elkin, Donald Gallup, Birgit Gast, Irene Gordon, Margrit Hahnloser, Esther Hecq, Johanna Hurwitz, Harwood Johnson, Edith Karlin, Nora Kaufman, Jacques Kelly, Emily H. Kunreuther, Claire L. Lyons, Joan Ramage Macdonald, Pierre and Maria-Gaetana Matisse, Carol C. Mattusch, James R. Mellow, Susan H. Myers, Philip T. Noblitt, Lauren M. O'Connell, Michael H. Ramage, John Richardson, Angela Rosengart, Siegfried Rosengart, Zick Rubin, John Russell, Elizabeth Sherman-Elvy, Hilary Spurling, Frances I. Stern, Ella Guggenheimer Ulman, Brenda Wineapple, and Susan Woodford; my students Theresa Jodz, Sasha Stefanova, and Heather Wagner; and especially Christopher J. Lane.

At the Artists Rights Society and at Art Resource, the staff facilitated our requests with good cheer, and we are also grateful to colleagues at the libraries and museums where we worked. Those at Northwestern University Press, including Susan Bradanini Betz, Serena Brommel, Henry L. Carrigan Jr., Mairead Case, Stephanie Frerich, Marianne Jankowski, Elizabeth Levenson, A. C. Racette, Lori Meek Schuldt, and especially Anne Gendler, made the work on the book a pleasure. At the Baltimore Museum of Art, many colleagues have helped us over the years; we would like to offer our deepest thanks to Doreen Bolger, Jay Fisher, and Sona Johnston, for so generously providing the photographs and for their enthusiastic support at every turn.

I am grateful to Ithaca College for several grants, including a Faculty Summer Research

Grant, a Gerontology Program Grant, an Academic Project Grant, support from Faculty Research and Development funds, and a Jewish Studies Grant; and I express my warmest appreciation to the following individuals for their generous backing of the publication of this book: Alan W. and Sally S. Cone; Barbara and Herman Cone; Benjamin Cone Jr.; Ceasar Cone III; Bryant and Nancy Hanley; Jeannette Cone Kimmell; James and Sue Klau; Richard and Jane Levy; Anne Cone Liptzin; Lois Stecker; Jean Stern Steinhart; Martha C. Wright; and my aunts Ethel W. Berney, Alice B. Hoffberger, and Margaret B. Mack.

Finally, I thank my husband, Andrew Ramage, for his unending support; my father, Paul M. Hirschland, whose belief in my mother's and my work, and in us, was boundless; and my brothers, Edward C. Hirschland and Roger B. Hirschland, to whom this book is dedicated.

Nancy Hirschland Ramage

PREFACE

How did two proper maiden ladies from a good Baltimore family find themselves in the young Picasso's apartment studio in 1905, forced to lift boots and petticoats to avoid stepping on risqué drawings strewn across the floor? What in the garish daubs of Matisse, so unlike the draped classical figures or sentimental landscapes that adorned the walls in a well-appointed Edwardian home, piqued their interest enough for them to linger, buy—and come back for more?

In the first decade of the twentieth century, Claribel and Etta Cone, then in their thirties and blessed with a limited but independent income, sailed to Paris. There they set up an establishment around the corner from their good friends Gertrude and Leo Stein, in whose house they met every radical artist, writer, and art dealer in Paris. Unchaperoned and with eyes and minds open, they went to the studios of disreputable young painters to search out rare treasures. Only in later years did they condescend to buy major works from dealers, and even then they trusted only a handpicked few in France and Switzerland.

The sisters acquired with abandon. With unblemished confidence, they bought what they liked. In this way, with little outside guidance, Etta and Claribel Cone (and to a far lesser extent their brother Fred) amassed a collection that contained 42 paintings, 18 bronzes, and 113 drawings by Matisse; 17 paintings, 43 drawings, and 2 bronzes by Picasso; 70 major works by other modern masters; assorted drawings by Ingres, Seurat, Toulouse-Lautrec, Manet, Degas, Rodin, Cassatt, Maillol, and Modigliani; and an astonishing 1,500 graphic works.

Back home in Baltimore, these purchases covered every available square inch of their adjoining apartments. But when it came to Van Gogh's *A Pair of Boots* (1887) or Matisse's *Woman with Hat* (1906) and *Blue Nude* (1907), opinion in the city was nearly unanimous: the Cone sisters had been crazy to waste good money on "infantile daubs." At the same time, the sisters' evident bias for beauty, which led them to prefer Picasso's Blue and Rose Periods to his later Cubist works, prompted more avant-garde critics to dismiss the ladies as sentimentalists whose taste was not modern enough.

Baltimore sniggered. Critics sneered. Claribel and Etta calmly carried on as they saw fit.

When Claribel died in 1929, she left her part of the collection to Etta with the direction to leave it to Baltimore "in the event the spirit of appreciation for modern art in Baltimore becomes improved."[1]

It took still another decade for the world to recognize what Claribel and Etta had seen all along. By the late 1940s, museums were courting the surviving Cone sister without shame—and the most fervent suitor of them all was the Baltimore Museum of Art, the same local institution that had earlier scoffed at the types of works they collected. Curators and directors came from around the world to pay obsequious homage to Etta Cone, praising the sisters' courage, will, taste—even their persons. Reveling in the long-withheld flattery, Etta encouraged it. But in the end she acted exactly as she and Claribel had always intended. Etta left everything she and her sister had amassed during their two remarkable lives to the Baltimore Museum of Art. Practical as ever, she also left the museum money to build a wing dedicated to the Cone Collection. In doing so she sought to ensure that this monument to the sisters' exceptional dedication and taste would not be divided but would remain a constant inspiration for generations to come.

This book, the work of the great-niece and the great-great-niece of Dr. Claribel and Miss Etta Cone, is a study of the lives and the collecting practices of two extraordinary women. They defied their place and time—conservative Baltimore in the late nineteenth and early twentieth centuries—to put together an avant-garde assemblage of paintings, sculpture, drawings, jewelry, laces, and furniture. Ignoring the ridicule of neighbors and friends, the Cone sisters used the funds available to them from their brothers' successful textile business to travel abroad, mainly to Paris and Munich. They established residences in elegant local hotels and socialized with old friends from home, like Gertrude Stein, and new friends, like Pablo Picasso and Henri Matisse. They knew the literary folk and art dealers, too, and wrote letters to each other, describing these people as well as the social scene and their purchases. The colorful circles in which the Cone sisters orbited and to which they contributed with such panache make up the texture of this story, which aims to show how, bucking the tide, the Cones assembled a remarkably forward-looking group of modern works for their collections.

Ellen Hirschland knew her great-aunt Etta Cone intimately, and she admired and loved her from her childhood until Etta's death in 1949. She knew Claribel less well, having been only a child when Claribel died in 1929. But she remembered her well enough to know that Claribel seemed forbidding to the children in the family, whereas Etta was warm and welcoming. As Ellen grew up, she developed a profound interest in art history, and it became the major focus of her studies at college as well as in subsequent years when she lived in New York City and went constantly to the museums. She and her husband, Paul, knew most of the contemporary artists, as well as the dealers and museum staffs, especially in nineteenth- and twentieth-century art, and they both became experts in the field.

Some years after Etta's death, Ellen Hirschland—then a teacher in the Adult Program of the Great Neck public schools—started to give lectures about her great-aunts, the Cone sisters, all over the country, in many venues; and she frequently took art groups to the Baltimore Museum of Art to see the collection. But it had been in the back of her mind to write about them as well, and when the Museum of Modern Art invited her to write an article on the subject, it was the beginning of the fulfillment of her plan to set out her own perspective on these remarkable sisters. Her essay, "The Cone Sisters and the Stein Family," appeared in *Four Americans in Paris* in 1970.[2] She intended, then, to write a book on the great-aunts and worked on it for many years, but the biggest stumbling block was the huge mass of archival material to be mastered and put into usable form.

In the early 1990s I volunteered to help my mother on this project, undaunted by the thousands of pages to be dealt with, since working in archives was something I had done and particularly enjoyed. I, too, am an art historian and had been interested for many years in the history of collecting, mostly in earlier periods. I found the study of the Cones as collectors to be a fascinating subject.

Growing out of this collaboration between mother and daughter (we had always gotten on particularly well) was an article we wrote on the Cone sisters, published in the *Journal of the History of Collections*.[3] The next logical step was to write the book that my mother had long intended to bring to fruition.

We decided to base much of the story on letters written by the sisters, especially those from Claribel to Etta. (Etta, with characteristic modesty, did not save most of her own.) Through the Cone sisters' writings, we have been able to glean their thoughts as they contemplated one purchase after another and to observe the ideas they had about the people who surrounded them. The Baltimore Museum of Art and the Beinecke Library at Yale University hold many of the Cone letters, and the collection of Ellen Hirschland had hundreds more letters, most of them unpublished. Unless noted otherwise, all letters derive from the Ellen B. Hirschland Archives. These letters have been given to the Baltimore Museum of Art by her children.

In addition, numerous stories told in this book are based on the recollections of Ellen, who, as she was growing up, spent endless hours with Aunt Etta. Ellen's intimate view provides a unique perspective on the Cone sisters and on Etta in particular, and those memories appear as italicized extracts in the pages that follow. Ellen also kept notes over the past half century on the interviews she conducted with many of the people who knew Claribel and Etta, and these reminiscences, too, help form the picture of the two women. The book thus provides a highly personal perspective on these remarkable collectors.

Ellen Hirschland knew that the book was more or less finished before she died in 1999, and it gave her great pleasure to know that it would come out in the end. I hope she would have been happy with the final product.

Nancy Hirschland Ramage
Ithaca, New York
March 2007

THE CONE SISTERS OF BALTIMORE

1

Presenting Miss Etta and Dr. Claribel

The Cone sisters exuded an aura of stateliness and dignity. In later years their old-fashioned formality, petticoats, and portliness—combined with the awe inspired by their unique collection of art—made them formidable indeed. Blinded by these trappings, people tend to speak of them as a unit. Yet it would be hard to find two people more different in personality, actions, or desires.

In her peculiarly impenetrable way, Gertrude Stein—a longtime friend of the Cones—proclaimed them to be quite different as early as 1912, when Claribel was forty-eight and Etta forty-two.[1] The differences separating the sisters also fascinated Gertrude's companion, Alice B. Toklas. In public Alice exchanged polite greetings with her lover's old friends, but behind their backs never missed the chance for a catty remark about Etta. Alice seemed particularly jealous of her because of Etta's early close relationship with Gertrude. In using Toklas as a source of information about the Cones, it should always be kept in mind that Alice fancied Etta to be her rival for Gertrude Stein's affections. "Dr. Claribel," she wrote of her first meeting with the Cone sisters, was "handsome and distinguished, Miss Etta not at all so."[2]

Dr. Claribel, who did not return the compliment, would often avoid going to functions when she knew Alice would be there. But too well-bred to indulge in open nastiness even in private, the Cones expressed their dislike rather by ignoring Alice or mangling her last name when writing to Gertrude.

For all of her ill will, Alice eventually admitted that Etta was an "astounding, colossal personality"—at the same time that she belittled Etta's great accomplishment by deeming the relationship between her and Claribel more fascinating than their collection, and assuming, inaccurately, that most of the important pictures were bought by Dr. Claribel.[3]

Claribel Cone—the older, bolder, and shorter of this interesting pair—made up in majesty and girth what she lacked in height. Her independent nature asserted itself early. At age twenty-three, she overcame her parents' resistance and entered medical school. Graduating just three years later, in 1890, she joined the select coterie of female physicians, which then numbered only a relative handful worldwide.

Claribel conversed with intelligence and spirit, not only about her profession (medicine) and her avocation (art) but also about politics and music. Fully conscious of her dignity as a "lady," she nonetheless cultivated idiosyncrasies that set her apart from the crowd. Her letters to Etta are filled with stories of how one distinguished person after another complimented her or sought her out. Perhaps her most characteristic trait was a seamless confidence in her own judgment, which gave her the courage to follow her own mind without regard for convention. She was active in women's suffrage, medical education for women, the drive for better conditions in maternity hospitals, and birth registration.

Yet the independent and intelligent Claribel was also considered self-absorbed and unapproachable. Within her family she overshadowed her eleven brothers and sisters alike. At age nineteen, one sibling taxed her with being "too self-satisfied," and she did not hesitate to make fun of her more retiring sister Etta in front of other people.[4] In such a mood she could be vitriolic and even cruel. Yet all her life she regarded Etta as her closest friend and confidante. Early on, she planned to leave everything she had to Etta, who enjoyed her complete trust.[5]

Flamboyant, egotistical, and self-assured, Claribel enjoyed the strong impression she made on others. Quoting to Etta a compliment paid to her by a new acquaintance, she demurred with pretended modesty, "Dare I repeat it?" and then went on to do just that, reporting that the lady thought she looked "like a queen."[6] Indeed, like a queen, Claribel took exceedingly good care of herself while remaining largely impervious to the needs and difficulties of those around her.

One such difficulty was caused by her abrupt defection into medicine, which left Etta, the last remaining girl in a large family, to oversee the

FIGURE 1.1

Dr. Claribel Cone at age twenty-seven as resident physician at the Philadelphia Hospital for the Insane, circa 1891 or 1892.

Photograph courtesy of the Baltimore Museum of Art (BMA), CC.2

In the illustration captions throughout this book, the abbreviation BMA indicates the Baltimore Museum of Art, specifically the Cone Collection formed by Dr. Claribel Cone and Miss Etta Cone of Baltimore, Maryland. The number that follows the abbreviation is the inventory number.

running of their aging parents' household. As responsible and caring as Claribel was independent and self-absorbed, Etta was not one to shirk her responsibilities.

Etta spent much of her life caring for relatives—her parents until their death, then her widowed sister-in-law. What time she had to herself she devoted to music—she was an accomplished pianist—and to the study and acquisition of modern art. In contrast to Claribel's marked preference for all things German, Etta preferred the people and culture of France. She spent most of her time abroad there and spoke reasonably good French, albeit with an American accent.

Etta's long face, heavy chin, and straight Cone mouth—so far from the Gibson girl ideal of beauty—ensured that she would never be considered pretty. Yet both artist and camera capture the beauty of her remarkable eyes—large, dark, and filled with sensitive and intelligent attentiveness. Photographed in her youth or in the company of her sister and their flamboyant friend Gertrude Stein, Etta appears dreamy and retiring. But in later years, when her white hair and dark eyebrows magnified the effect of her fine eyes and her straight carriage underscored her quiet dignity, the impression was of a woman who was sensitive, yet handsome and strong.

For the most part, Etta accepted her subordination to Claribel. She once wrote jokingly to Gertrude Stein that something would happen "if all goes my way—which is mostly my sister's way."[7] Claribel, too, knew that she tended to overpower Etta and may have been referring to such an incident in this brief and somewhat cryptic note to herself:

> P.M. 2 o'clock — to Etta's room
> Housemaid Cleaning brushing 7 pieces of clothing for me
> Etta nervous over Mrs. G and perhaps me . . .[8]

An incident in Paris in 1927 illustrates the sisters' very different ways of handling an awkward situation. One day Gertrude Stein asked her friend Etta Cone to visit the composer Virgil Thomson. Gertrude assured Etta that Thomson had real talent, in the hope that the tenderhearted Etta might offer him assistance in his poverty. Not long thereafter, the Cone sisters and their friend Nora ("Mac," as Etta called her) Kaufman visited Thomson in his sparsely furnished room, which contained his bed, a chest, an upright piano, and two chairs.

Claribel and Etta occupied the chairs while Mac sat on a third, borrowed chair, which had been placed in the doorway. Virgil Thomson sat

FIGURE 1.2

Ben Silbert, Portrait of Etta Cone, *1926.*
Etching. 10 x 7 in. Etta is shown here at age fifty-six wearing a favorite necklace, which she left to the Baltimore Museum of Art.
Collection of Nancy H. Ramage

Ben Silbert
Paris · 1924

on the piano stool and played for them the music that he was just then composing for Gertrude's opera, *Four Saints in Three Acts*. Both Cone sisters drifted off to sleep. Just in time for the end of the performance, Mac cleared her throat and woke them. With her characteristic quick wit, Claribel immediately came up with a gracious comment about the music, while the slower and clearly embarrassed response of her more sensitive sister only made her inattention more obvious. The incident is preserved for us only because it made enough of an impression on Nora that she remembered it across the years and relayed it to Etta's great-niece Ellen Hirschland, who noted the retelling thus:

Nora Kaufman recollected this story to me about forty years after it occurred. Oddly enough, shortly thereafter I had the opportunity to spend an evening with Virgil Thomson at the home of the artist Robert Indiana. He remembered well the visit of my aunts but made no comment—whether from politeness or from not having remembered it—of their inattention to the music.

In their later years, when both Claribel and Etta grew portly and their unique style of dress became ever more out of step with the times, strangers may be forgiven for failing to distinguish between them. The sisters designed their own clothes and had them made in Paris by a Madame George. Both dressed conservatively—although they drew the line at the Victorian bone collars favored by their still more austere sister-in-law, Bertha, the wife of their brother Moses.[9]

In her youth, Etta generally wore white, lavender, or black. When traveling, both sisters, as well as their friend Gertrude Stein, favored the dark skirt and shirtwaist (a full-sleeved, high-necked white blouse) worn by fashionable young women in the years preceding World War I.

In later years, both Cone sisters almost invariably dressed in black. Their dresses were made of the best-quality fabric and adorned with braid or other fine trim. Impervious to changes in fashion, they yet appeared perfectly groomed in every detail, giving a polished effect.

Throughout the flapper days, when skirts went knee high, Claribel and Etta modestly continued to wear their dresses floor length. No part of the legs showed above the black stockings and heavy black walking shoes.

FIGURE 1.3

Left to right: *Claribel Cone,
Gertrude Stein, and Etta Cone at
a table in Fiesole, Italy, June 1903.*
Photograph courtesy of BMA, CG.12

Voicing a rather modern complaint, Etta claimed she needed flat shoes for comfort and wondered how other women managed to walk in high heels. Once while traveling with her great-aunt, Ellen Hirschland tried an experiment:

I persuaded her, in a hotel room, to try on a pair of my high–heeled shoes, and she walked around the room merrily like a child with a new toy. Perhaps she had hankered to make this experiment for a long time. But despite her obvious delight, her style in footwear never changed.

Claribel occasionally sported a dramatic broad-brimmed hat but more frequently preferred the tailored narrow-brimmed style. She would drape a scarf aristocratically around her throat and accent it with a colorful pin, selected with care from her extensive collection. The tableau was completed by black gloves and a slim black umbrella with an engraved silver handle. This last not only served the customary purpose of protecting her from the rain but also was used on occasion to ward off bats. In one of her few surviving letters, Etta describes such a scene to Gertrude Stein:

> Sister C. has a new method of seeing cathedrals, [take, for instance,] Ely Cathedral. She goes through with her umbrella open over her . . .
> Now the reason why my sister goes through Ely Cathedral with her umbrella raised, is because several bats have selected the Ely Cathedral as the scene of their wanderings also.
> You can picture the scene.[10]

The impression of massiveness produced by both sisters was due in part to their habit of wearing voluminous petticoats. The outermost of these remarkable undergarments contained a large pocket, just below the knee, for keeping money and keys. Ellen Hirschland recalled that when it came time to pay, this arrangement—combined with Aunt Etta's preference for newly printed bills—led to some amusing situations.

FIGURE 1.4 *(left)*

Etta Cone in London, circa 1922.
Ellen B. Hirschland Archives

FIGURE 1.5 *(top)*

Photograph of Claribel Cone, circa 1922.
Ellen B. Hirschland Archives

In restaurants Etta would rustle about under the table, reaching beneath her dress into her petticoat for her money. Both slip and dress were black, making it difficult for a curious outsider to observe what was going on. Since Etta almost always used newly printed money, however, the bills had a tendency to stick together. Instead of paying $20, for instance, she would hand out $40 or $60 by mistake. Waiters astonished in the first place to see this hoard appear mysteriously from under the tablecloth were dumbfounded when the amount was so wrong. But in my experience they invariably pointed out the error.

When venturing out, Etta also carried a black leather purse to keep tickets, a handkerchief, and other such items. She did not use cosmetics. But at home, whenever the household help asked for change for a deliveryman, the skirt search would commence in the open. The ample coverage provided by the next layer of petticoat ensured complete modesty during this rummaging in what Etta called her "underground pocket."

Whatever tensions existed between the Cone sisters, they chose to travel and live together much of their lives, and the active correspondence they maintained with each other when apart bears eloquent testimony to the strength of their friendship.

In the first years of the twentieth century, two young women—one timid, one bold—ventured across the ocean into a world unknown to the Baltimore

of their youth. In the beginning they sought little more than a glimpse of the Old World, a privilege granted to a few well-to-do Victorians before they settled down. They sailed headlong into the turmoil surrounding the birth of modern art and a revolution in Western aesthetics. At first accompanied by their friends the Steins and later alone, Claribel and Etta followed the true plumb line of their taste. Every year they searched artists' ateliers and dealers' shops and chose one modern masterpiece after another. Only Etta lived to see their life's work appreciated, but both sisters experienced deep and abiding pleasure in amassing their great collections and in living with them in their crowded, art-filled apartments.

FIGURE 1.7

*Claribel and Etta Cone,
probably in Paris,
early 1900s.*
Ellen B. Hirschland Archives

2

Impoverished Peddler
to Prosperous Merchant

When writing his inspirational stories for boys, Horatio Alger could well have been describing Herman Cone, for Herman's life can fairly be said to embody the American dream. Yet on June 3, 1828, the day Klara Marx Kahn gave birth to her tenth child in the small Bavarian town of Altenstadt-am-Iller, no one would have suspected the child was destined for great adventure. Klara and her husband, Moses (1781–April 28, 1853), named the child Herman. But Klara never recovered from the birth, and not long into the following year, she died. So life began for the man who would found the remarkable Cone dynasty.

HERMAN CONE'S EMIGRATION FROM GERMANY TO AMERICA

In the first half of the nineteenth century, much of Europe was in political and social upheaval,[1] but in Germany the twin evils of poverty and repression were particularly severe.[2] Faced with dismal prospects for the future, young people and even whole families packed up and left for the New World. In 1840 an estimated thirty thousand Germans sailed for the United States; by 1854 that number had grown to two hundred thousand.[3]

If times were hard for all Germans, for German Jews they were wretched. Bavaria's laws ensured that its large and largely poor Jewish community stayed poor. Quotas were set on the number of Jews allowed to settle in any one area. Those permitted to stay were restricted to certain professions and forced to live in ever-more-heavily taxed ghettos.[4] In addition to these age-old injustices, Jews faced the prospect of being conscripted into an army that made no provision for kosher foods or observance of the Saturday Sabbath. For the devout, army life meant an inescapable descent into sin.

As the century progressed, more and more Jews—especially young, single men—ventured across the ocean to seek a better life.[5] Among them was the seventeen-year-old Herman Kahn, who left Germany to join his married sister Elise in Richmond, Virginia, in 1846.

Before he departed, young Herman received a letter from his brother-in-law Joseph Rosengart, married to another of his sisters. With profound sympathy for the teenager forced to leave home and family—perhaps never to see them again—Rosengart wrote eloquent words of comfort and advice (see appendix A for full text of letter).

> You may shed tears because you are leaving your parents'
> house, your Father, Brothers and Sisters, relatives, friends and
> your native land, but dry your tears, because you may have
> the sweet hope of finding a second home abroad and a new
> country where you will not be deprived of all political and
> civil rights and where the Jew is not excluded from the society
> of all other men and subject to the severest restriction, but
> you will find a real homeland where you as a human being
> may claim all human rights and human dignity.

Armed with little more than a wise, eloquent, and loving letter—which he would treasure all his life, as did his descendants after him—the penniless young Herman arrived in Richmond. For a short time he stayed with the family of his sister Elise Kahn Hirsh, fifteen years his senior.

Not one to be held back by such small obstacles as the lack of money and a limited command of English, Herman soon struck out on his own. He moved to Lunenburg County, Virginia, found a room in a boardinghouse, and traveled around the countryside selling items small enough to be carried with him.[6] In honor of his new language and country, he also changed his name from Kahn to Cone.

Early in 1851, Herman's sister Sofie, by then also living in the United States, married Jacob Adler, and Herman and Jacob decided to open a retail store in Lunenburg. What they sold is not recorded, but the business apparently did not prosper. In short order they moved from Lunenburg back to Richmond and from Richmond to Jonesborough, Tennessee.[7]

THE CONES IN TENNESSEE

In 1853, Tennessee appeared to offer the would-be merchants more fertile ground than they had found in Virginia. Ready-made clothing was still a rarity in the South and much in demand in Tennessee. By offering clothes along with other necessities in their new general-merchandise store, the brothers-in-law finally achieved commercial success.

Perhaps as important as the business climate was the fact that, although they were the first Jews ever to settle in Jonesborough, they encountered no anti-Semitism.[8] Throughout their nearly two decades in Tennessee, the two families found the townspeople welcoming and friendly.[9]

In September 1856, Cone and Adler's business was well established, and Herman—by then twenty-eight years old—returned to Virginia to marry Helen Guggenheimer (March 8, 1838–December 17, 1902). The Guggenheimer family had arrived in Virginia from their native Württemberg, Germany, in 1848, two years after Herman, and settled in Gilmer's Mill near Natural Bridge. Like Herman, Helen had been forced to leave her native country behind, but unlike him, she had grown up in

FIGURE 2.1

Herman [Kahn] Cone, circa 1860.

Photograph courtesy of Alan W. Cone

FIGURE 2.2

Helen Guggenheimer Cone, circa 1860.

Photograph courtesy of Alan W. Cone

the company of her parents and her nine brothers and sisters. After the wedding the couple returned to Jonesborough.

Twenty-six years and thirteen children later, Herman and Helen Cone decided to go back to Germany on what Helen facetiously called their "bridal trip." This venture in 1882 was their first—and would be Helen's only—return to the land of their youth.[10] Happily, by this time their children ranged in age from three and a half to twenty-four years, so the older boys and girls could help take care of the younger ones.

From the deck of the steamship *Nürnberg*, Herman and Helen wrote to the family back home in Jonesborough. The many mistakes in spelling and grammar in these letters bear testimony to the fact that these were immigrants whose native tongue was not English and—at least in Herman's case—whose education had been cut short. The letters suggest that the Cones were having the time of their life.

> You will excuse poor writing the Steamer is rocking
> considerable. Pa thinks I am napping had me easily fixed in
> the stateroom, but I preferd writing, just you should hear Papa
> sing for to amuse the crowd, each Gentelmen is trying to cut
> up as much as possible; cracking jokes for passtime.[11]

In addition to the letters, the "bridal trip" resulted in a much-prized memento. One day when Herman and Helen were out shopping, she records in her diary, he surprised her with a pair of diamond earrings (and later a diamond brooch; see figure 2.3).[12] Ellen Hirschland recalled,

My mother gave me a pair of diamond earrings and a brooch—as Etta had asked her to—which Herman Cone had bought his wife on their trip to Europe. Etta wanted me to have them because I was named after my great-grandmother, whose husband always called her Ellen. Aunt Etta occasionally used to refer to me as "Ellen II," but it was only on the occasion of my marriage and the consequent elimination of Cone from my name altogether that I realized how much it had meant to her that my name, Ellen Cone Berney, was so much like her mother's. She wrote me a warm, nostalgic letter about this on the eve of my wedding.

FIGURE 2.3

*Ellen B. Hirschland wears
her great-grandmother
Helen Cone's diamond
brooch at an exhibition
opening at the Baltimore
Museum of Art,
November 2, 1974.
Next to Ellen is a bronze
head of her made in
1941 by the sculptor
William Zorach (fig. 8.6).*
Photograph courtesy of BMA

The oldest Cone son was originally named Moses Ceasar after his paternal and maternal grandfathers. But on the birth of a second son two years later, his parents took his middle name for the new child and gave him the name Moses Herman after his father. The unusual spelling of *Ceasar* originates from the name Seeskind (or *Süsskind*, meaning "sweet child"), the given name of Helen Guggenheimer Cone's father.

Carrie, the first girl in the family (and grandmother and great-grandmother of the authors) was named after Helen's sister Carlyne Guggenheimer. The only other girls in the family were Claribel and Etta. Claribel was at first nicknamed Clara, and as a girl Etta was called "Lette."[13]

In the early years of their marriage, Herman and Helen lived in a large house in Jonesborough next to the Cone and Adler store on Main Street. But during the Civil War, when Herman Cone and Jacob Adler were forced to shut the store, both families moved to farms in the neighboring countryside where they could grow their own food, keep livestock, and better look after their families.

This move opened an unfortunate chapter in the Cone family history. Unskilled at rural life, the two businessmen bought three slaves to work the farm. In addition to the overriding problem of the morality of this decision, the purchase was tainted for another reason as well: the slaves' former owner, Judith Lee, accused Herman and Jacob of having stolen her property. Although the brothers-in-law were able to produce a valid bill of sale and a third party was eventually charged with the theft, the court still forced them to pay what Mrs. Lee was judged to have lost in services from the slaves.[14]

After the Civil War, Cone and Adler took on a new partner, the county sheriff, and reopened the store in town. The sheriff provided welcome protection during those unsettled postwar years, when many local citizens were impoverished. Cone and Adler were often obliged to accept goods instead of cash for payment, but over time the two immigrants who had arrived penniless in their new country became quite comfortable. In addition to supporting their large families, they were also able to acquire many foreclosed and bankrupt farms, and eventually they came to own large tracts of real estate in Tennessee.[15]

But Herman Cone's business dealings were not all smooth sailing. In 1866 and 1867, a court in Leesburg, not far from Jonesborough, found him guilty of fraudulently ignoring debts incurred by Samuel Guggenheim when he took over the man's failed business.[16] The judge ordered that all property gained from the deal with Guggenheim be auctioned off and, in a second suit, required that Cone pay off still more debts.[17] Embarrassing and expensive as these judgments must have been, when Herman Cone moved away from Jonesborough, he nonetheless left behind him a reputation for integrity and fair dealing.

The Cones Settle in Baltimore

In 1870, after seventeen fruitful years in Tennessee, Herman Cone decided to move his growing family to the larger and more sophisticated city of Baltimore. The Civil War had so damaged Norfolk and Richmond that Baltimore was now the major hub for southern commerce. Another attraction was Baltimore's substantial German Jewish community, which would provide a welcome social milieu for the Cone children and parents alike.

Making a clean break, the partners sold their business to a Dr. M. S. Mahoney,[18] and Herman put up his goods for auction. The event was advertised in the *Jonesborough Herald and Tribune* on January 20, 1870:

AUCTION

Intending to move from this place to Baltimore by the first
of March next, I will sell my entire Household and Kitchen
Furniture, consisting of Bureaus, Wardrobe, Bedsteads,
Chairs, Sofa, Lounges, Tables, Looking Glasses, Clocks,
Carpets, Matting, Cook and Parlor Stoves, Cooking utensils,
China and Glassware. Also, Horses, Cows, Harness, Wagons,
Saddles, Buggies, Carryall [covered wagon], Sulky [open two-
wheeled vehicle], Hay and corn, and a great many desirable
articles, too numerous to mention. Terms of sale liberal, and
will be given and made known on day of sale.

H. Cone[19]

In May 1870 when the Cones moved to Baltimore, the family already
had seven children, and Helen was nearing the end of another pregnancy.
Claribel was then five years old, and a few months after they arrived in
Baltimore, Etta was born.[20]

It appears that the people of Jonesborough regretted the Cones'
departure. When Herman returned in 1873, the *Jonesborough Herald and
Tribune* reported the visit, calling him "one of our staunchest, wealthiest,
and most enterprising citizens."[21] Three years after the Cones left
Jonesborough, the Adlers, too, departed for Baltimore.[22]

In Baltimore Herman Cone went into partnership with some of his
wife's relatives and established Guggenheimer, Cone and Company, a
wholesale cigar and grocery business; but when Jacob Adler moved to
Baltimore in 1873, Herman immediately took his old partner and friend
into the business and renamed it Cone and Adler.

Later that summer, when Jonesborough was struck by a devastating
cholera epidemic, Cone and Adler sent a generous donation to the relief
fund in their former hometown.[23] Perhaps Herman was thinking of his
brother-in-law Joseph Rosengart's advice, from so many years before, to "be
particularly liberal toward the poor, and charitable to the needy. Be glad
to help and give part of your bread and give assistance to the distressed."
After so many years, he finally had the means to follow it.

The Baltimore partnership between Herman Cone and Jacob Adler
lasted five years; however, as their children grew, both men came to rely
more and more on their sons. Like their father before them, young Moses
and Ceasar Cone traveled the South searching out customers. They went

by train as far as it would take them and then proceeded to outlying districts by horse and buggy or even on foot.[24] People in these remote areas welcomed the enterprising young traders and placed orders for their goods.

Their ample supply of what Moses called "go-aheaditiveness" allowed them to make many contacts across the South. Among their customers were owners of mill stores, many of whom were strapped for cash and would use bales of local cloth to pay for their goods. Selling the cloth to other customers gave the Cone brothers their first taste of the textile market.[25] The wide net cast by their travels during this period would also serve them well during their later expansion of the Cone family business.

When Moses Cone turned twenty-one in 1878, his father bought out Jacob Adler's share and took Moses officially into the firm, changing the company's name to H. Cone and Sons. Eventually all nine of the surviving Cone sons would participate in the business. But while Herman continued to concentrate on wholesale groceries, his two enterprising eldest sons had a far bolder plan for the future. The Cone sons' involvement in the textile industry began in earnest when C. E. Graham, a mill owner and a customer of H. Cone and Sons, approached the firm for financial backing. The Cones agreed to invest in the company on condition that Moses be made an officer. Graham accepted the deal, and thus in 1887, Moses was helping to run the C. E. Graham Manufacturing Company, a working cotton mill in Asheville, North Carolina.

At the same time, in partnership with two other enterprising young men from the local Jewish community, Moses and Ceasar established Cone Brothers, Lowman and Burger Clothing Manufacturers in Baltimore. Following in their father's footsteps, the young Cones would benefit from the growing popularity of ready-made clothing.[26]

Cotton Mills in the South

Over the next few years, Moses realized that cotton factories in the South had no good way of finishing their goods or of marketing them in the northern states. In 1890, therefore, the Cone brothers formed the Cone Export and Commission Company with headquarters in New York City. Their father liquidated his wholesale grocery and turned over the capital to his sons to support their new venture.[27] Then, in 1892, the brothers opened the Southern Finishing and Warehouse Company, a factory for finishing the edges of woven cloth, in Greensboro, North Carolina. They also acquired the Asheville Cotton Mill[28] and moved the headquarters of the Cone Export and Commission Company from New York City to Greensboro.

Their business was in urgent need of expansion because the mills working for the Cone Export and Commission Company had begun to produce denim. Ever alert to new opportunities in the market, Moses and Ceasar had noticed that Levi Strauss and Company, in New England, was virtually the sole producer of that material. At the same time, they saw that locating cotton mills close to the fields would give a cotton textile producer a clear economic advantage.

The Cones therefore asked one of the best plant managers they knew, W. A. Erwin, to make denim for them at the mill owned by the Duke family of Durham, North Carolina. Over the next three years, Erwin supplied vast quantities of denim to the Cone Export and Commission Company for marketing and distribution. However, when he declined to produce the

FIGURE 2.4

Asheville Cotton Mill in 1993, two years before it burned to the ground.

Photograph by Nancy H. Ramage

FIGURE 2.5

*Stereoscopic view of
female workers at the
White Oak Cotton
Mills, Greensboro,
North Carolina,
circa 1909.*

H. C. White Company
stereoscopic photograph
courtesy of Susan H. Myers

cloth thereafter, the Cones saw no alternative: if they were to fulfill their customers' orders for denim, they would have to make it themselves.[29]

Greensboro offered abundant cheap labor, low-cost real estate, and proximity to the cotton fields that provided raw material for the mills. Women as well as men worked in large factory spaces in the White Oak Cotton Mills and others. New railroads fanning out from the city linked it with markets all over the country. Even more important, the new investors had access to vast tracts of undeveloped land just northeast of the city. A few years earlier the North Carolina Steel and Iron Company had purchased this land with the idea of mining and refining coal, iron, and limestone, but the quality of the local materials turned out to be below commercial grade, and the project folded. The Cone brothers were able to buy most of the land owned by the failed mining venture as the site for a new cotton mill.

By 1895 Moses and Ceasar had built the Proximity Manufacturing Company—a new plant for spinning and weaving denim. Proximity (so named for its location in the midst of cotton fields) was the Cones' first real venture into textile production. Not only did they purchase the land and pay all the costs of construction, but they also took charge of the production plant and associated community activities.[30] Then, in 1898, they opened Revolution Mill, dedicated to the manufacture of a new product for the South: flannel.

As was common in their day, the Cones maintained a paternalistic concern for their employees not unlike the all-encompassing model of Pullman's Palace Car Company in Illinois.[31] The Cones provided their mill workers with houses and schools, company stores, churches, and YMCAs. They even set up an employee summer camp, "Camp Herman," and sponsored parades and other public events for their amusement.[32] In return, workers were expected to behave properly, avoid drinking, and— most important of all—stay clear of labor unions. The drawback of this

FIGURE 2.6

View of one of the Cone Mills factories with company workers' houses in the foreground, circa 1900.

H. C. White Company stereoscopic photograph courtesy of Susan H. Myers

FIGURE 2.7

White Oak Cotton Mill School, Greensboro, North Carolina, "built and maintained by the Mill,"
circa 1909. The original caption further described the school as built "at a cost of $25,000.00,
and . . . maintained by [the Mill] as a graded school, for the exclusive benefit of children of the
operatives, who are given a free education. The present faculty numbers nine teachers. Special
teachers are employed for instruction in manual training, singing, cooking, and sewing."
H. C. White Company stereoscopic photograph courtesy of Susan H. Myers

arrangement was that employees who did not obey company rules faced losing not only their job but also their house. Poverty was so widespread in the region that few dared argue with the boss.[33]

Workers often referred to Moses, the more politically adept of the two brothers, as "Gov'ner." Ceasar, meanwhile, ran the business end with an iron hand. A confrontation between the Cones and the unions came in 1900, when Ceasar discovered that 150 Proximity Mill workers had joined the National Union of Textile Workers. Acting without delay, he shut down the mill (throwing more than one thousand workers out of their jobs) and threatened to tear it down rather than deal with a union. At the same time, he and Moses began evicting the families of union workers from company housing and closed down the company store, which also housed the post office.[34] With no salary, no access to credit, and no mail station closer than Greensboro, two miles away, the workers were quickly brought to their knees.[35] The lockout lasted a week. When the Cone brothers began rehiring, they refused to take on any worker who would not sign a yellow-dog contract guaranteeing that he or she would never join a union.[36]

In the years 1902 to 1905, the Cones built yet a third factory, the White Oak Cotton Mills in Greensboro, North Carolina. This was the largest factory they would own and became the largest producer of denim in the world. Eventually, in 1948, these factories would be amalgamated under the name of Cone Mills Corporation to produce printed fabrics, corduroy, flannelette, and numerous other materials. This company is still in business as part of the International Textile Group.

Moses and his wife, Bertha, built a magnificent twenty-three-room house, which they named Flat Top Manor, in Blowing Rock, North Carolina (see figure 5.1, p. 90). Constructed between 1900 and 1904,[37] the house boasted two butler's pantries, huge bathrooms (each with tiles of different colors), a grand columned entryway, porches, balustrades, and a magnificent view of the Cones' 3,600-acre estate. Not one to do things halfway, Moses also planted ten thousand apple trees of twenty-five varieties and eventually became a prizewinning apple grower. It was said that Moses laid out the carriage roads at least in part for the sake of Etta, whom he adored and who was an indefatigable walker.[38]

Moses's servants, who lived in the thirty or so small cabins that were rented to them at low cost, were required to show the same kind of loyalty and behave in the same upright manner as the workers in the Cone mills.

FIGURE 2.8

Workers at the lapper machines of the White Oak Cotton Mills, Greensboro, North Carolina, circa 1909.

H. C. White Company stereoscopic photograph courtesy of Susan H. Myers

Anyone who broke the rules by drinking too much or otherwise violating the code of decorum would be fired and would lose his or her house.[39]

Yet Moses was good to the people who met his requirements. The cabins he provided were clean, and each tenant had space for a small garden. In Greensboro he built many schools for his workers' children and paid the teachers' salaries for four months of schooling beyond the two months a year paid for by the state. In addition, he founded Appalachian Teacher's College in Boone, which is now part of the state university system.[40]

While Herman Cone's sons concerned themselves with the family business, his three daughters were also growing up. In 1884, just after her twenty-third birthday, Carrie, the eldest Cone girl, married Moses David Long. In 1888 the couple moved to Asheville, where Moses Cone hired his brother-in-law to work at the C. E. Graham Manufacturing Company.[41]

In Asheville the Longs lived in a charming frame house at 70 Park Avenue, located on a hill overlooking the mill—as was the common

Etta Cone and her young niece Dorothy Long in Asheville, North Carolina, circa 1897. Dorothy was Ellen Hirschland's mother.
Ellen B. Hirschland Archives

FIGURE 2.10

Moses Cone,1890s.
Courtesy of BMA

practice for mill executives. They were probably already renting and living in the house when Moses Cone bought it for $5,300 on July 5, 1889. In 1897 he sold it to Carrie and her husband for $3,500,[42] although she undoubtedly never knew that he had paid more for it than he asked her to pay.

Carrie Cone Long and her husband, Moses, had three children: Irving (who committed suicide just before his thirty-eighth birthday), Edna, and Dorothy (mother of Ellen B. Hirschland and grandmother of Nancy Hirschland Ramage). In the 1890s, Claribel and Etta came now and again to visit the Long family and enjoyed playing with the children. Visiting Asheville when Dorothy was a year old, Claribel became totally soppy about the child.[43] Etta, too, adored Dorothy and always maintained this affection for her. Once when the young Dorothy's mother, Carrie, became ill, Etta begged to be able to adopt the little girl. Short of that, she always treated her niece like a daughter. Etta was also tremendously attached to her eldest brother, Moses, whom she affectionately called "Mosie" or "Mo." Mosie was his shy sister's most constant supporter, praising and encouraging her at every turn. Her devotion to him would last all her life.

As the business prospered, the shares inherited from their father as well as additional contributions from their brothers provided the two unmarried Cone sisters with a steady and comfortable income. The assurance of this income—which in later years grew substantial—gave Claribel and Etta the freedom to seek out and acquire the works of art they loved.

3

Etta Opens the Door

Etta Cone was the shy sister, the hesitant and self-reflective one who always came second. Claribel was a doctor, the one people remembered. Yet it was Etta and not Claribel whose winter in Paris would launch the sisters' memorable careers.

When Etta was born on November 30, 1870, she came into a thriving family in the booming commercial town of Baltimore. Her father's fortunes had improved steadily over the past quarter century, and by 1870 this German Jewish immigrant who started life as an itinerant peddler had been able to move his large family to Baltimore. Ten years later the family moved to a large and elegant brownstone at 1607 Eutaw Place. Baltimore was the first town Etta knew, and for all her growing sophistication and extended stays abroad in later years, she always returned to the city of her birth.

After nearly two decades in Tennessee, the elder Cones particularly appreciated Baltimore's large Jewish community, which contained many immigrants from Germany. In addition to Helen Cone's family, the Guggenheimers, the Cones' social circle included the Franks, Gutmans, Bambergers, and Bachrachs. Helen attended the Baltimore Hebrew Congregation every week, and Herman gave generously enough to the synagogue fund to have his name engraved on a gold-plated pew plaque dated to the opening of the new synagogue in 1891.[1]

Yet Herman and Helen's enthusiasm for Jewish life did not pass down equally to all their daughters. While their eldest daughter, Carrie, and her family were active members of their synagogue in Asheville, neither

Claribel nor Etta showed much interest in religion. Both supported a number of different Jewish charities, yet both (along with their brother Fred) chose to be buried in a mausoleum in Baltimore's nonsectarian Druid Ridge Cemetery.

Not much is known about the early life of the Cone children. It was, however, comfortable enough for the girls to take riding lessons.

Etta's formal education ended with her graduation from Baltimore's public Western Female High School, a level of educational attainment quite respectable for girls at that time. She had also become proficient at the piano, an instrument she played seriously all her life. Music was in fact one of her great and enduring passions, exceeded only by love of family and art. But as the last remaining girl in a Victorian family with eleven surviving children, Etta must have known that her career was already determined: she was to manage her parents' household.

It appears that she accepted this duty without a murmur. Chores mounted when the parents became partial invalids in old age. Visits by the large family led to an incessant stream of comings and goings, which prompted one Cone brother to dub the parental home a "boardinghouse." Through it all the young Etta remained competent, self-effacing, and uncomplaining. She would in fact resume the role of homemaker for her family later in life, when she managed the household and meals for herself, her sister Claribel, and her youngest brother, Fred.

Gertrude Stein and Brother Leo Come to Baltimore

When Etta was twenty-two, an event occurred that would change her life: eighteen-year-old Gertrude Stein moved to Baltimore. After the death of her mother and father, Gertrude and her older sister, Bertha, came to live with their aunt, Fanny Bachrach, wife of the illustrious portrait photographer (see figure 4.3, p. 84). The elder Stein brothers, Michael and Simon, remained behind in California to handle the family business interests, while Leo, then a college sophomore at Berkeley, transferred his studies to Harvard.[2] A year later Gertrude left Baltimore without finishing high school and followed Leo to Cambridge, where she enrolled in the Harvard Annex (later called Radcliffe College) as a special student. When Leo returned to Baltimore to attend Johns Hopkins, Gertrude came with him to study medicine.[3]

FIGURE 3.1

Etta Cone at age eighteen or nineteen, wearing her riding outfit, circa 1889.
Photograph courtesy of
BMA, EC.1

At Johns Hopkins Medical School Gertrude befriended Claribel Cone, a woman ten years her senior, who was teaching a course in pathology. Gertrude knew the Cone sisters slightly from an earlier Baltimore stay, and now the three became fast friends. Claribel and Gertrude traveled to school together every day on the tram, and Etta often invited Gertrude to their parents' home.

Gertrude and Leo must have provided an exciting new window into a different kind of life for Etta. Her own family was oriented more toward business than culture. And while Etta was diffident about her own abilities, she clearly hungered after the delights of the arts. Perhaps because of this modesty, she listened with open ears and studied intensely. Busy as she was at home, she never skipped her piano lessons or failed to practice. She also studied French and approached her twin loves of history and art with the diligence of a natural scholar.

In all of these efforts, as in everything she did, her most fervent and affectionate booster was her eldest brother, Moses. It is easy to imagine the shy young Etta's blush of pleasure upon reading the closing line of a letter from her adored Mosie, filled as it is with unstinting admiration: "I find there are so few really high toned sweet cultured ladies that it is a pleasure to me to recognize my sister as one and I don't think it will hurt her to hear this once in awhile . . . take much care of my dear sweet sister Etta, one of the finest women living."[4]

Etta's innate grace and charm also struck those outside the family circle. In a letter to her then twenty-year-old sister, Claribel candidly compared the very different impressions the two of them made in society. After much encouragement, Claribel wrote, she finally got a medical colleague to admit that she "used to think so and still thinks I 'put on airs'—but she likes me any way." But when the same lady was asked what she thought of Etta, she spontaneously blurted out, "Oh, Etta is a perfect child of nature!"[5]

Like her charm, Etta's feeling for the visual arts also seems to have been instinctive and innate.[6] For while her knowledge of modern works grew substantially over the years, during which she made the most of every opportunity to study and learn, an incident that occurred when she was twenty-seven suggests that the celebrated Cone taste was even then already at work.

FIGURE 3.2

Etta Cone at the piano in her apartment on Eutaw Place in Baltimore, circa 1920. She was an avid pianist all her life.

Photograph by Bertram S. Berney, Ellen B. Hirschland Archives

ETTA'S FIRST PURCHASES

Following her father's death in 1897, Etta thought to cheer up her mother by redecorating the front parlor. A photo taken a few years earlier shows the elder Cones seated in the Eutaw Place house. The room is undistinguished, with typically overpowering Victorian wallpaper relieved only by a scattering of small framed photographs. It seems clear that for Etta, "redecorating" had nothing to do with carpets or furniture. Her intention was to buy original works of art.

The ever-generous Moses contributed three hundred dollars, a large sum at that time, for the project, and Etta and her sister-in-law Bertha Cone (wife of Moses) set off for New York. On March 24, 1898, the two women attended an exhibition of paintings to be auctioned from the estate of the American Impressionist Theodore Robinson (1852–96). Etta then returned to her mother in Baltimore, leaving Bertha to bid for her.

In fact, Bertha went to a concert instead and authorized a Mr. Randolph to act as her agent, passing on Etta's instructions to "get as many

for the money as possible." Mr. Randolph bought five small oil paintings by Theodore Robinson, including the picture Etta wanted most, which depicted an old man with his horse (figure 3.4).[7]

To put Etta's purchase in perspective, it should be noted that in the closing years of the nineteenth century, even so avid a student of art as Leo Stein was only dimly aware of the existence of the Impressionists. Leo was then in Europe expressly seeking out new experiences in art. In addition, he had the advantage of advice from his friend Bernard Berenson, the premier art critic of the day. In 1898 Etta had never been to Paris and therefore would not have seen the few Impressionist or Post-Impressionist works on exhibit there. But even Leo—who would one day spearhead the collecting of modern art—did not discover Toulouse-Lautrec until 1904 or Van Gogh until 1905.[8]

Etta's decision to spend a large sum of money on oil paintings by a relatively unknown modern artist suggests an unlooked-for determination and independence of mind. At the time the purchase was made, no one else in the large Cone family displayed any interest in or appreciation for the visual arts. The move was daring, and it is likely that Etta felt much as did Leo Stein in 1902, when he bought his first oil painting: "I felt a bit like a desperado. Oil paintings were for the rich; that was part of the

American credo . . . [But this purchase showed me that] one could actually own paintings, even if one were not a millionaire."[9]

Theodore Robinson's roller-coaster reputation in the world of art casts a revealing light on the sureness of Etta's taste and the boldness of her first purchase. For decades, the Baltimore Museum of Art kept the four Robinsons Etta had bequeathed to them[10] in 1949 in its basement. It was not until three-quarters of a century after Etta bought them that the artist began to be widely admired. Finally, in 1973, the Baltimore Museum held a one-man Robinson show, and the artist's reputation has only grown since.[11]

In addition to the inheritance Herman Cone left to each of his eleven surviving children, Etta and Claribel also had the benefit of shares belonging to Moses and Ceasar, which the two brothers generously signed over to their unmarried sisters. This gave Etta and Claribel an independent income of some $2,400 a year each. With these assets, the Cone sisters were comfortable rather than wealthy. But having an assured income freed them of the necessity of supporting themselves—a problem women generally resolved at that time by marrying.

ETTA'S FIRST TRIP ABROAD

Etta used her new independence to take a break from her family duties. On May 10, 1901, at the age of thirty, she embarked with her cousin Hortense Guggenheimer and friend Harriet Clark for Europe. Leo Stein, Etta's old friend from Baltimore who had been living abroad for several years, surprised them by meeting them on their arrival in Naples. That same day they set out for the National Archaeological Museum, the first of many such visits. Over the next weeks the four traveled to Pompeii, Capri, Sorrento, Rome—and finally to Leo's beloved Florence.

Leo, then twenty-eight, had settled in Florence the year before to write a book on the Italian Renaissance painter Andrea Mantegna. While that project was soon abandoned, he spent the time becoming well versed in the art of the period.

Leo loved to teach, and Etta was an eager pupil. Her journal tells a rapturous tale of discovery. She did not go around to the museums just to have seen the pictures but rather went back over and over again, studying the same works, and truly learning about the painters and their output.

FIGURE 3.5

Left to right: *Etta Cone
and Harriet Clark in
Florence, 1901.*
Ellen B. Hirschland Archives

The group's endless round of visits to museums, churches, and gardens
indicates better than words the unquenchable hunger for beauty felt by
Etta and Leo. Increasingly, too, Etta's romantic interest in history and
stories about artists was balanced by an informed and analytic assessment
of what she saw. Two years after this grand tour of Europe, Harriet Clark
was still marveling at her friend's ability to absorb and understand art.
Writing in 1903, she thanked Etta for contributing so much to her own
enjoyment of their trip and said she was "overwhelmed at the way you
learned pictures and names."[12]

Romance may also have entered Etta's life at the time of her 1901 trip in quite another way. For after a dash through Italy, Switzerland, Germany, and Paris, she would find herself returning to the United States with her friend Gertrude Stein.

Arriving in Paris at the end of August 1901, Etta was amazed to find there Leo (who had split off from the group in Florence) and his sister Gertrude. In Paris the two women spent virtually every day together—shopping, going to galleries, museums, and the opera, visiting friends, and above all talking. On September 13, while touring the shops of Paris with Gertrude, Etta made her second venture into the world of collecting fine art by purchasing a small bronze relief by Antoine Louis Barye called *Walking Panther* (1831). Each day's entry in Etta's journal contains a reference to Gertrude:

> [September 15, 1901, Paris.] . . . Talked with Gertrude on her pet subject of Human intercourse of the sexes. She is surely interesting . . .[13]

Although Leo continued to be Etta's mentor in matters of art—she would later credit him for laying the basis for her own aesthetic[14]—it was Gertrude's approval she sought. Etta's relationship with Gertrude Stein has occasioned much speculation.[15] Gertrude's flagrant predilection for women and Alice B. Toklas's obvious jealousy suggest that Etta was more to Gertrude than a friend. Yet the Victorian propriety that prompted Etta to leave no clear indication of her feelings makes the difficult task of interpreting a private life over a century after the fact in this case a near impossibility. For all Etta's desire for privacy, Ellen Hirschland's girlhood diary contains a surprising tidbit dated September 4, 1935:

"Went to Aunt Etta's for lunch . . . She told me lots of things about her love affairs, etc."

One wonders what the sixteen-year-old Ellen could have meant. Sixty-four years later, the mature Ellen Hirschland could only lament, "How I wish I had made detailed notes about that discussion!"

Still, one hint does survive. In early October 1901, Etta, her cousin Hortense, and Gertrude (Harriet Clark stayed on in Paris) sailed for the United States. The weather was gloomy, and Etta's journal entries were terse. Suddenly left with nothing to do but read and stroll, she felt low, and her thoughts turned to home.

[Thursday, October 3, 1901, Ocean, day 1] Uneventful in every sense of the word . . .

[Monday, October 7, 1901, Ocean, day 5] I fear that I am not in a sociable mood. I want awfully to get home . . .[16]

Yet the next day brought a change in both weather and mood—recorded only in this tantalizingly enigmatic journal entry:

[Tuesday, October 8, 1901, Ocean, day 6] Clear beautiful day which I spent mostly below in a most <u>beautiful state of mind</u>, but one which brought out the most exquisite qualities of Gertrude. My vanity . . .[17]

The diary entry breaks off, leaving the mysterious last two words dangling. Although the relationship between Etta and Gertrude was undoubtedly intimate, there are only a few suggestions—including this one—and the fact that Alice B. Toklas was extremely jealous of Etta in later years. But Gertrude's word portrait of the Cone sisters, "Two Women," helps fill out the picture a little. The text itself carries on in the following manner:

There were others connected with them, connected with each of them, connected with both of them. There were some connected with both of them. There had been a father and there had been a mother and there were brothers and quite enough of them. They each of them had certainly duties toward these connected with them. They had, each one of them, what they wanted, Martha [Claribel] when she wanted it, Ada [Etta] when she was going to want it. They had brothers and a mother and a father. They were quite rich, all of them. They were sometimes together, the two of them, they were sometimes traveling. They were sometimes alone together then. They knew it then. They were sometimes not alone together then. They knew that then. They were, the two of them, ones traveling and they were then ones buying some things and they were then ones living in a way and they were then ones sometimes living in another way. They were very different the one from the other of them. They were certainly very different.[18]

In one of the notes that Gertrude wrote in the margins of the original manuscript, she wrote, "Sex in both," adding to the implications of lesbian leanings.[19]

ETTA AND CLARIBEL IN EUROPE TOGETHER

Left to right: Gertrude Stein, Etta Cone, and Claribel Cone in Vallombrosa, July 1903. Vallombrosa is a forested area twenty miles southeast of Florence.
Courtesy of BMA, CG.10

Late in 1902, Helen Cone died. Finally, at age thirty-two, Etta was free to follow her own inclinations. She and Claribel set sail for Europe in the early summer of 1903. On arriving in Florence, Etta found a letter from Gertrude inviting her to come to Rome. Etta declined, but Gertrude came to Florence instead and they all took long walks in the hills and valleys of Tuscany, and had warm and intense discussions. Far from being obsessed with Gertrude, however, Etta's diary shows her once again engaged in the tireless search for new experiences in architecture and art.[20]

When fall came, Claribel went to Germany to do research at the Senckenberg Institute in Frankfurt am Main, and Etta headed for home. Gertrude too went back to the United States. But by the next summer, 1904, Etta and Gertrude were sailing back to the Continent once again.

When they arrived in Genoa, Claribel joined them, and the trio traveled together to meet Leo in Florence. That was the year Bernard Berenson had steered him to the works of Paul Cézanne, and Leo was bubbling over with his new discovery. By that time he was established in Paris at 27 rue de Fleurus. Gertrude decided to move in with him; their elder brother Michael Stein, his wife, Sally (Sarah), and their young son Allan were installed a short walk away at 58 rue Madame. In the fall of 1905, Etta rented an apartment in the same house on the rue Madame.[21]

For Etta, Paris meant piano lessons from her landlady twice a week,[22] exploring the city, attending weekly salons at Gertrude and Leo's or, more frequently, at Michael and Sally's, and typing Gertrude's first novel, *Three Lives*, from the handwritten manuscript. Most of all, it meant freedom.

For the first time in her life, Etta was on her own. By then a confirmed single woman of thirty-five, she became friendly with the sculptor Mahonri Young, grandson of the Mormon leader Brigham Young. But when Young proposed,[23] Etta turned him down. To others she maintained that she could not marry because she could find no one as wonderful as her brother Moses. But within the family it was believed that one of her brothers refused to allow her to marry a non-Jew.[24] An essay Ellen Hirschland wrote in 1937[25] describes her own thoughts on her great-aunt's plight:

About Mahonri, it has been said that "a thing is important by its absence as well as by its presence." I have often debated, in my mind, whether such is true of a husband for Miss Castleby [Etta Cone]. She might have married; in fact at one time was ready to but did not because her brothers, not intolerantly, but rather in reverence toward their ancestors, persuaded her not to because of his religion [strict Mormonism] which is different from hers.

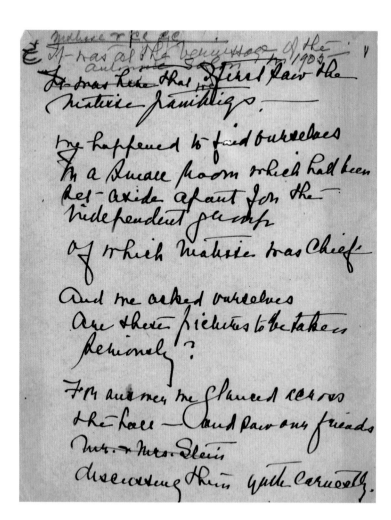

FIGURE 3.7

*One of several almost identical
sheets on which Claribel Cone
set out her recollections of the
opening of the Salon d'Automne
of 1905.*

Ellen B. Hirschland Archives

As ever, it is hard to judge Etta's own feelings about men, marriage, and Mahonri in particular. Writing to Gertrude two years after the proposal, having heard that Mahonri was married, she adopted a tone of mock regret: "Gee! Don't tell me Young is married! My last hope."[26] Then in her letter she drew a woman's face with lines coming down from the eyes and, in parentheses, the words, "These are tears."

THE SISTERS' FIRST EXPOSURES TO MODERN ART

If the record is virtually silent on the subject of love, it is eloquent on Etta's and Claribel's entry into the world of modern art. Claribel, who had come to Paris from Germany to visit her sister, joined Etta in attending the opening of the exposition of avant-garde art displayed at the Salon d'Automne on October 18, 1905. Years later Claribel recalled the shock of coming into the room reserved for modern works, whose slashing brushwork and violently juxtaposed colors caused one critic to dub their creators *Fauves* (wild beasts):

> Having passed through several of the larger halls we soon
> found ourselves in a small room . . . which had been set . . .
> apart for the independent group of which Matisse was
> chief . . . We asked ourselves are these things to be taken
> seriously. As we looked across the room we found our friends
> [Gertrude, Leo, Michael, and Sally] earnestly contemplating
> a canvas—the canvas of a woman with a hat tilted jauntily at
> an angle on the top of her head—the drawing crude, the color
> bizarre.[27]

At first Matisse's *Woman with Hat* repulsed Leo, who called it "a thing brilliant and powerful but the nastiest smear of paint I had ever seen." But after a few days of thinking about it and talking it over with his sister-in-law Sally, he bought it.[28]

Within the next two weeks the art dealer Clovis Sagot,[29] whose shop Leo visited regularly to browse and chat, introduced Leo to the work of a then-unknown Spanish painter named Pablo Picasso.[30] The dealer showed Leo *Acrobat Family with an Ape*[31] and, taken immediately by the fine draftsmanship, Leo bought the painting.[32] (The animal is a baboon, not an ape, but the name has stuck.) Fernande Olivier, Picasso's live-in mistress, described the relationship of the animal to Picasso:

> A little monkey called Monina, who had taken a great fancy
> to him, used to eat all her meals with Picasso and pester him
> incessantly; he bore with this and even enjoyed it. He would
> let her take his cigarette or the fruit he was eating. She would
> nestle up to his chest, where she felt quite at home. He loved
> to see this animal being so trusting and was delighted by the
> tricks she used to play.[33]

The baboon served as a model in Picasso's work around 1905.

A few days later when Leo visited the young artist in his studio in the "Bateau Lavoir" ("Floating Laundry"),[34] he took Gertrude and Etta with him, and Etta would soon purchase a study of the baboon related to Leo Stein's drawing. It was not long before all three became regular visitors. When Claribel later came to Paris and accompanied Etta on her visits to Picasso, he dubbed the sisters the "Miss Etta Cones." This was a pun on the Spanish, "¡Eh, tacones!" ("Hey, high heels!").[35] The comment is particularly amusing when one remembers that the sisters always wore flat shoes.

On November 5, 1905, Picasso asked Etta to give him the comics section of an American newspaper and in exchange invited her to help herself to the sketches and etchings lying about on the floor. Wondering about the truth of this oft-repeated story, Ellen Hirschland decided to ask her great-aunt about it:

When I asked Etta if this was accurate, she replied that she did, in fact, occasionally give Picasso comics, but that she insisted on paying for any of his drawings that she got.

FIGURE 3.8

Pablo Picasso, The Monkey, *circa 1905. Pen, ink, and gouache. 19 ¾ x 12 ¾ in. Baltimore Museum of Art. This drawing may be one of those Etta Cone bought directly from Picasso on March 3, 1906.*

Courtesy of BMA, 1950.271

Etta's strict sense of propriety would not allow her to accept any gifts from the artist, and her expense book duly lists "1 picture, 1 etching Picasso" for 120 francs—about twenty-three dollars in 1905. By early spring, having studied the situation for five months, Etta was ready to buy Picasso's work in earnest. On March 3, 1906, she noted in her expense notebook: "11 drawings and 7 etchings" by Picasso, purchased for 175 francs—about thirty-four dollars at the time. This means that Etta paid a little less than two dollars apiece for the Picasso drawings and etchings that she acquired that day.[36]

At this point something needs to be said about another persistent legend—the idea that the Cone sisters were in the habit of picking up drawings randomly from Picasso's studio floor. Since only Etta was involved at this time, and she was a cautious buyer no matter how small the sum, it can be assumed that "random" is a word particularly ill suited to describe her selection process. Etta certainly chose with great care and a distinct sureness of taste.[37]

Picasso

FIGURE 3.9

Pablo Picasso, Boy Riding
Sidesaddle, *circa 1905.*
Pen and ink. 9 ⅜ x 12 ⅛ in.
Baltimore Museum of Art.
Picasso's first mistress, Rosita
del Oro, was a well-known
bareback rider in Barcelona's
Tivoli–Circuo Equestre. He
met her in 1896 when she was
just fifteen years old, but he
was still fascinated by the grace
of circus riders nine years later.
Etta bought this drawing
in 1905.
Courtesy of BMA, 1950.12.479

In addition to rumors, another source of disinformation about the
Cones is the autobiography of Gertrude Stein, written long after her
friendship with Etta had soured. This work gives a mean-spirited version of
events in which Gertrude, not surprisingly, is the éminence grise prompting
Etta's actions:

> Etta Cone found the Picassos appalling but romantic. She was
> taken there by Gertrude Stein whenever the Picasso finances
> got beyond everybody and was made to buy a hundred francs'
> worth of drawings. After all a hundred francs in those days
> was worth twenty dollars. She was quite willing to indulge in
> this romantic charity. Needless to say these drawings became
> in very much later years the nucleus of her collection.[38]

Despite Gertrude's pressure, Etta would go only so far to help Picasso.
But she was quick to lend substantial sums to Gertrude herself. Rather than

cementing the friendship, this generosity only earned her the reputation among the Steins of being a patsy.[39]

PORTRAITS

By this time Gertrude and Picasso had become good friends, and the young painter asked if he might paint her portrait. Despite his renowned ability for speed, he took, by her report, *ninety* sittings for the portrait, suggesting that her visits to his studio had more to do with conversation than with art. Around this time he also made portraits of Leo and Allan Stein, which eventually entered Etta's collection.

FIGURE 3.10

Pablo Picasso, Portrait of Gertrude Stein, *1906. Oil on canvas. 39¼ x 32 in. Metropolitan Museum of Art, New York. When told that Stein looked nothing like Picasso's picture, the artist wittily replied, "She will." Stein herself treasured the portrait as a most accurate and pleasing representation, keeping it until she died and willing it to the Metropolitan Museum of Art.*

Reproduced by permission from Metropolitan Museum of Art. Image copyright © Metropolitan Museum of Art/Art Resource, New York (image reference ART321366)

Shortly after Picasso finished his portrait of Gertrude Stein, an older artist, Félix Vallotton, also asked her to pose. Sitting for her portrait suited Gertrude, who liked being the center of attention, and her autobiography contains the following self-serving note: "He [Vallotton] asked Gertrude Stein to pose for him. She did the following year. She had come to like posing, the long still hours followed by a long dark walk intensified the concentration with which she was creating her sentences . . ."[40]

Vallotton chose a canvas of the same size as Picasso's and used a similar color scheme. Like Picasso, he shows a corner of the room and emphasizes Gertrude's bulk and the roundness of her shoulders. In both paintings she wears dark clothes against a lighter background, and her hands stand out prominently—though they look wider and fatter in Vallotton's portrait than in Picasso's. Where Gertrude wears a brooch in Picasso's painting,[41] Vallotton shows her in a long string of beads reminiscent of Hans Holbein the Younger's portraits of Henry VIII. He succeeds mightily in capturing the size and mass of the woman but, even though his painting is more lifelike, it is less dynamic than Picasso's.

In the end it appears that Gertrude Stein did not like Vallotton's portrait of her, as the painting does not appear in the early photographs of her studio.[42] Yet she appears to have been fascinated by Vallotton's technique:

> When he painted a portrait he made a crayon sketch and
> then began painting at the top of the canvas straight across.
> Gertrude Stein said it was like pulling down a curtain as
> slowly moving as one of his swiss [sic] glaciers. Slowly he
> pulled the curtain down and by the time he was at the
> bottom of the canvas, there you were. The whole operation
> took about two weeks and then he gave the canvas to you.
> First however he exhibited it in the autumn salon and it had
> considerable notice and everyone was pleased.[43]

Around this time there was also talk of Picasso painting a portrait of Etta. Worried about the strained circumstances of their painter friend, the Steins urged the Cone sisters to have their portraits done. But when Etta went to Frankfurt to see a specialist about her persistent stomach problems (which both she and Gertrude called "bum gut"), she wrote Gertrude that her medical problems had taken up all of her disposable funds.[44]

FIGURE 3.11

Félix Vallotton, Portrait of Gertrude Stein, *1907. Oil on canvas. 43 ⅜ x 32 in. Baltimore Museum of Art.* Courtesy of BMA, 1950.300

In her next letter, the unstoppable Gertrude apparently once again mentioned Picasso's poverty, for Etta replies: "Poor little Picasso! but then I'd swap all around with his health and genius, where [sic] it possible, but as it is not, I've just got to fight it out [the 'bum gut'] to the end and its [sic] not unhappy I've been lately, pain and all included."[45]

In the end, Etta never sat for a portrait by Picasso, although it is rumored that *Woman with Fan* of 1909 is meant to represent her.[46] The Picasso biographer John Richardson first speculates that the impecunious young painter put out the rumor himself as a ploy to get Etta to buy the painting. But he then lays that notion to rest by recording that although Etta had not been in Paris for three years when the picture was painted, Picasso told him he had in fact had her in mind when painting it.[47] In any case, the Russian art collector Sergei Shchukin, who must have known Etta from the Stein salons in 1905 and 1906, bought the painting as a portrait of her.[48]

ETTA MEETS MATISSE

At the same time that Etta was becoming acquainted with the rakish young Spaniard and his work, she was also getting to know a slightly older modern painter, Henri Matisse. At the time when she met him, Matisse, in his early thirties, must have looked much as he does in his self-portrait (figure 3.13).

In 1905 there were few Americans in Paris, and the Stein salons, which offered avant-garde pictures and good conversation without the necessity of a formal introduction, became the favorite gathering place for the city's intellectual set. From the time of the Salon d'Automne in October, Henri Matisse became a regular at Sally Stein's, and Sally became one of Matisse's most ardent promoters. The Steins in fact bought Matisses only during these early years.[49] But from 1905 to 1907 virtually the only place to see Matisse's work was at the apartments of Leo and Gertrude and Michael and Sally.

On January 15, 1906, just three months after she had first seen his shockingly bold paintings at the Salon d'Automne of 1905, Etta accompanied Sally Stein to Matisse's studio and bought two drawings, one of which she gave to her friend. Soon thereafter she also bought her first Matisse oil painting: *Yellow Pottery from Provence*, also called *The Yellow Jug*.[50]

FIGURE 3.12

Pablo Picasso, Woman with Fan, *1909. Oil on canvas. 39 ⅜ x 31 ⅞ in. Pushkin Museum of Fine Arts, Moscow. Although not painted from life, this painting resembles Etta Cone, and Picasso claimed to have had her in mind when creating it.*

Reproduced by permission from Scala/Art Resource, New York

Henri Matisse, Self-Portrait, *1901–3. Drypoint. 5½ x 7⅞ in. Baltimore Museum of Art. Purchased as the gift of Edward T. Cone in memory of his mother, Laura W. Cone, and of Jeanette Kimmel in memory of her father, Benjamin Cone.* Courtesy of BMA, 1986.72

Henri Matisse, Yellow Pottery from Provence, *formerly called* The Yellow Jug, *1906. Oil on canvas. 21⅞ x 18⅜ in. Baltimore Museum of Art.* Courtesy of BMA, 1950.227

A perfect example of the Fauvist style, *Yellow Pottery* is characterized by its striking swaths of intense color unabashedly juxtaposed. The simple foreground shows a bare tabletop and has an unfinished look. On the table sits a dish of eggplants and squash sketched in outline and oddly not filled in, in contrast to the rest of the color-drenched canvas. Behind the dish sits the yellow vase of the title, marked with two round white spots of reflected light. The background consists of seven vertical bands of seemingly unrelated colors, which yet interact successfully to hold the composition together.

Bold and modern even today, *Yellow Pottery* must have seemed revolutionary, and even mad, in 1906. It is not possible to imagine the impact it would have had on contemporary viewers. What can be said is that Etta's purchase of the painting marked the beginning of her enduring preference for Henri Matisse's work.

During the fall and winter she spent in Paris, Etta Cone engaged fully in the discovery and encouragement of modern art. She met and formed friendships with several artists. Both with her friends and on her own, she visited their studios and bought works from them on the spot. She browsed in dealers' shops and haunted the halls of the great museums.

Henri. Matisse

Most important for artists grown accustomed to public scorn, she did more than look and talk. Offering them the true test of approval, she bought.

PARIS LEFT BEHIND

During a span of half a year in Paris in 1905 and 1906, Etta acquired twenty-eight works of art by six artists, at least two of whom were virtually unknown at the time (Cézanne and Picasso) and one who was violently rejected by the art establishment (Matisse). Then in the fall of 1906, just as suddenly as she had plunged headlong into this exciting new world, Etta abruptly left it. Apparently stowing her brilliant new Matisse with her friends Leo and Gertrude Stein (a 1907 photograph shows it hanging on the wall at 27 rue de Fleurus),[51] Etta—together with sister Claribel and brother Moses and his wife, Bertha—set out on a grand tour. Their trip around the world would last an entire year.

In a letter to Gertrude from Cairo, baby talk and the addition of an unconvincing disclaimer cannot disguise Etta's longing for her old Paris life:

> Has my successor [Alice B. Toklas] done her duty by my place
> what she usurped & does she your typewriting & takes she
> care of that nice Mikey man [Michael Stein]. I am sometimes
> envious, but I guess am greedy, cause so far this trip has not
> been all a bad stunt.[52]

Paris missed Etta, too. Upon her return to Baltimore, she was astonished to find a whimsical pencil self-portrait by Picasso enclosed with a letter from Gertrude. Thoroughly charmed, she wrote back immediately (couching her reply in the "cute" dialect she and Gertrude used regularly):

> A funny coincidence—here I am at my desk having come to
> tell you that it was about time for you to be writing to me,
> and here comes your dear old letter with this delightful sketch
> of Picasso and Fernando's [Fernande's] wishes. Dey sure am
> nice folk and I hope to see them in the near future; so thank
> them for their respects and please give them mine and tell
> Pablo that Fernando [sic] ought massage his tummy into shape
> again. I love his picture for it is just like him.[53]

Still, life at home was not entirely dull. In 1907 Etta developed a passionate interest in a younger woman in Baltimore named Ida Gutman. Although she makes no mention of her inflamed feelings in her letters to her sister Claribel, she writes openly about them to Gertrude in January 1908: "Ida too is still my pet adoration & my heart still beats hot when her letters come so what are you going to do—advise me to go to Balto & get a surfeit—no I'm coming to Italy & get weened [sic] again."[54]

Still lovesick four months later, she pours out her heart to Gertrude again: "Sad to say I loves Ida as much as ever. I see very little of her, for the poor thing is so walled in with an excited household & when she gets out, she goes by her lonesome to the park and needs to be alone to get her poise & that's how it stands between Ida & me."[55]

However deep Etta's feelings, a typically cryptic note by Gertrude strongly suggests that Etta never acted on them—which Gertrude puts down to her friend's soul-destroying cowardice:

> Spinster quality, lacke [sic] of generosity and sentimentality.
> Conceive themselves heroes but do nothing heroic. Etta

Cone perfect type with all her splendor and richness and possible disspinsterising quality, when she was in love with Ida Gutman least it, she became almost generous in her nature, for her love became heroic, now she is her own hero and spinster state is complete . . .[56]

Etta had typed Gertrude's first book and knew well her friend's habit of taking her characters directly from life. She appears to have had momentary second thoughts about sharing too many confidences but as it turns out allowed her great affection for Gertrude to overcome any such scruples.[57]

THE DEATH OF MOSES CONE

If Etta's passion for Ida Gutman turned her internal world upside down for a time in 1908, that year later brought an event that would cast a pall over her life for all the years to come. On December 8, 1908, Etta's beloved brother Moses died suddenly at age fifty-one. After his death Etta spent many months at a time at his home in Blowing Rock, North Carolina—in part to help her widowed sister-in-law, Bertha Lindau Cone, and in part to be near her brother, who was buried on a hilltop near the manor house.

Moses Cone died intestate, despite his fascination with the details of every negotiation, contract, deal, and business plan. By law, then, his wife, Bertha, inherited half of his fortune—including Flat Top Manor, where she continued to live for nearly forty years, until her death in 1947.[58] Soon after Moses died, Bertha put all of her assets into a trust to fund the building of a Moses H. Cone Memorial Hospital in Greensboro as a monument to her late husband.

Over the next few years, Etta spent summers in Blowing Rock and winters in Baltimore, where social pressure to do charity work was heavy. To Gertrude she noted that her two alternatives were "philanthropy and woman Suffrage—questions that have put old Baltimore in a state of real turmoil."[59]

In Blowing Rock she did her best to help Bertha while sending bleak letters to Claribel in Europe. Etta felt that Claribel alone, of all the people in the world, could understand what she had lost. In July 1910 Claribel wrote sympathetically that she understood how lonely Etta was;[60] but

FIGURE 3.16

Pablo Picasso, Bonjour Mlle Cone, *1907. Ink on paper. 8¼ x 5½ in. Baltimore Museum of Art. In pen and ink on the back of the fold, Picasso's mistress wrote (in French), "I send you my remembrances, Fernand [sic] Picasso."*
Courtesy of BMA, 1950.12.481

Bon jour Mlle Cone

the next summer was a repeat of the last, and it seemed that as the years dragged on, nothing could lift Etta's mood. Indeed, she seems to have been deeply depressed, as a 1910 letter she wrote to Claribel shows:

> Your dear letter from Frankfurt with its details of your doings gave me much pleasure. It makes me very sad indeed to realize that while I am deeply interested in the things you write of, I have lost courage and feel that it is useless spending energy to get all the information etc that one does in travelling around. I actually have not the energy either mental or physical . . . Do continue to have a good time. You are a very fortunate makeup. I am a desperate one and would like to go to sleep & not awaken. Sounds awful to send across the ocean.[61]

One satisfaction for Etta at Blowing Rock was her newfound persuasive power to influence Bertha. In the same letter in which she admits to being "a desperate one," she relates with evident pleasure how she convinced her sister-in-law to enlarge the workers' cottages to make sure parents and children were not sleeping too close together for propriety's sake.[62]

ETTA, GERTRUDE, AND OTHER WOMEN FRIENDS

Another source of continuing pleasure for Etta was the interest both she and Claribel took in Gertrude's growing reputation as a writer. When *Three Lives* appeared in the summer of 1909, Etta immediately wrote to congratulate Gertrude and to wish "your book the great success it deserves."[63] In view of the fact that she had typed the manuscript four years earlier, she added in a subsequent letter, "It is a real happiness to see Tena and Anna and Melanctha all in print and I feel a real proprietor's pride in them. They read famously well."[64]

In a December 1909 letter to Gertrude, she returned to the subject of *Three Lives*: "I have tried to write you about your book. I have only just succeeded in reading it through. It is truly in literature what Matisse's painting and sculpture are in art. It was like being with you and it did me good."[65] And in a January 1910 letter to Gertrude, Etta reported, "Your *Three Lives* has stirred sleepy Baltimore up more than a bomb could have done."[66] A month later she wrote again, reporting that Baltimore readers thought Gertrude had a lack of style and that her departure from the "rules of rhetoric" as well as her immoral tales made the writing unacceptable; but Etta herself gave these readers a piece of her mind and told them they didn't know what they were talking about.[67]

As Etta was writing these lines, the publisher reported that "only 73 of the 500 bound copies had been sold and 37 of these to bookstores at 75 cents per copy," and that "many copies had gone to friends."[68] But the faithful Etta continued to send clippings about *Three Lives* to Gertrude for years. Much later Gertrude asked Etta to subscribe to a clipping service (at Gertrude's expense) so that she would hear of any further reviews.[69]

In her many letters to Gertrude in 1909 and 1910, when the affair between Gertrude and Alice B. Toklas was ripening, Etta did not mention Alice at all.[70] Although she certainly knew of Alice, it is possible that she did not yet know the extent of the relationship. Then in the summer of 1910, Claribel wrote Etta that Gertrude, most uncharacteristically, was not answering her letters. Later that summer, shortly after Alice moved in with Gertrude,[71] Claribel wrote Etta that Gertrude and Alice had come to see her.[72] When Etta next wrote Gertrude she dutifully included a note to "take lots of love and give some to Leo and remember me to Miss Taklos."[73] Other letters from both Claribel and Etta leave Alice out altogether ("love to you and Leo") or continue to perpetuate the unflattering "Taklos." Other spellings, such as "Taklas," "Toaklos," "Tachlos," and "Tacklos," appear in their letters too; and furthermore, the ending *-los* in German, meaning "less" or "without," tends to have a negative connotation. This is akin to misspelling *Toklas* in English as "Takless," with more than a hint of a derogatory tone.

Etta's failure to acknowledge Alice's very public bond with Gertrude has sometimes been put down to her "delicate sensibilities." Although letters between the two sisters suggest that neither Etta nor Claribel particularly liked Gertrude's friend, rudeness was so out of character for Etta that jealousy or prudery may well have played a role.

For Etta was first and foremost a lady. In an age that condemned the "woman who lives her own life" as either a "trollop" or masculine,[74] her delicate sensibilities and fine manners were much admired. It was these qualities, among others, that had prompted her brother Moses to compliment her lavishly.[75]

A scene from Gertrude's 1933 *Autobiography of Alice B. Toklas* captures Etta's absolute and scrupulous rectitude in social dealings. Writing in the third person, Gertrude describes how her own attempts to type *Three Lives* invariably ended in failure:

> It was no use, it made her nervous, so Etta Cone came to the rescue. The Miss Etta Cones as Pablo Picasso used to call her and her sister. Etta Cone was a Baltimore connection of Gertrude Stein's and she was spending a winter in Paris. She was rather lonesome and she was rather interested . . .
>
> Etta Cone offered to typewrite *Three Lives* and she began. Baltimore is famous for the delicate sensibilities and conscientiousness of its inhabitants. It suddenly occurred to Gertrude Stein that she had not told Etta Cone to read the manuscript before beginning to typewrite it. She went to see her and there indeed was Etta Cone faithfully copying the manuscript letter by letter so that she might not by any indiscretion become conscious of the meaning. Permission to read the text having been given the typewriting went on.[76]

An incident from the early 1920s shows that the Cones' relations with Gertrude and Alice had thawed considerably. Both sisters were ending their letters to Gertrude with "lots of love to you both" and had begun calling her companion "Alice." By 1922 Etta could write about her with humor:

> Dear Gertrude, Don't be shocked, but we are in Brittany still and we [Nora Kaufman and I] have been through—if I weren't afraid of shocking Alice, I'd say "Hell" but with consideration for her, I'll say "Purgatory."[77]

Whether or not it was true, Etta certainly fostered the impression that she was totally naive about matters related to sex. Speaking with Laura Cone's daughter, Frances, Etta said she had heard a rumor that Gertrude and Alice were lovers, then asked Frances, apparently mystified, "But after all, what can two women do?"[78]

Interestingly, Etta gave Claribel a book entitled *How Women Love and Other Tales*, written in 1896. The book has Etta's signature, in ink, and then, written in pencil, is the notation "to CC Dec 1924."[79] The book is not about lesbian relationships but about women's passions. The title, and the lavender cover with gilded decoration, must have been appealing to one or both of them, but the stories within have nothing to do with lesbians.

Proper and prim as she was, Miss Etta maintained lifelong friendships with a number of people notorious for loose living. It was Laura Cone's opinion that Etta allowed artists to behave any way they wished because she thought they operated on a level high above the mundane.[80] From her own and her mother's observations, Ellen Hirschland is not so sure:

It was ironic that lady guests at Etta's elegant dining table might find themselves being tickled under the table by the famous American artist, teacher, and frequent guest Leon Kroll, whom Etta deemed a bland and cultured person. He often whispered improper stories. But it was Mother's opinion that had the hostess heard them, he would have been immediately banned from her salon.

It has also been said that when certain guests came Etta placed a tea caddy over a nude sculptured figure by Degas that used to stand on the piano.

Whatever her real attitude about sex, it is certain that between 1913 and 1939, Etta shared many happy hours with her friend and frequent traveling companion Nora Kaufman, and after 1939, with her piano teacher and close friend Lilly Schwarz. Like the many women who remained unmarried during the early years of the twentieth century, Etta depended for emotional sustenance on her family and close women friends.

Although Etta generally stood in the shadow of the more outgoing Claribel, the older sister clearly recognized the younger's superior ability to inspire love. Shortly before she returned home from Germany, where she spent all of World War I, Claribel wrote Etta a rare appreciation, referring to her "Charmed Circle of friends and admirers."[81]

She could not help contrasting Etta's full life with her own lonely independence.

4

The Decided Doctor Claribel

Dr. Claribel Cone was a woman of presence—so much so, it is difficult to imagine her young (but see figure 4.1). She is aptly captured by Picasso's drawing (figure 5.6), which shows her plump and imperious at age fifty-eight, with her feet resting on a pillow. Yet Picasso's deft hand also managed to convey a surprisingly engaging elegance and an aura that could not be ignored.

People particularly remarked on Claribel's lovely voice and captivating delivery when she read aloud. Gertrude Stein encapsulated her like this:

> Doctor Claribel Cone of Baltimore came majestically in and
> out. She loved to read Gertrude Stein's work out loud and she
> did read it out loud extraordinarily well. She liked ease and
> graciousness and comfort. She and her sister Etta Cone were
> travelling. The only room in the hotel was not comfortable.
> Etta bade her sister put up with it as it was only for one night.
> Etta, answered Doctor Claribel, one night is as important
> as any other night in my life and I must be comfortable . . .
> Everybody delighted in Doctor Claribel.[1]

Ellen Hirschland remembered her elderly relative as

an imposing personality—short, stout, and regal. When she spoke, I was mesmerized by her melodic voice. But magnetic as she was, she was also austere and not as likable to me as her sister Etta.

By the standards of the day, Claribel was prettier than Etta, with her round face, large eyes, regular features, and beautifully wavy hair. Once her hairdo was in place, she usually used a silver skewer, which served also as a handy letter opener, to hold it in place. Punctilious about grooming, Claribel never failed to give her long hair a nightly "100 licks" with a brush.[2]

It was in fact her habit wherever she lived to emerge sometime around noon, and her toilette never took less than two hours. At the Green Park Hotel in Blowing Rock, North Carolina, where Ceasar had arranged for an additional bathroom to be built to accommodate Cone family gatherings, it soon became necessary to forbid Claribel the use of the new bathroom altogether. Once in, she stayed for hours, not permitting access to anyone else. According to her sister-in-law Laura Cone, "She was physically and mentally unable to meet an appointment or to finish a job." This somewhat acid assessment may well have been true with regard to family and social engagements but clearly does not reflect the discipline Claribel needed to become a distinguished medical educator and researcher.

Claribel Cone had a tremendous flair for clothes. While both she and Etta invariably dressed in black in their later years, Claribel's effect was always dramatic, whatever the color choice. She had the romantic habit of wearing a black ribbon around her throat and always carried an elegant, silver-framed black purse. During World War I, which she spent in Germany, she reported to Etta that she stood out in a crowd—a visibility she obviously fostered and enjoyed. She also explained that by putting on a scarf from Liberty of London, she managed to dress up her old and worn clothes.[3] Although Claribel was a Victorian lady to her roots, she liked to experiment with effects outside the common mold: "Yes I am a bit unconventional—but I need not assure you very very dignified."[4] She also claimed that artists called her "pittoresque" and reported that an actress in Munich asked whether she could copy some of Claribel's clothes to wear onstage.[5] On occasion she wore striking cloths from the Far East—acquired on her tour around the world in 1906 and 1907—either made into colorful robes or draped around her in the manner of a sari or some other type of Oriental dress.

Generally satisfied with her appearance, she was yet self-conscious about her hands, which she considered unattractive. Once she gave a rare glimpse of self-deprecation, explaining that she wore ruffles on her sleeves

FIGURE 4.1

Claribel Cone at about age eighteen, in a fashionable dress of that time, circa 1882.

Photograph by the Cummins Studio, Ellen B. Hirschland Archives

to obscure her hands, a practice that she claimed was like Queen Elizabeth I wearing a ruffled collar to hide her goiter.[6]

CLARIBEL'S EDUCATION AND MEDICAL CAREER

Claribel Cone graduated from Western Female High School in Baltimore in 1883, at which time she announced the desire to become a doctor. In addition to the intellectual challenge, she may have found it a convenient way to wiggle out of the expectation that she would take over the household duties from her older sister, Carrie, who had left home to get married.

Claribel's father tried unsuccessfully to dissuade his daughter from so "unladylike" a profession, even offering her an extraordinary opportunity to travel abroad as an alternative. In the end Claribel—as was her habit throughout life—got everything she wanted. Not only did she take up her father's offer of the trip abroad (the first of many such overseas journeys) but she also persuaded him, a few years later, to fund her passage through medical school.

But first, for several years after high school, Claribel spent time enjoying herself. Voluble, intelligent, and lively, she frequently took center stage. She attended many masked balls and "sociables," most often escorted by one of her many brothers. Her more serious pursuits included studying German, which was spoken at home by her parents. She also studied singing and piano, although she was never as serious a musician as her younger sister Etta and would give up both as an adult. On the scientific side she studied botany about an hour and a half before breakfast each day, grew special plants in the garden, and met weekly with her cousin Flora Adler,[7] at the home of one or the other, to pursue their mutual interest in plants.

Part of the summer after graduation from high school Claribel spent in Atlantic City, where she enjoyed the attentions of various young men from Philadelphia and Baltimore. Her letters written at that time to her sister Carrie reveal a real spirit of fun.[8]

Eventually, in 1887, Claribel entered the Woman's Medical College of Baltimore.[9] Opened in 1882, this institution was at the time the only college south of the Mason-Dixon Line where women could receive training in medicine. Although Johns Hopkins had incorporated his university in 1867 and the hospital would open in 1889, the School of Medicine did not open until 1893.

Claribel obtained her medical diploma in 1890, graduating first in her class. Moving to Philadelphia, she did graduate work at the Woman's Medical College of Pennsylvania (1890–91) and served as resident physician at Blockley Almshouse (1891–92), which was part of the Philadelphia Hospital for the Insane.[10]

The first sign of Claribel's fascination with the visual arts comes in a letter to Etta that she wrote in 1891, at the age of twenty-six. In it she describes her efforts to decorate the reception room at the Blockley where she and the other young doctors spent a good deal of their time.[11] In the same letter, Claribel also describes how she decorated her own room at the Almshouse. This fascination with decor and minute attention to detail would continue throughout her life.

Claribel made friends at Blockley House, although she had to overcome—as she truthfully reported to Etta—the impression of arrogance she invariably conveyed. Dr. Pollock, at the hospital, said that Claribel "put on airs" and was "affected" or "stiff" or a "society woman," which are not particularly flattering remarks, as Claribel herself noted.[12] Nevertheless, by the age of thirty, Claribel was a respected and well-established professional in a highly competitive field. This may in some way account for her imperious attitude, for even at that age Claribel could not understand why anyone would not accede to her wishes. Horrified that a maid had the temerity to refuse her demands, for instance, as she describes in a letter to Etta, she abandons her highly prized "dignity," complaining that Mary refused to come to work for her: "a fact terrible but true . . . Mary will not come—will not." She goes on to call Mary a liar and a "choicy negress" and after three and a half pages of complaints drops the problem in Etta's lap with the words, "If you manage the servant question, I will manage father."[13]

In 1893 Claribel returned to Baltimore to lecture on hygiene at her alma mater for two years. In 1895 she was elevated to professor of pathology and pathological histology and acted, with Dr. W. Milton Lewis, as curator of the museum there.[14] She continued teaching at the college, on and off, for fifteen years. The opening address she gave to students entering Woman's Medical College in October 1895, written when she was thirty-two, shows something of her philosophy and beliefs about medicine, as well as her attitude regarding women in medicine (see appendix B). She praised the assembled students for their continuing self-sacrifice and suggested that, despite opinions to the contrary, women can still fulfill their "social duties" even as they serve as physicians. She also argued that women physicians may marry and still uphold their medical responsibilities.

At the same time that Claribel taught at the Woman's Medical College of Baltimore, she served on its board of trustees, acting as the board's president from 1899 to 1900. She also worked from 1895 to 1910 as a pathologist at the Good Samaritan Hospital, which was the hospital attached to the college. In addition, Claribel served her alma mater through its Alumnae Association—first as corresponding secretary (1893–94) and then as president (1894–98). From 1893 to 1903 and again from 1907 to 1914, she conducted research at Johns Hopkins in the laboratories of the distinguished doctors William H. Welch, William Osler, and Simon Flexner[15] and became quite friendly with all of them.

To give an idea of the distinction of Dr. Welch, Herbert Hoover credited him as being "our greatest statesman in the field of public health."[16] It was Welch who, in 1893, reviewed the applications of the first students to be admitted to the Johns Hopkins School of Medicine. For Dr. Welch's festschrift, prepared for him by his students in 1900, Claribel contributed a paper titled "Multiple Hyperplastic Gastric Nodules Associated with Nodular Gastric Tuberculosis." Welch was complimentary and thanked her enthusiastically:

> Your paper is certainly one of great interest and the case
> reported you have worked up admirably. Your interpretation
> seems to me the correct one, and at any rate the observation
> is so clearly described and illustrated that future investigations
> can identify the lesion, which after all is the most important
> matter.
>
> . . . For your own good, conscientious scientific work I
> entertain the highest opinion, and it has always been a source
> of gratification to me that you have worked so faithfully in
> my laboratory, where in many ways, including the work of
> instruction, you have been of much assistance. For all of
> this I thank you very heartily.[17]

Claribel's first extended stay in Germany took place from 1903 to 1906, when she settled in Frankfurt am Main to attend the Senckenburg Institute as a special research student in pathology. At the institute she worked with Professor Karl Weigert[18] until his death in 1904, then stayed on until 1906 to conduct pathology research with Professor Eugen Albrecht and Dr. Paul Ehrlich. Back in Frankfurt am Main again in 1910 to work with Dr. Hermann Strauss,[19] Claribel excitedly reported to Etta Dr. Ehrlich's discovery of Salvarsan, the only treatment for syphilis—"a disease we do not usually speak of in polite society"—until the advent of penicillin.[20]

In 1904 Claribel also did pathology research work with Drs. Metchnikoff and Borel at the Pasteur Institute in Paris.[21] But for her, Germany was the intellectual mecca as perhaps the only place on earth gentlemanly enough to recognize the true intellectual worth of a woman.[22]

Despite her plaintive rhetorical question, "What else is there for me?" Claribel did indeed make a name for herself in medicine. Perhaps because she recognized that it was her lot to remain a single woman, she worked hard and treasured every distinction and compliment she received.

Claribel spoke German fluently and remarked how much she enjoyed being mistaken for—if not a native speaker—at least not an American. She spoke German most of the time and was even taken for a foreigner, such as a Hungarian, Austrian, or Slav.[23] Claribel always felt comfortable in Germany. Returning to Frankfurt in 1910 after a break of a few years, she wrote Etta that she felt more at home there than in America.[24] So much was Germany to her liking that she opted to stay there—as an acknowledged enemy alien—throughout World War I.

Contrary to the rumor that Dr. Cone was the first woman ever to teach medicine in the United States, she followed by almost thirty years Dr. Ann Preston, who taught at the Woman's Medical College of Pennsylvania as early as 1865.[25] Other female physicians were also actively teaching at the time in other institutions.[26] But while Claribel taught medicine for years and did important research, especially on tuberculosis, she was never a clinician. As Ellen Hirschland remembers:

She liked to tell the story that she had had but one single private patient in her entire career. I enjoy passing on the story, for the patient was my mother, whose life—when she was an infant—was saved by her Aunt Claribel. A nurse had fed the days-old baby barbiturates to keep her quiet. Aunt Claribel discovered the emergency but, though a physician, had no medical equipment with her. Accordingly, she told my grandmother to hold the infant upside down until further treatment could be provided, and ran at full speed into the city of Asheville to get another doctor.

Although Dr. Cone never aspired to private practice, at one time when street fighting broke out during the post–World War I stress in Weimar, a general call was issued for doctors. Claribel reported to Etta that she remembered "with some surprise" that she was a doctor and lent her services to bandage the wounded.

Claribel was well aware of the unusual role she filled as a professional woman working in a man's world (see appendix C). She confined herself to the more rarefied circles of research and scholarship where women were more easily accepted and felt little hostility. She wrote numerous scientific articles that were published both in the United States and in Germany throughout her life (see appendix D) and was a member of several medical societies: the American Medical Association, the Medical and Chirurgical Faculty of Maryland, the Baltimore City Medical Society, the American Association of Pathology and Bacteriology, and the American Association for the Study and Prevention of Infant Mortality. From 1925 to 1927 she served as president of the Society of Woman's Medical College of Baltimore.

Early in her career Claribel became interested in establishing a new association for the study and prevention of infant mortality. When such a society was eventually formed around 1910, Claribel marked the notice about it in the Baltimore *Sun*[27] and kept that day's issue for the rest of her life. She was also active in the cause to register births and in 1910 delivered an address on this subject to the Maryland Society for the Prevention of Blindness.[28]

CLARIBEL'S SOCIAL VIEWS

Not only was Claribel Cone a recognized luminary in Baltimore's medical community, but by the time she reached middle age, she was also well known as a social dynamo. In 1911 her fame as a hostess for the intellectual set even made news at the Baltimore *Sun*, which claimed that her "Saturday parties . . . came as near being a salon as anything the city has ever known."[29]

Claribel was sociable, however, only when she chose to be. She was also an unabashed snob. The more unsophisticated types of Americans abroad, for instance, came in for her particular scorn. She bitterly lamented the growing number of Americans to be found in Europe and grumbled that it was bad enough to be with Americans at home but worse that those very same people she tried to avoid seemed to end up in Paris.[30]

Successful and well satisfied with herself, Claribel supported charities as a well-heeled lady should, but she maintained an aloof attitude when it came to welcoming members of the poorer and less-educated classes into her own social circle. Her snobbery came out particularly strongly with regard to poor Jews. Writing to Etta from shipboard in 1910, for instance, she tells how she found a spot on the sunny side of the deck next to the

FIGURE 4.2

Claribel Cone, circa 1910.
Ellen B. Hirschland Archives

family of a businessman who knew the Cone brothers and spoke well of Moses. She then went on to talk about the "long line of illiterate good natured bad mannered Jews" who sat on the other side, a group that she wanted nothing to do with.[31] On this same voyage, Claribel befriended the ship's senior doctor, a German whom she described as "well-educated, cultured . . . narrow-minded . . . and <u>very exclusive</u>."[32] Of one mind in their snobbery, the two passengers discussed "the Jew question" at length.[33]

Claribel's thinly veiled disdain for poor (and poorly educated) Jews may have stemmed from the Cone family's thoroughgoing sense of superiority. Claribel was notably haughty, and though Etta was less so, both felt keenly the distinction of being a Cone. All of the family were convinced that being a Cone was the equivalent of being royal and that, like royalty, you could only become a Cone by birth—an attitude understandably not much appreciated by their spouses. Ellen Hirschland's mother told her the following story, which illustrates the exclusivity of the Cone family circle:

On April 15, 1930, Etta and Fred bought a mausoleum in the Druid Ridge Cemetery just outside Baltimore, for $5,600, and Claribel's body was transferred to it. Etta offered the fourth spot in the mausoleum to my mother [Etta's niece], Dorothy Long Berney, who respectfully declined. Etta found it hard to understand Mother's rejection of an honored resting place in the Cone mausoleum. It had not occurred to her that Mother would wish to be buried next to her husband, even though Etta spoke constantly of her admiration for their mutual devotion.

In a revealing letter to Etta in 1919, Claribel exalted those inborn qualities that she felt set their family apart, barely disguising her elitist views by expressing them in scientific terms. Admitting that she might sound "somewhat chauvinistic," she explained what she called "a Cone quality" that was "more or less generally distributed throughout the Cone-Guggenheimer families—and possibly developed and enhanced through the southern influence and training." This quality she described as "fineness sensitiveness refinement—consideration—goodness," and she went on to say, regarding one of her less-successful brothers, that "deep down in his nature, I believe [he] possesses the same excellent fundament of the Cone Constitution."[34]

When it came to her personal relationships with other people, Claribel left few clues. We know that she viewed her work as an impediment to friendship. In 1910—a year that appears to have been difficult for her— she reflected on the social costs imposed by her dedication to medicine, and she admitted that her work prevented her from having the time to think of others. Her plan, she continued, was to take the time to think about other people in the unlikely circumstance that she might get to be an old lady and not be able to work any longer.[35]

Throughout that year, Claribel's letters home are filled with the subject of loneliness. Although she cannot leave the subject alone, her most common tack is to insist that she is *not* lonely—or to distance this delicate issue from herself.[36] Claribel points out how contented she is to be alone in Europe, while in the United States she is doomed to loneliness by the constant presence of uncongenial people—a comment that raises questions about her relations with her family and others she knew back home.[37]

On another occasion, when a young man whom she liked was hiking with her in the mountains, she sent him away, admitting to Etta that this was a normal practice for her: sending away people whom she liked.[38] Later that year she proclaimed, "What good friends I am getting to be with myself," and remarked that she would be quite sorry to die, given how much she liked her own company.[39] But despite her insistence that she was happiest when alone and alone by choice, the hard brightness of these letters and her inability to let go of the topic suggest that even the magnificently self-sufficient Claribel Cone sometimes knew what it was to be lonely.

It was just at this time, in 1910, that Claribel also found herself beginning to question her commitment to medicine.[40] By 1915 she had given up serious research in both Germany and the United States, and we see that both her time and her social connections were drifting toward the arts.[41]

Claribel's one constant, intimate relationship in life was with her younger sister Etta. Already as young women, when they had been the two girls remaining at home in a houseful of boys, Claribel and Etta were close. Although they had their differences—Claribel was demanding and Etta deferential—they remained the best of friends throughout their lives. Whenever Claribel wanted to let her hair down, she talked to Etta; and when Etta was not near at hand, Claribel wrote to her.

When the sisters were first separated, they wrote each other once a week. Later they wrote daily or, on some occasions, several letters in one day. Their correspondence tells us most of what we know about the sisters' private thoughts and lives. Unfortunately, most of Etta's responses to Claribel's letters do not survive—either because Claribel discarded them (unlikely given her compulsion to save everything) or because Etta herself destroyed them after Claribel's death.

Some of Claribel's letters to Etta were extremely long, often carrying on for as many as thirty-eight pages. She would continue the same letter, putting the new pages in another envelope. She referred to these as "diary letters." She would write at all hours of the day or night, even in the wee hours of the morning. Pages were numbered in both top corners—with black at top left, and red at top right. It's not clear what the various numbers and colors meant.[42]

There is only one blank page in all of the hundreds of letters preserved. Once, Claribel commented on her need to fill all the available space, noting that since there was a half page empty, she must fill it, "not being able to think of letting a <u>bare space</u> cross the ocean."[43]

Claribel must have been conscious of the fact that her letters might be kept for posterity. On one occasion she noted, "My sleepy letters remind me of an over-corrected literary manuscript."[44] She would also spend pages telling her sister the dates and numbers of other letters received and sent. To give a sense of the complication and length of Claribel's letters, here is a quotation from one, in which she sets out some of her own observations on how she wrote a particular letter: "I am now sending the second part (B) of the 'Diary-letter'—so-called—begun November 25 and written on the Dates Nov. 25, 26, 30, Dec. 3 successively. It grew to be so long that I felt forced to divide it into 3 parts—of which the first 6 sheets with an introductory one in addition were sent off Dec. 4 last Thursday. On the same day I sent dear Sydney [her brother] a 4 page letter—. . . In case this part B of the letter comes 1st—as happened once before in our epistolary experience I believe you will understand the patchwork."[45]

Etta, for her part, was well organized and kept the letters and fragments of letters in order. She would number the envelopes in the order received, write the content of each letter on the envelope, and add "ans" when she had answered it. Claribel often wrote a letter and dated it, then sent it off days or even more than a week later. She also tantalized Etta with the beginnings of stories, then wrote, typically, "more of him if I think of it in my next"—which of course she rarely did.

Claribel's social and professional success only confirmed her high opinion of herself. Her letters to Etta are filled with incidents in which she is the star, picked out for special attention by the brightest and the best. Her invincible self-confidence gave her an emotional strength and consistent optimism that her more sensitive younger sister could only envy.

In her self-absorption, Claribel frequently wrote Etta—who was too depressed to travel abroad after the death of Moses—of her "Collection" of admirers in Munich, one of whom referred to her as "electric" and who caused her to exclaim, "Oh, how I have been giving myself words of approval today—you must really excuse me."[46] Apparently feeling a twinge of self-consciousness the following day, she wrote, albeit with characteristic absence of remorse, "I wrote you a long letter yesterday—it is so full of <u>myself</u> and <u>my</u> doings!"[47]

In Paris in 1923 another incident occurred that exemplifies how Claribel's strong self-regard protected her from humiliation. She had made a big scene in a shop and admitted to having caused trouble for one of the employees. But upon returning to the shop a year later, she not only felt no remorse but actually congratulated herself that the employees welcomed her back—presumably because of the likelihood of large purchases—despite the earlier ruckus.[48]

CLARIBEL AND GERTRUDE STEIN

Claribel could not abide Alice B. Toklas, and after Alice and Gertrude Stein moved in together, Claribel greatly reduced her contact with Gertrude.[49] One senses that Claribel did not gauge how enduring the relationship between Gertrude and Alice would be, since she told Etta that "Miss T. is living with Gertrude this winter."[50] Claribel's antipathy for Alice sometimes caused her to decline Gertrude's invitations, but on other occasions they would get together, normally with Alice tagging along.

Despite their dislike for Alice, both Claribel and Etta remained in touch with Gertrude and kept her apprised of her work's reception in the United States. In 1914 Claribel wrote to Gertrude about her "fast growing American fame" and described a reading of Gertrude's work she had heard in Baltimore.[51]

When in Paris, Claribel liked to acquire things out of the Stein household, and she was much more brazen about it than Etta ever was. It worked liked this: Gertrude would hem and haw about perhaps wanting to dispose of a certain piece, as she needed the space as well as some money to buy something else, and she wondered if Claribel might perhaps be interested in it. Claribel would then exclaim how interested she was, at which point Gertrude would invite her over to look at the piece. Not only that, but Claribel would then encourage Gertrude to let her know of other pieces that she might have for sale.[52]

CLARIBEL IN MUNICH DURING WORLD WAR I

Not only was the amazing Dr. Cone remarkable in trying to acquire objects out of the home of her friend, but another of the oddest facts about her is that she spent all of World War I in Germany. Claribel was in Munich in 1917 when Germany went to war with the United States, and most of her fellow Americans were going home any way they could. Claribel herself tried to secure passage home on a westbound steamer, but on finding that a private stateroom could not be guaranteed, she decided to remain where she was.

Meanwhile, in the United States, her brother Ceasar was doing his best to secure passage for her from his end. He got in touch with all his political contacts, including high-placed individuals in President Wilson's administration, and he finally was able to make arrangements for Claribel to travel on a train reserved for the diplomatic corps, only to learn that she would not accept the terms since it would mean sharing a compartment on the train and coming without the ten to fifteen trunks that she always required when traveling. Her brother is said to have "hit the roof" when he learned of her stubbornness even in the face of the Great War.[53]

In any case, Claribel had too many possessions to pack quickly, and there was no one to help her. Claribel would not leave her collection and could not take it all along. Throughout the war, then, she lived openly among the Germans as an American, was treated well, and on the whole avoided being branded as "the enemy." She regarded herself as neutral between the two parties and was indeed quite sympathetic toward the plight of the Germans.[54]

What was it like in Germany for an American? Perhaps because of her fear of censorship, we get little hint of political problems in Claribel's wartime letters. In 1915 she blamed the shortness of her letters—what Etta was "good enough to call literature"—on the fact that it was illegal to write long ones because of the strain on the censors.[55]

On one occasion she explained to Etta how she was awakened by a knock at the door and was told it was the police. Although the ensuing encounter was not pleasant, it was nowhere near as awful as when she was "hauled up in the middle of the night."[56] The record is silent on exactly what that involved.

Claribel spent the war years living in the residential Regina-Palast Hotel in central Munich, which she found deliciously unconventional and basically very comfortable. She had three lovely rooms to live in and a balcony, as well as an extra room on another floor without charge for storage of her belongings. She felt that this place was a splurge worth treating herself to, reckoning that it was all right to "leave less to my heirs" in order to cater to her own comforts.[57]

Claribel benefited still further from the fact that few tourists came to Germany during the war, which made it possible for her to monopolize more space in the hotel to house her ever-growing mountain of possessions. Writing home at the end of 1919, she reported that the end of the war also brought an end to this happy state of affairs. As the hotel was full again, she either had to pay for the spare storage room or give it up. She chose the latter course.[58]

At least in the beginning, Claribel seems to have viewed the war as something of a lark. The country had not yet experienced years of grinding hardship, and Claribel—along with most of the German population—felt a jolt of new vitality at the prospect of war. In 1915 she described the German nation and its people as "inspiring"[59] and expected them to succeed in winning the war.[60] Like most people, too, she idealized the common soldier, and she enjoyed being able to supply the soldiers with cigarettes. On one occasion she gave a hundred cigarettes to a young woman for her husband at the front because the lady always saved the best places at concert halls for Claribel.[61]

In 1915 even the food situation seems to have been more or less normal. Claribel wrote to Etta of dining at a fashionable restaurant in the course of her normal social rounds and went on to explain that since the war began, names of dishes were no longer in French on the menus, but there was plenty of food to go around.[62] But the supply of food seems to have worsened soon thereafter. In 1916 she described how people were losing weight, which was not entirely a bad thing, she pointed out.[63] A few months later, she persisted in this optimistic view. Even as she admitted to having been hungry, she claimed to recall her hard times in Germany with pleasure at having improved her figure, although she also confessed that thin people were actually dying from lack of food. As she put it, "During the war all the fat people had disappeared from Germany—more correctly expressed—all the fat of the people had disappeared from Germany."[64]

Cut off from the United States and her family during the war, Claribel was quite naturally concerned about money and the amount she was spending. In Germany she had no easy way to replenish her funds. She continued to rely on the Cone Mills, which did extremely well during World War I, when the need for army uniforms greatly increased the demand for fabric; yet no one could send money to Claribel from abroad, and for some reason she always felt poor. She admitted that the cash limit had its good sides "to keep one in check when one is possessed of the ever-increasing love of antique 'objets'—and a passion for auction sales."[65]

She was quite concerned as to how much money she could afford to spend each day, and she asked Etta to inquire of brother Ceasar what his opinion was.[66] She was worrying about this issue partly because it affected how much she could afford to tip people. In any case, the problem was solved by her cousin Heinrich Rosengart[67] of Munich, who offered to support her with the understanding that she would reimburse him after the war—which of course she did.

While food may have been scarce in Germany during World War I, art and music were not. Claribel continued going to concerts and visiting art museums, auctions, and dealers, perhaps even more than before the war. It was at this time that she began thinking of setting up a small museum in her apartment, as the Steins had done so successfully in Paris.

By regularly attending professional lectures and concerts, looking for art, and dining out with friends, Claribel occasionally encountered people of high station. One day she even ran into—and bowed to—the prince regent, Luitpold.[68] On another occasion, she reports with glee, her majestic appearance drew the attention of the kaiser himself.

Only very occasionally did the real horrors of war intrude upon her active social life. Yet for all her acceptance by and goodwill toward the German people, being an enemy alien in time of war cannot have been easy. A rare self-criticism captured in a letter written in the summer of 1916 suggests that, despite her rosy letters home, years of reclusiveness were hardening Claribel's naturally misanthropic bent: "With my bad habit of isolated exclusiveness—perhaps the fear of having other bad habits intruded upon or interfered with, I go about for the most part alone. I am growing more and more a recluse and sometimes I wonder when I get back among my own friends again—will I know how to carry on a conversation."[69] In the same letter Claribel goes on to indulge in some very dark thoughts about the expendability of people—thoughts that horribly presage the coming decimation of her fellow Jews in her beloved Germany.

One privation of war that she certainly felt—because it only increased her isolation—was the fact that for more than two years Claribel could not receive letters from home. Although her brother Ceasar died on March 1, 1917, she only learned about the event a year later, when a message sent through Spain finally reached her.[70] Ironically, the first letter to arrive after the war, dated May 9, 1916, was a letter from Ceasar himself.[71]

In her first letter back to her family after the war, in August 1919, Claribel reports that she is beginning to get things to eat from the United States and sends affectionate greetings to a list of family members so long that she jokes about wearing out the censors. Yet even her light tone cannot conceal the social withdrawal that the war's disruption of her correspondence had caused.[72]

Incredibly, although Claribel had been well served by her cousin Heinrich during the war, she seemed to have forgotten his generosity when the war was over; for by 1920 their relationship appeared to have become strained. Claribel resented her cousin's continual requests for food and goods from the United States, and she spoke about him ungenerously as acting as if he needed food when he didn't.[73] Annoyed as she was with her savior, Claribel was punctilious about repaying her debt. Moreover, she dutifully relayed Rosengart's requests for money and goods and again asked that food boxes be sent to him as quickly as possible.

Claribel's Return to the United States

By late 1919, World War I was at an end, and yet Claribel was still in no rush to return to the United States. Even after being cut off for nearly six

FIGURE 4.3

Claribel Cone, circa 1920.

Photograph by the Bachrach Studio,
Ellen B. Hirschland Archives

years from family and friends, she used any excuse to delay her passage home. She came up with such explanations as not being able to book a whole room on a ship (rather than just a berth); having to get on a long waiting list for passage; her unwillingness to travel in cold weather; and the fact that she had put down such deep roots "that it will take more than horses to drive me away."[74] Claribel also wrote home that she could not travel because an abscessed tooth had caused an enlargement of her thyroid gland, and she did not feel "physically nor mentally equal to cope with the difficulties and indecencies of travel in these troublous times."[75]

The year 1919 drew to a close and Claribel still did not return. She was by then fifty-five years old, and her letters speak of her having aged (although couching this news as a compliment to herself), almost as if to prepare her family for changes in her appearance: "I am an old lady now—with almost white hair—I have gotten to the point where people say of me—'What a —— woman she <u>must have been</u>!' Do not expect to find me young and charming. Remember Rip Van Winkle and his long sleep."[76]

She also thanked Etta for offering to give her a bed in her own apartment, which Claribel said she would accept for her first night, but she did not want Etta to prepare her apartment for her in any way, explaining that she could not "think of inflicting you with my idiosyncrasies." She went on to say that she would love to take a hotel and to use her apartment as an "office," and she dreaded the notion of having someone ring the doorbell when she was in the bathtub. Hotels, she claimed, could provide protection against unwanted visitors.[77]

As usual, Claribel left everything to the last minute—even the renewal of her passport. And she was still hoping to have the luxury of traveling in her own stateroom.

Writing from Munich, supposedly on the verge of going to the Netherlands to embark, she complained of all the red tape and the running around to arrange this and that.[78] Late in 1919 she was still making purchases, doing Christmas shopping, and thinking about how to get all her possessions home.

Etta must have been responding to this or a similar comment when she wrote back, in one of the rarely preserved letters from her to Claribel, "I only hope you are not letting your things bother you, for you are far too important a human being to be worn out & hampered by the care of your possessions."[79]

Etta's advice doesn't seem to have done any good, however, for soon thereafter she received a letter from Claribel summing up the situation: "My things are piled up about me—and this is symbolic of my mental state—confusion."[80]

By March 1920 she was really, finally, making arrangements to come home, albeit with strict stipulations as to how she was willing to travel. Here are the requirements she set out for the travel agency, insisting that she have physical comforts at any cost: "Conditions 1) comfort above all else—an airy well-lighted outer room—to myself somewhere about the middle of the ship—and as near the top (i.e. Deck A) as possible."[81]

Now that Claribel had a room booked on the boat and all was clear for her return passage, she was obviously still daunted at the thought of packing. The necessity of getting herself back was causing her much anguish, especially in regard to the practical details. Writing to Etta, she expressed it like this:

I am so rushed—This unpacked mass of material with which I have been living—and which has been developing in geometrical ratio the last few years . . . "hangs over my head like a sword of Damocles" I was about to say. Better perhaps would be—is threatening me like a Frankenstein monster . . . anyway I hope to get out of this mess alive. You are right— do not let <u>things</u> consume you. But on the whole I find <u>things</u> so much more satisfactory than people.[82]

She reported that she had not used her return ticket from the last time she went to Germany (although in the intervening years she had lost it) and had convinced the North German Lloyd shipping company to refund the $150 to her. In general she was making progress but still overwhelmed; she admitted to being *technically* ready to leave, but in practical terms, the

FIGURE 4.4

One of Claribel's trunks, at the Baltimore Museum of Art.

Photograph by Nancy H. Ramage

things continued to bog her down.[83] And in an outburst of nervousness, she worried about inventorying her objects, claiming that German law required her to write down every single item she possessed and planned to take out of the country, on pain of having items confiscated if they did not appear on her list.[84]

Finally, on April 25, Claribel wrote, "I am off for Holland—after a struggle with the growing monster Frankenstein—my belongings—and shall be most happy to see you soon I hope—"[85]A week later Claribel wrote from The Hague, "I <u>am on the way home</u>!—so far so good. altho. last days of packing a nightmare! Mr. Laming has gotten me just what I want on Deck A—Room 33—of the boat . . . A Room for 3 people—that is <u>a room for C. C.</u>—it will cost between $500–$600. but I shall no doubt be comfortable."[86] The next day she wrote further details of her passage and of the required taxes she had to pay, even on objects she had brought back and forth with her from the United States several times before.[87]

When Claribel Cone sailed from Europe, she closed an exciting and remarkably comfortable chapter of her life. After World War I she continued to be interested in medical policy but was no longer personally involved in teaching and research. During her long medical career, she was a successful pathology researcher, professor of medicine, and writer. Her characteristically bold career choice shows her courage and willingness to buck the tide at a time when few women of means had careers at all, and her success is an indication of her exceptional vigor, intelligence, and stamina in pursing her unusual choice. In later years, when she tired of medicine and shifted her focus to art, Claribel showed the same strength of character by never looking back. Without compunction she abandoned a field in which she had achieved eminence for one in which she had as yet no standing. And she pursued this new career with such vigor that her accomplishments in medicine pale beside the name she made for herself as a collector of modern art.

The Roaring Twenties

During World War I and for several years before and after, Claribel and Etta added little to their collections of art. Etta's severe depression following the death of her brother Moses in 1908 lasted for years, draining her will to study and learn. Nor was she attracted by the idea of European travel but rather centered her life around her family in Baltimore and Blowing Rock.

Yet the flame that had glowed so brightly in her breast just a few years earlier was not entirely dead. In 1910 Etta wrote to Michael Stein asking him to buy her a Renoir lithograph.[1] And another letter written to Gertrude around the same time shows that Etta still longed for her Paris life and friends.

A year later, Etta began teaching school in Blowing Rock, increasing her commitment to the area and to her widowed sister-in-law, Bertha. Yet she pleaded for news from Gertrude, asking about "the Matisses and Picassos and other people I know and admire in Paris."[2]

In 1914 Europe disintegrated into war. For the next four years travel abroad was impossible, making moot the question of whether Etta would have recovered enough to begin collecting again. For her part, Claribel was only mildly interested in art and collecting at that time. Living in Germany on a reduced income throughout the war, she was in any case in no position to make large-scale purchases.[3]

When Claribel finally returned to Baltimore in May 1920, she, Etta, and their brother Fred took up residence together in three adjoining apartment suites on the eighth floor of the Marlborough Apartments. This

FIGURE 5.1

Flat Top Manor, the home of Moses and Bertha Cone, built from 1900 to 1904 in Blowing Rock, North Carolina.

Photograph by Nancy H. Ramage, 1993

solid Beaux-Arts apartment house still stands at the corner of Eutaw Place and Wilson Street, in what was then a fashionable section of Baltimore. The Cones' front windows looked out on Eutaw Place, a wide and gracious avenue with a parklike mall in the center, where the sisters were often seen sitting and taking the air in their long, old-fashioned dresses.[4]

Fred Cone bore a strong family resemblance to his sisters but was less determined and more retiring. In his youth he had worked in the family's cotton mills and earned himself a certain reputation for daring by buying a car when few people had one. In his later years he exhibited some of that same temerity by buying artworks on his own. Claribel was enraged with her brother for not having consulted his sisters, and it took all of Etta's diplomacy to smooth the rift. Yet eight years after Claribel's death, when Fred again bought paintings on his own—including two Bonnards and a Vuillard—Etta was as annoyed as Claribel had been earlier.[5]

Fred's apartment was a continuation of Etta's, with a door connecting them. Claribel originally also lived next door, in the apartment adjoining

FIGURE 5.2

*The Marlborough
Apartments, at the corner
of Eutaw Place and Wilson
Street, in Baltimore.
Three adjoining eighth-floor
apartments that belonged
to Etta, Claribel, and Fred
Cone housed the entire Cone
art collection, uninsured,
from 1920 to 1949.*
Photograph by Nancy H.
Ramage, 1990

on the other side, but after she filled her large apartment with paintings, sculpture, furniture, books, mementos, and piles of supplies, she left it as it was and took another suite on a lower floor for sleeping. Their three apartments on the eighth floor were designed like railroad cars, long and narrow, with seventeen rooms all together, most of them quite small, opening off snakelike halls. After Claribel died in 1929 and Fred in 1944, Etta retained the three original apartments, leaving them very much as their occupants had furnished them.

Etta's apartment was the center of activity, and it was there that the three Cone siblings dined together. Both Fred and Claribel paid Etta for each meal—and for those that they missed if they canceled too late. Claribel enjoyed the stability and convenience of the joint household but felt immune to any restrictions of routine. She seldom arrived on time, leaving Etta and Fred to sit down irritably without her at their punctually served meals that had been prepared by the cook. When Claribel finally did show up to join the group, an argument invariably ensued. Adamant about her right to independence, Claribel would declare, "Etta, if my way doesn't suit you, I will dine elsewhere!" The wounded Etta would dissolve in tears—much to the discomfiture of any guests who chanced to be present.[6]

In the summer of 1922, Claribel and Etta set off for Europe in search of art, establishing a pattern that they would follow until Claribel's death seven years later. It was fifteen years since Etta's last visit to the Continent, but it appears that her interest in the old life had finally reawakened. By this time, too, Claribel was also deeply interested in art. Though not so knowledgeable as her sister, she turned the full attention of her keen mind to its study and was soon as heavily involved in the art scene as Etta. Following World War I, moreover, the Cone sisters were far better off financially than before. For all of these reasons, 1922 was the year when their buying of modern art deepened from a serious hobby into a passion.

In July 1922 the sisters bought several works directly from Picasso and Matisse, six paintings from the Paris art dealer Bernheim-Jeune, and one from Durand-Ruel. The following year they bought ten works—most of them recently completed—by Matisse.[7]

Oddly, the sisters' accounts of those heady days convey no sense of the excitement they must have felt—and that Etta certainly felt later in life—when making their momentous acquisitions. In fact, in Claribel's account books, the purchase of major works of art is mixed in randomly with those of the most mundane items of daily life. In one list, for instance, Claribel puts the purchase of a major painting from Bernheim-Jeune somewhere between buying shampoo, picking up skirts at the department store, and getting a number of small items from the drugstore:

Remember

1. Hairwash
2. Bernheim Jeune pay 32500 fr.
3. Cohen pay 1665
4. Bon Marché skirts
5. Drugs 20 fr

      alcohol 1 pt. 1850

      borax 1.00

Another list of Claribel's gives a rare view of the rather strange activities she felt needed to be done. We know from her own and others' accounts that Claribel was a compulsive hoarder, and the following list may represent her desperate attempt to stay organized:

List of things to do
1. Look for corsets
2. Place bed room slippers in [?]
3. Look over scarves
4. Look over white lace
5. Look over black lace
6. Alcohol in bottles
7. Change corset old pink for new salmon
8. Count lace - white
9. Count lace - black
10. Count jewelry
11. Place jewelry
12. Place silver boxes[8]

First Major Purchases in Paris 1922

During their first summer in Europe following the war, Claribel and Etta frequently viewed paintings together and consulted each other before making a purchase. Among the first acquisitions was Matisse's *La Malade*, or *The Convalescent Woman*, a painting that had been in Leo Stein's collection. In July 1922 Claribel or Etta—it's not clear which one—bought the painting through the Bernheim-Jeune Gallery in Paris for four thousand francs.[9]

Ellen Hirschland, who often visited her great-aunts at the Marlborough Apartments, recalled:

I remember being told by Etta as a youngster that the subject of this painting was Madame Matisse. Since the canvas was painted in Toulouse, where Monsieur and Madame Matisse had gone to stay with her parents during her pregnancy,[10] I speculate that the woman is indeed Madame Matisse lying in bed resting, possibly just after the birth of her first child, Jean Gérard, who was born on January 10, 1899.

The Convalescent Woman is a departure from Matisse's traditionally Impressionist pictures of the 1880s. His travels with his bride in 1898 to Corsica and in 1899 to the south of France near Toulouse greatly influenced his use of color, which became ever more brilliant. With its large swaths of remarkably intense colors, the painting verges on the abstract.

At around the same time as the previous purchase, Claribel bought a painting with a totally different subject by Matisse, *The Pewter Jug*. Etta put down the initial two thousand francs, and Claribel later paid the balance of the painting's cost—twenty thousand francs.[11]

The artist painted this lean, powerful still life around 1917. His pleasingly muted colors—gray, puce, lavender, grayish green, and black—highlight a silver dish holding orange and yellow fruit. The tabletop tips up in Cézannesque manner to display the objects, including a pair of sandals, and the folds of cloth and the shadows depart from a strictly representational style. Matisse reinforced the spatial oddities of the picture by showing the base of the pewter jug distorted by the glass. He particularly liked the jug's swirling lines, and he used the object in several paintings over the years.[12]

Claribel may have been attracted to *The Pewter Jug* in part because she loved the color lavender. Until some years ago, the storerooms of the Baltimore Museum of Art contained laces and fabrics still in the lavender tissue paper in which Claribel and Etta had wrapped them more than half a century earlier.[13]

Among her purchases in 1922, Claribel bought a Matisse that was a difficult picture to appreciate: *Woman with a Turban*.[14] This brutally aggressive painting had belonged to Leo Stein, which may in part account

FIGURE 5.3

Henri Matisse, The Convalescent Woman, *or* La Malade, *1899. Oil on canvas. 18 ⅝ x 15 ⅛ in. Baltimore Museum of Art. The artist hyphenated his signature at this time because another artist, Auguste Matisse, was painting then too, and Henri wanted to make sure that the public did not confuse the two. Henri Matisse stopped hyphenating his name, for the most part, when Auguste died in 1931, but occasionally he continued the practice, as on* Interior with Dog *(see fig. 7.11).* Courtesy of BMA, 1950.225

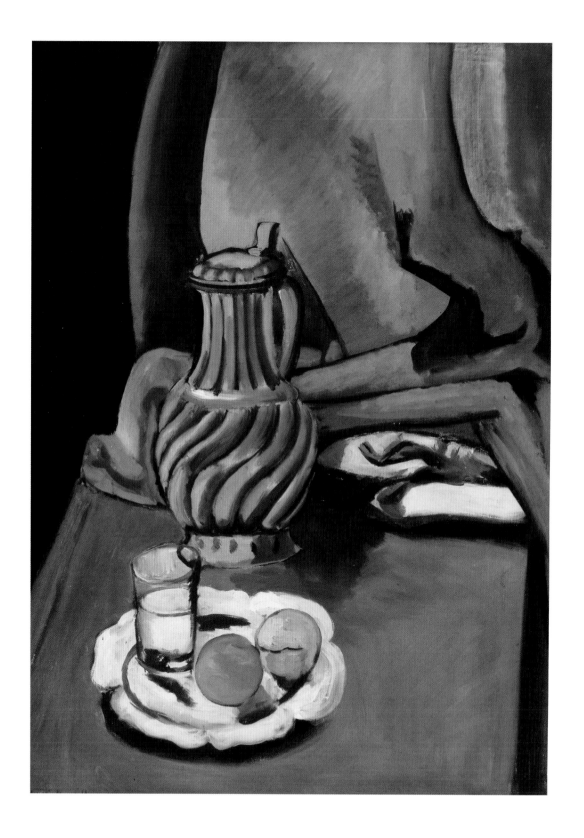

for Claribel's interest in it. Yet even with Leo as her guide, it was a rare person in 1922 who would have spent more than five thousand dollars on such a painting. Matisse's model Lorette stares back here at the viewer with iconic features subtly askew. Framed starkly by the white turban, black hair, and dark green background, her pale over-life-size head fairly leaps off the canvas.[15]

Surely the great highlight of the summer of 1922 for Claribel Cone must have been having her portrait drawn by Picasso. Etta's friend and companion Nora Kaufman, who survived her by many years, recollected that she had accompanied Claribel for the single sitting with Picasso.[16] But if we needed proof of how insufficient documentary evidence can be, we have it in the fact that neither of the Cone sisters' diaries or letters contain so much as a mention of this momentous event.

FIGURE 5.4

Henri Matisse, The Pewter Jug, *or* Le pot d'étain, *1916–17. Oil on canvas. 36 x 25 ⅝ in. Baltimore Museum of Art.* Courtesy of BMA, 1950.230

FIGURE 5.5

Henri Matisse, Woman with a Turban, *1917. Oil on canvas. 32 x 25 ¾ in. Baltimore Museum of Art.* Courtesy of BMA, 1950.229

In 1976 Ellen Hirschland heard about the making of the portrait from Siegfried Rosengart, son of Heinrich Rosengart (a cousin of the Cone sisters, mentioned in the previous chapter) and an old friend and art dealer in Lucerne, Switzerland. With huge enjoyment, Siegfried and his daughter, Angela, recounted Picasso's description of the event, told to them many years earlier, which Ellen in turn recalled:

Picasso described Claribel looking under her petticoats, reaching for the 1000 francs from her underskirt to pay for the drawing. He had fun imitating Claribel, and must have been laughing about it, as Siegfried did in the retelling.

Ellen Hirschland also liked to tell the story about how the director of the Baltimore Museum of Art mimicked Claribel:

After the Baltimore Museum received the Cone Collection and household possessions by bequest, I remember seeing Adelyn Breeskin sitting at her desk with her feet on one of the embroidered pillows from the Cone establishment, imitating the benefactor Claribel Cone as seen in Picasso's drawing.

One of Matisse's drawings that Etta bought in 1923, entitled *The Plumed Hat*, came from Matisse's son Pierre, who had a gallery in New York. The subject is the model Antoinette Arnoux wearing a wide-brimmed hat,[17] which Matisse himself fashioned using a straw foundation, black ribbons, and feathers he had bought.[18] This work was one of a series of sixteen drawings and three paintings that Matisse made of her in 1919. (One is a picture of only the hat.) Etta's drawing is a particularly sensitive rendering of Antoinette's face looking forward, with light shadows on her left cheek and chin, and the hat sitting securely on her head. Etta was particularly fond of this drawing and hung it in her bedroom.[19]

By the summer of 1923, Claribel and Etta began buying newer works by Matisse rather than concentrating on those he had painted in the earliest years of the century, as they had done the previous summer. Back in Baltimore that year the Cone sisters delivered a joint lecture on Matisse and Cézanne to an art forum. By this time they were both taking aesthetics courses at Johns Hopkins University from the art historian and philosopher Dr. George Boas. Moreover, Claribel's fascination with art had all but replaced her interest in a medical career. She may have regretted

leaving medicine to a certain degree, but claimed that "art seems to attract me more than medicine these days—which is bad—for I know little of art—and more of medicine."[20]

Lest we take the sisters' chosen path for granted, it should be remembered that until quite recently the critics almost universally dismissed Matisse paintings from the 1920s and 1930s as "decorative." The period was considered his least important—a sort of blank space separating his radical early Fauve style from his late and spectacularly innovative cutouts. Put off by Matisse's failure to follow his contemporaries into Cubism, critics dismissed him as stale, lacking in courage, distinctly unmodern. It was not until 1986—when the National Gallery of Art in Washington, D.C., mounted a groundbreaking exhibition, *Henri Matisse: The Early Years in Nice*—that the artist's pre-Depression-era reputation emerged from the doldrums.

OTHER PAINTINGS OF THE 1920S BY MATISSE

Matisse's *Anemones and Chinese Vase*, purchased by one or the other of the Cone sisters in 1923, was the kind of picture the critics long regarded as "just pretty." But if one looks at it objectively, it is an extraordinary work. At first glance, the subject seems simple: the interior of a room with a vase of flowers on a table, a large chair, and the corner of a bed. But nothing is haphazard about the composition. The table is presented to us at an angle, with the near corner cut off. This tactic, an idea that Matisse adapted from Cézanne's unusual way of showing perspective, was typical of his work. The vase and lemons on the table would seem at first to be falling off, but in fact they are sturdily set on the table. The humorously sketchy bottom half of one of Matisse's women in Middle Eastern pantaloons[21] merges with the striped yellow wallpaper, which in turn merges with the flowers and their stems.

Matisse adds to this commotion by putting a red tile floor to the left of the table, a flowery green and yellow rug to the right, and diagonal green and red stripes on the pillow and caramel-colored chair behind. He holds the composition in check, however, with the black bedspread and broad gray baseboard leading back to the lighter gray table from the right. A surprising flat wall of pink takes up much of the left background. Nothing

FIGURE 5.7

Henri Matisse, The Plumed Hat, *1919. Graphite. 20 ⅞ x 14 ⅜ in. Baltimore Museum of Art.* Courtesy of BMA, 1950.12.58

Henri Matisse, Anemones and Chinese Vase, *1922. Oil on canvas. 24 x 36⅜ in. Baltimore Museum of Art. This painting evidently was bought not from Matisse himself but rather from the Bernheim-Jeune Gallery, probably by Claribel Cone, while she and Etta Cone were in Paris together between June 14 and June 25, 1923. Artworks in the Cone Collection were purchased by one or the other sister, individually.*
Courtesy of BMA, 1950.248

if not audacious, this wildly patterned and colored interior yet manages to pull together so pleasingly that the casual observer might dismiss it as unplanned and merely "decorative."

The Chinese vase of the title, now in the Matisse Museum in Cimiez near Nice, was a favorite prop and appears in many other paintings, and the vivid and unpredictably branching anemones were Matisse's favorite flowers. Etta also loved anemones, which may in part explain why she would have been attracted to this painting. And by 1923 Etta and Claribel had both developed a deeply felt appreciation for what Matisse was trying to do. Unlike so many others both then and now, they understood and were attracted to the artist's innovative experiments with composition, color, and point of view—combined so intriguingly in *Anemones and Chinese Vase.*

In *Odalisque Reflected in a Mirror,* Matisse was clearly fascinated by the idea of the double image seen at different angles—as were many other artists both before and after him.[22] We therefore see two views of the

FIGURE 5.9

Henri Matisse, Odalisque Reflected in a Mirror, *1923. Oil on canvas. 31 ⅞ x 21 ⅜ in. Baltimore Museum of Art.*
Courtesy of BMA, 1950.250

model, who wears nothing but low-slung, poufed trousers and a necklace. After the young woman's slightly pouting face from the front, the profile in the mirror comes as a surprise. The rich array of checks and patterns, verticals, horizontals, and diagonals plays against the solid pink curves of the woman's body.

Unlike Claribel, Etta preferred dealing with artists rather than dealers, especially when it came to her old friend Henri Matisse. On this matter, the Lucerne art dealer Siegfried Rosengart reported that Matisse would set out pictures for Etta to consider, proposing to her that this or that would be a good addition to the Cone collection of Matisses.[23] *Odalisque Reflected in a Mirror* is one of the paintings that Etta bought directly from the artist in the year he painted it.

However, Etta did not always buy Matisses from the artist himself. In September 1923, she bought a work he had painted three years earlier called *Grande falaise, les poissons*, or *Large Cliff, Fish*, from the Bernheim-Jeune Gallery in Paris. Like Gustave Courbet and Claude Monet before him, Henri Matisse loved to paint the jagged rocks at the resort town of Étretat on the Normandy coast. During the summers of 1919 and 1920 he painted many renditions of this scene, including three executed at the same spot, showing fish lying on the sand. One shows an eel; a second, two rays. Etta bought the third painting, which shows a pale lavender cliff and beach and sun-bleached blue sea set off by assorted fish on a bed of brown-green seaweed. Etta is said to have hesitated to buy the painting because she was afraid the fish were suffocating as they lay on the beach with no water. But Matisse himself is said to have reassured her, claiming that he had had someone water the fish frequently so that they would not die.[24] Whether the fish had been kept wet or not, the transaction went forward.

In 1925, on her annual pilgrimage to Paris, Etta bought *Interior, Flowers and Parakeets* from Pierre Matisse, the artist's son, on July 6,[25] a few months after it was completed. The painting's ravishing colors and feeling of deep space fit in with the sense of taste reflected in Etta's other purchases of the period.

Matisse portrays the interior of his apartment on Place Charles-Félix in Nice.[26] In a reversal of the usual light receding into dark to give the impression of perspective, he contrasts the bright sunlight of the back rooms and window with the filtered light falling on the table, wall, birdcage, and hangings in the foreground. This layered use of light to draw our eye back to a window or door leading to the outside puts *Interior, Flowers and Parakeets* in the company of seventeenth-century Dutch painters, most particularly Pieter de Hooch.[27] Matisse also draws our eye rearward with the zigzag from the canted angle of the table in the foreground to the rug in the room behind, while a vertical screen suggests still a third room beyond.

FIGURE 5.10

Henri Matisse, Large Cliff, Fish, *or* Grande falaise, les poissons, *1920. Oil on canvas. 36 5/8 x 29 in. Baltimore Museum of Art.*
Courtesy of BMA, 1950.233

Matisse loved birds and often kept them around wherever he was. Familiar with this painting from her great-aunts' home, Ellen Hirschland recalled that she was amazed to see a huge birdcage in the Matisse home in 1936. This painting, in fact, held a special importance for her, because it was through it that she first came to understand just how unusual her great-aunt Etta was:

I had always taken Aunt Etta's fascinating home for granted. No one ever told me that she was known for anything but being a special aunt, for whom one dressed up, especially when visiting her apartment. My sisters and I always had what we called "an Aunt Etta dress."

In 1933, when I was fourteen years old, some relatives took me to Chicago to see the World's Fair, and I was astonished to see Aunt Etta's Interior, Flowers and Parakeets *hanging on the wall of the Art Institute. How did they know about it? How come they borrowed it?*

That was when I first became aware of the fact that my aunt's artworks were more than pleasant decorations and that she was an art collector of note. Her modesty ensured that it never came up in our conversations. It was typical of her not even to mention anyone else's interest in her or her possessions.

CLARIBEL AND THE DECORATIVE ARTS

Claribel's serious if somewhat haphazard interest in the decorative arts had begun in Germany during the war. Then, in the summer of 1923, while Etta was visiting Milan, Claribel stayed in Paris to visit museums—especially the Musée des Arts Décoratifs—for Claribel wanted to become a connoisseur like her sister but by her own admission was unwilling to sacrifice her creature comforts for learning's sake. For example, she always left time for leisurely bathing in the morning before going out to study art.[28]

Her shopping expeditions began to center on places that specialized in decorative items. Claribel reported to Etta that when she was buying a shawl for her, the shopkeeper asked "12000" francs for the item, but then

Claribel in her letter crossed out the final zero, complaining that "one gets so mixed up with these large figures that a 0 more or less seems to make little difference."[29]

In August 1924, while Etta was traveling in the south of France, Claribel met an Oriental-rug dealer in Paris, a Jew from Turkey whom Claribel promptly dubbed "the Arab." In describing fellow Jews to Etta, Claribel invariably refers to them as "they" rather than "we." This may have been due to religious reasons as much as snobbery, for when registering at the Regina-Palast Hotel in Munich in 1919, she wrote in the space for religion the German word *Freigläubig* (agnostic).[30]

In the time-hallowed manner of his profession, the rug dealer flattered her shamelessly, and Claribel loved it. After buying several Turkish rugs from him, she wrote to Etta about the encounter with obvious relish and apparently no second thoughts, telling her that "the Arab from Constantinople" had invited her to go into business with him.[31]

The "friendship" blossomed apace, with Claribel placing ever-greater confidence in this man although he was offering her carpets at what she called "fabulous" prices.[32] It was not long before Claribel's new friend introduced her to another Jewish dealer, a Mr. Ararat, whom she found less than honest. Whatever her beliefs, it is clear that she held herself apart from (and above) these Jewish businessmen from the Middle East. It is equally clear that she thoroughly enjoyed their attention and their show of esteem.[33] "The Arab" told her that his son was in love with her and told her, too, that he liked how she beat him at a bargain, offering to take anything she would offer because he needed the money. In the end, Claribel decided against the "bargain rug" since she decided she did not need it.[34]

PURCHASES FROM THE STEINS

In the 1920s Michael Stein frequently served as the conduit for sales from Gertrude Stein to Claribel and Etta Cone. While the Cones regarded him as a close friend who was entirely impartial, private communications among the Steins show that the whole family thought the Cone sisters were pushovers and easy marks.

Claribel trusted Michael completely. In 1923 she wrote to Etta that "he hates to see us stung—he hates to see us put big money in things which are not worth it."[35] Going on in the same vein, she declared that Michael's wife, Sally, was just as protective of them. Had they ever caught wind of the Steins' real opinion of them or found out how the Steins connived behind their backs, both sisters presumably would have been tremendously hurt.

The Steins' correspondence is filled with sly reports of how they were using their friendship to soften up the Cone sisters. In an undated letter from the early 1920s, for instance, Gertrude wrote to Michael, "I am practically sure that Etta is not prepared for any big deal this year; but shall try to pull off a small one."[36] In the same vein, Michael wrote to Alice Toklas in 1925:

> The Cones came last night & Sally at once got busy for Gertrude. She has sold 9000 francs worth without the Favre pictures. Pretty swifty as Allan [son of Michael and Sally] would say. I also spoke to them about the Laurencin and they seemed interested.[37]

Yet for all of the Steins' maneuvering, it was certainly the Cones who profited in the end.

Gertrude tried to tempt Etta to buy the manuscript of *Three Lives*, her first published book, which Etta had so laboriously typed for her in 1905 and 1906. In June 1924 she wrote Etta that she was planning to sell the manuscript of *Three Lives* for one thousand dollars, and she wondered if Etta might want to buy it, considering the fact that she had a "connection" with it. "I think it's kind of foolish but I wouldn't want you to think that I would sell it to any one else without telling you about it first."[38] Insulted by the offer, Etta responded coolly, saying that she needed the money to buy a Renoir instead. Yet Etta was incapable of being overtly nasty, and her letter rejecting Gertrude's offer ends graciously, saying that she appreciated Gertrude's remembering her interest in the book.[39] Michael tried again two years later, writing Gertrude that he would "try to work her for the manuscript of *Three Lives*."[40]

Despite her rift with Gertrude, Etta would always treasure her friendship with the Stein family. Both sisters admired their insightful opinions on art, and both sought out pictures that had been in their collections. Etta bought art from the Stein collections in part because she liked the pictures and in part to help her friends out financially. But not wishing others to know that they needed money, she remained secretive about these purchases all her life.[41]

In 1925 Claribel acquired a painting from the Stein collection, paying Michael Stein and his wife ten thousand francs (roughly $460 at that time) for Gertrude's Laurencin. In her expense book she noted that the Thannhäuser Gallery wanted the picture she had just purchased. At the same time two other dealers, Messrs. Flechtheim and Kahnweiler, were trying to sell the painting on Gertrude's behalf.[42] This is a good example of how, by the 1920s, dealers were vying with one another for good modern paintings with a respectable provenance, and association with the Steins made a work even more appealing.

Marie Laurencin's clever 1908 portrait *Group of Artists* distinguishes each of its famous subjects with a characteristic trait.[43] As a nod to Picasso's experiments with point of view, Laurencin paints him in profile with his eye facing frontally. Picasso's friend Henri Rousseau used to say to him, "We are the two great painters of the age, you paint in the 'Egyptian' style, I in the modern."[44]

Laurencin, who was nearsighted, shows herself squinting. Gertrude Stein describes her first meeting with Laurencin like this:

> Guillaume Apollinaire brought her to the rue de Fleurus, not on a Saturday evening, but another evening. She was very interesting. They were an extraordinary pair. Marie Laurencin was terribly near-sighted and of course she never wore eyeglasses, no french woman and few frenchmen did in those days. She used a lorgnette.[45]

Fernande Olivier later also recalled Marie's myopia as well as her long nose and beautiful long hair, shown here tied up in a bun.[46] The less-charitable Alice B. Toklas wrote about her thick lips.[47]

In the painting, Laurencin appears to be offering the flower she holds to her lover Guillaume Apollinaire, a heavyset man who looks like other portraits of him at the time.[48] Gertrude said he was "very attractive and very interesting. He had a head like one of the late roman emperors."[49] Fernande Olivier described him as having "a rather pear-shaped head, the features pointed, kindly and distinguished, with small eyes very close to his long, thin hook of a nose, and eyebrows like commas."[50] Fernande Olivier herself, at right, looks coy, and her notably long fingers are conspicuous. Again, Gertrude Stein provides the description in a word portrait:

FIGURE 5.12

*Marie Laurencin,
Group of Artists,
1908. Oil on canvas.
25½ x 31⅞ in.
Baltimore Museum of Art.*
Left to right: *Pablo
Picasso, seated, with his
dog, Frika, on his lap;
Marie Laurencin, standing
and holding a flower; the
poet Guillaume Apollinaire,
Laurencin's lover, seated;
and Fernande Olivier,
Picasso's mistress, with her
chin resting on her hand.*
Courtesy of BMA, 1950.215

She had the Napoleonic forefinger quite as long if not longer than the middle finger . . . her voice was lovely and she was very very beautiful with a marvellous complexion. She was a big woman but not too big because she was indolent and she had the small round arms that give the characteristic beauty to all french women."[51]

Laurencin makes a playful reference in this painting to Fernande Olivier's love for elegant hats by placing the flower vase behind her so that the stems seem to decorate the top of her head. On the same subject, Gertrude Stein wrote:

Fernande was the first wife of a genius I sat with and she was not the least amusing. We talked hats. Fernande had two subjects hats and perfumes. This first day we talked hats. She liked hats, she had the true french feeling about a hat, if a hat did not provoke some witticism from a man on the street the hat was not a success. Later on once in Montmartre she and I were walking together. She had on a large yellow hat and I had on a much smaller blue one. As we were walking along a workman stopped and called out, there go the sun and the moon shining together. Ah, said Fernande to me with a radiant smile, you see our hats are a success.[52]

Gertrude Stein claimed to have bought *Group of Artists* directly from Marie Laurencin and said that this was the first picture the artist ever sold. Fernande Olivier gave a more low-key account, uncolored by Gertrude's inevitable self-promotion and fanfare. She reported that "it was mainly for fun, and due to Picasso's encouragement, that the Steins bought a painting by her: quite a large composition, consisting of a seated group of some of the artists she knew."[53]

In 1926 it was Etta's turn to buy a painting from Gertrude, and she chose Cézanne's *Bathers*. In keeping with her desire for complete discretion regarding purchases from her friend, no price for the transaction is recorded. Leo and Gertrude had bought the painting from the art dealer Ambroise Vollard in 1904 for about $250,[54] and it was one of the first Cézannes in their collection. Writing in the third person (as was her habit), Gertrude describes their finding the painting in Vollard's shop:

> They began to take an interest in Cézanne nudes and they
> finally bought two tiny canvases of nude groups . . . They
> frequently bought in two's because one of them usually liked
> one more than the other one did.[55]

A photo dating to around 1907 shows the painting conspicuously displayed in the Steins' studio on the rue de Fleurus,[56] where it remained until 1913 or 1914, when Gertrude kept it after the division of their household.[57]

Later, during World War I, when both Gertrude and Alice were in the south of France driving ambulances for the French army, Paris came under attack from bombs, and they began to worry about the safety of

their paintings. Michael Stein went to their apartment and took several paintings, including Cézanne's *Bathers*, and sent the package to them in Nîmes via American Express. He advised them to put the paintings in a bank vault where "at least you will have them where they need cause you no anxiety."[58] After the war the painting was returned to Paris, and in Man Ray's 1922 photograph of Gertrude and Alice, it is hanging once again in the rue de Fleurus studio.[59]

Gertrude Stein, who had owned *Bathers* for so long, spoke about Cézanne at the Baltimore Museum of Art in 1934, as part of a lecture trip.[60] When Etta Cone realized that Gertrude was coming to Baltimore, she wrote to offer her apartment for Gertrude to use as a meeting place to see people, if she wished. Etta wrote that she looked forward to entertaining both Gertrude and Alice, offered to make arrangements for them, and planned to postpone her trip to the South until after Gertrude's lecture.[61] Gertrude replied that she would have no time to be with Etta, whereupon Etta made reservations to go south before Gertrude's arrival. Ellen Hirschland later recalled the situation:

FIGURE 5.13

Paul Cézanne, Bathers, *1890s. Oil on canvas. 10 ⅝ x 18 ⅛ in. Baltimore Museum of Art.*
Courtesy of BMA, 1950.195

FIGURE 5.14

Alice B. Toklas and Gertrude Stein in their apartment on the rue de Fleurus, Paris,
1922. Photograph by Man Ray. Note Cézanne's Bathers *(fig. 5.13) hanging on*
the wall above the jug at the left end of the mantelpiece.
Courtesy of BMA, 1950.1985.5

In my diary of 1936, I wrote that on December 23, 1934, we drove in town
to see Aunt Etta and to say good-bye, as she was leaving Baltimore because
Gertrude Stein was coming. This was so that she would not have to endure
this slight in person.

It was because Etta went to see her family in Greensboro to avoid being
further snubbed by Gertrude that I was lucky enough to attend the lecture that
Gertrude Stein gave at the Baltimore Museum of Art on December 28, 1934.

Tickets were scarce as there was great interest from the public and the capacity of the area where the talk was to take place was limited.

Having no auditorium, the Baltimore Museum of Art had chairs set up in the large open area used as an entrance hall. The audience was seated on folding chairs, not designed for comfort, and there was a spirit of anticipatory restlessness. As I was seated in the front row, both Gertrude Stein and Alice Toklas brushed past me before and after the lecture and I got a close look at them. The speaker was dressed in a masculine way, had a short haircut, and made an altogether manly impression.

When this massive-looking woman began to speak, a hush came over the crowd, and everyone was suddenly attentive; we were all captivated by the magnificence of Gertrude Stein's voice. For the next hour, there was no coughing or chair shuffling; everyone was totally absorbed; her delivery was like a diva singing, with beautifully modulated cadences rising and falling.

To return to Cézanne's *Bathers:* it was widely seen in the Stein atelier and had a great influence on other artists. The art critic Leo Steinberg claimed that Picasso had this little painting in mind when he produced *Three Women* (now housed at the Hermitage in St. Petersburg, Russia),[62] and it bears a clear relation to his seminal *Demoiselles d'Avignon* in the Museum of Modern Art.[63]

Cézanne's paintings of bathers also inspired Henri Matisse. In 1899, five years before Leo and Gertrude Stein bought their little painting, Matisse bought a Cézanne *Bathers* he would treasure all his life. Even when mired in poverty, he refused to sell it. Finally, in November 1936, he donated his *Bathers* to the Musée de la Ville de Paris (housed in the Petit Palais) and wrote to his friend the museum director:

> Yesterday I consigned to your shipper Cézanne's *Baigneuses*. I saw the picture carefully packed and it was supposed to leave that very evening for the Petit Palais.
>
> Allow me to tell you that this picture is of the very first importance in the work of Cézanne because it is a very solid, very complete realization of a composition that he carefully studied in various canvases, which, though now in important collections, are not the studies that culminated in the present work.

I have owned this canvas for 37 years and I know it fairly well, I hope, though not entirely; it has sustained me spiritually in the critical moments of my career as an artist. I have drawn from it my faith and my perseverance: for this reason allow me to request that it be placed so that it may be seen to the best advantage. For this it needs both light and perspective. It is rich in color and surface and only when it is seen at a distance is it possible to appreciate the sweep of its lines and the exceptional sobriety of its relationships.

I know I do not need to tell you this but nevertheless I think it is my duty to do so; please interpret my remarks as a pardonable testimony of my admiration for this work which has grown ever greater since I first acquired it. Let me thank you for the care you will give it for I hand it over to you with the deepest confidence . . .

Henri Matisse[64]

When viewing the picture in the Petit Palais in Paris, Ellen Hirschland, who knew this story, was always touched by the caption, *Don de* [*Gift of*] M. *Henri Matisse*, which acknowledged in a simple way how much this work by one great artist had meant to another. Yet in the spring of 1982 she was amazed to find that

the caption, modest as it had been, was gone. I wrote to the administration of the Petit Palais expressing my disappointment and astonishment that after Matisse had expressed so movingly what Bathers *had meant to him, there was not even a word of acknowledgment of him as the donor. By return mail, I received a letter of apology, assuring me that the omission had been rectified.*[65]

In 1926 Gertrude Stein sold her Cézanne *Bathers* to Etta. The sale was complicated, but because Gertrude kept everything—including visiting cards and every letter she ever received from anyone (because "you never knew who would become famous")—we know a great deal about it.

It appears that in July 1926 both Claribel and Etta were in Paris but Gertrude was away. Knowing that his sister was in need of cash, Michael

Stein agreed to negotiate with the Cones for the purchase of various items. By the end of July, all was amicably concluded, and Michael wrote Gertrude that in addition to facilitating the sale, he had helped the sisters (especially Claribel) transport their many acquisitions:

> The Cones leave tomorrow for Lausanne and of course I had
> to go today and pack off our car full of Claribel's truck so that
> she will get off. Her room was full of it as usual.[66]

Etta particularly loved the Cézanne, which she kept in prominent view in her dining room, hanging alone on a narrow wall. Since she took out no insurance, she used to hide the tiny *Bathers* under her bed when she went away on a long journey.

CLARIBEL'S MOST MONUMENTAL PURCHASES

"Not since Moses has anyone seen a mountain so greatly," wrote Rainer Maria Rilke of Cézanne's many representations of Mont Sainte-Victoire.[67] On June 26, 1925, Claribel purchased Cézanne's *Mont Sainte-Victoire Seen from the Bibémus Quarry* from Bernheim-Jeune in Paris, just one day after the gallery bought it at the Gangnat sale at the Hôtel Drouot. With her typical sangfroid, Claribel paid the colossal sum of 410,000 francs, about $18,900 on the day of the sale[68]—the highest price either sister ever paid for a painting.

The painting is one of about sixty Cézanne studies of this mountain, which looms over the town of Aix-en-Provence where Cézanne was born, grew up, and lived most of his life. Both sisters loved the painting, and Claribel gave it pride of place in her apartment. Although *Mont Sainte-Victoire* was one of her favorite paintings, Etta because of her exquisite rectitude would not move it from her sister's apartment after Claribel's death.

Why is Cézanne's portrait of the mountain so monumental? In his unique way, the artist makes the mountain appear to hover *over* rather than *behind* the orange rocks of the quarry, so that the far distant mass becomes close and dominating. As always in Cézanne's work, the composition is beautifully organized, with the diagonal of the mountain's left side balanced not only by the asymmetrical line of its right but also by the tree at the far right. The placement of trees against the rocks makes for a

nearly abstract pattern of colors. Yet the objects have three-dimensional
form, with highlights and shadows that make them recognizable as well as
abstract. With his simple palette of colors—blue, green, orange—Cézanne
manages to re-create the whole spectrum of nature while giving a sense of
solidity and stability to the scene.

In 1926, Claribel Cone purchased what is perhaps the most daring work
of art in the entire Cone Collection—Matisse's *Blue Nude*. Just four years
after she began studying and buying modern painting in earnest, Claribel
had the audacity to acquire this painting, which she bought from the John
Quinn estate sale at the Hôtel Drouot in Paris, at a cost of 101,000 francs
(around five thousand dollars at that time).[69]

Twenty years earlier, Leo Stein had bought the painting, in the year it was painted, 1907. When he moved out of the apartment where he had been with Gertrude for some years, at the rue de Fleurus, he took *Blue Nude* with him. About five years later, he sold the picture to a French dealer, after which it changed hands several times until the prominent New York lawyer John Quinn bought it in December 1920 for six thousand dollars.[70] In 1926 Claribel's purchase price was a relatively low one for a major painting by Matisse, which may reflect its lack of appeal for most buyers.[71]

Claribel obviously felt no qualms about it. Back in Baltimore, she hung *Blue Nude* in a prominent position in her narrow apartment at the Marlborough Apartments, where it produced a stupendous—if largely negative—effect on the unwary visitor, much to her enjoyment.

Blue Nude was originally exhibited with the title of "Tableau No. III" in the Salon des Indépendants of 1907.[72] Leo Stein saw it there and bought it—the last of his remarkable Matisse acquisitions. Describing his purchase much later, Leo called it *Blue Woman* "but really a pink woman in blue scenery."[73]

The painting, hanging on the wall of Gertrude and Leo's Paris atelier in 1907, had struck most visitors speechless. One of Gertrude's friends found herself at a loss for words, wondering what to say about it in the presence of the artist. When she blurted out, at last, that she did not think she herself could take the position of the model, Matisse is said to have replied, "Neither could I!"[74] But if most visitors to the Stein studio were appalled by *Blue Nude*, Gertrude Stein records that the painting had one instant admirer not afraid to flout conventional taste:

> One day the five year old boy of the janitor who often used
> to visit Gertrude Stein who was fond of him, jumped into her
> arms as she was standing at the open door of the atelier and
> looking over her shoulder and seeing the picture cried out
> in rapture, oh là là what a beautiful body of a woman. Miss
> Stein used always to tell this story when the casual stranger in
> the aggressive way of the casual stranger said, looking at this
> picture, and what is that supposed to represent.[75]

Etta and Claribel's nephew Edward Cone, who later came to appreciate the picture, recalled that when he first went to visit his aunts, Claribel insisted that he not enter her apartment until she could accompany him because she wanted to be present when he first saw *Blue Nude*. He reported that he thought it was "revolting" and said so.[76]

Contemporaneous artists, on the other hand, did not despise the painting. According to the German painter Hans Purrmann, who joined Matisse's art class in 1907, Matisse and André Derain had had a friendly bet as to who could paint the best figure in blue. When Derain saw Matisse's *Blue Nude,* he immediately conceded defeat and destroyed his own painting.[77]

Five years after Leo bought *Blue Nude,* he loaned it to the Armory Show of 1913, an exhibition that provided the American public with its first real exposure to modern art.[78] The show created a hostile explosion in New York, and viewers who saw it at the Art Institute in Chicago proved even more irate. According to the president of the Chicago Law and Order League, "The idea that people can gaze at this sort of thing without it hurting them is all bosh. The exhibition ought to be suppressed." Local critics chimed in with, "Our splendid Art Institute is being desecrated," and, "Matisse has examples of the nude that should be turned to the wall." On the last day of the exhibition, students from the School of the Art Institute expressed their disgust by burning copies

of *Blue Nude* and Matisse's *Le Luxe II* in effigy.[79] An art critic described Matisse's works as "the most hideous monstrosities ever perpetrated in the name of long suffering art." [80]

What was all the fuss about? The painting is, in fact, still difficult to understand but incredibly daring, powerful, and dramatic. Matisse creates momentum by leaving preliminary lines visible, suggesting that the model's elbows have only recently moved. Even the upper body seems to have just shifted, as again we see the shape of the woman's left breast reflected in paler colors behind her. Yet Leo Stein stopped buying Matisse works after his purchase of *Blue Nude* because he implausibly found the rhythm in his paintings insufficient.[81]

Matisse had a habit of making a model in clay before undertaking a large painting in oil. But when the large figure for *Blue Nude* fell and broke, he completed the painting without finishing the sculpture.[82] Afterward, in a reversal of his usual process, he made a smaller study of the reclining nude, which he later cast in bronze.

The knowledge Matisse brought to this work included an intimate acquaintance with the long series of reclining nudes painted by Giorgione, Titian, Goya, Courbet, Manet, and many others before him.[83] He also

FIGURE 5.17

Henri Matisse, Reclining Nude I (Aurore), *1907; this cast circa 1930. Bronze. 13 ½ x 19 ⅝ in. Baltimore Museum of Art. This is the bronze that was modeled after* Blue Nude.
Courtesy of BMA, 1950.429

brought a reverence for Cézanne, who died the year before *Blue Nude* was painted. Cézanne had pioneered the technique of combining different points of view that would later serve Matisse, Picasso, and other modern painters so well.

PURCHASES FROM DEALERS

In 1928 the Cone sisters bought no fewer than thirty-eight works of art made by eighteen artists. Breaking somewhat from their marked preference for Matisse, they struck out boldly in new directions. Etta no longer held back in making large purchases. Upon reaching Paris in June, she promptly bought Renoir's *The Washerwomen* from the Bernheim-Jeune gallery for a large sum, roughly equivalent to six thousand dollars.

The Renoir oil depicts country women doing their laundry in a stream in the town of Essoyes, where Madame Renoir had lived before her marriage. From Renoir's letters we know that he was attempting to emulate eighteenth-century painters (in his words, "like Fragonard, only not so good") and had returned to his softer and more painterly style after having worked on linearity for some time.[84]

Familiar with all of her aunt's paintings, in 1946 Ellen Hirschland made the following discovery of a study for the painting:

At Etta's request, my husband and I were always on the lookout for works of special interest to her. In the spring of 1946, I noted the similarity of a Renoir watercolor at the art dealer Otto Gerson's gallery. We asked him to reserve the picture. I phoned Etta, introduced Gerson, and arranged for him to visit her. On the following Monday morning, Gerson took the sketch to Baltimore to show it to her. After her customary research on any picture's pedigree, she purchased it.

From the early days of their friendships with Matisse, Picasso, and Gertrude Stein to their acquaintance with the art dealer Dikran Kelekian, whom Claribel met only two years before she died, dealers, artists, and collectors formed a large part of the Cone sisters' social contacts. In Paris they patronized the Galerie Durand-Ruel, the auction houses, and, most

often, Georges Bernheim of the Galerie Bernheim-Jeune. In Lucerne they bought from Siegfried Rosengart. And in Lausanne they bought from Paul Vallotton, brother of the artist Félix Vallotton.[85]

The sisters' correspondence is filled with analyses of these people's personalities and lives as well as with the valuable works they sold. Both Etta and Claribel paid close attention to the character and reliability of their sources, and the quality of their collection suggests that they got at least as much benefit out of the dealers as the dealers got of them.

By 1927 Claribel had become quite friendly with Paul Vallotton and his wife, Marianne. Mrs. Vallotton was beautiful and one of the few women Claribel admired without reserve. She also enjoyed the attention the Vallottons showered on her, and she shared their boundless appetite for gossip about the art world.

While visiting Lausanne in the summer of 1927, Claribel wrote her sister, "It seems I do nothing these days but write letters and talk with the Vallottons, and get up late in the morning."[86] Claribel recognized that Paul was quite a talker, and she noticed that he was far more interested in a story if *he* was telling it than if she was.[87]

Perhaps because her own life was so strictly "proper," Claribel especially liked to dwell on social improprieties. She would often relay stories to Etta that both sisters would have considered racy. One of these had to do with a model Paul Vallotton called Bonnard's "wife" but Claribel thought should be called his mistress: "Why can I not call a spade a spade?" Claribel went on to talk about Félix Vallotton's "harmless little flirtation" with a beautiful American girl "that made him more interesting even than his pictures do."[88]

Claribel clung to the friendship with Paul Vallotton but must have had some lingering uneasiness about their client-salesman relationship. Perhaps to allay these qualms, she again sang his praises and claimed he had unlimited devotion to the Cones, and she touted his utter and unquestionable trustworthiness. She liked how he called attention to the faults (as well as the merits) of the paintings he was trying to sell to her, and she claimed he was devoted to the sisters—"not only commercially."[89]

Another dealer, Dikran Kelekian, who was knowledgeable about decorative arts and therefore someone Claribel could not ignore, was not a person she liked—an opinion the Vallottons apparently shared. Claribel wondered if Mrs. Vallotton's visit to see her one day might have been partly to get out of the house while the Kelekians were visiting, since "they appear to be very trying guests—however important commercially, artistically, and financially!"[90]

As with "the Arab," Claribel was well aware that she was a potential buyer and Paul Vallotton a wily businessman. Eager to believe in him, however, she threw caution aside and touted his virtues to Etta, calling "this good man" commercially shrewd and natively honest.[91] Etta's understated comments are considerably less enthusiastic. In 1927 she wrote Claribel, "Miss K. [her companion Nora Kaufman] says she does'nt [sic] envy you any V's but Paul—and I not even Paul."[92]

Although Etta did not like Paul Vallotton personally, that did not stop her from buying from him. In August 1927 he billed her for several works, and a few weeks later, she bought a pastel by Degas and an oil painting by Paul's brother, Félix Vallotton, called *The Lie*.

In 1927 *The Lie* was a rather daring subject. A couple is locked in an embrace on a sofa at the left side of the picture, while a small vase of

FIGURE 5.19

Félix Vallotton, The Lie, *1897 or 1898. Oil on canvas. 9 7/16 x 13 1/8 in. Baltimore Museum of Art.*

Courtesy of BMA, 1950.298

flowers stands on the right. As inextricably intertwined as the lovers, the picture's reds and reddish browns cause furniture, tablecloth, wallpaper, and the couple to meld together in a semiabstract pattern fascinating to the eye. The artist has indicated the corner of the room by a subtle shift in the spacing and color of the wallpaper's stripes.

The Lie is the first of a series of Vallotton oil paintings depicting such intimate scenes, although an earlier group of woodcuts and ink-and-gouache sketches on similar themes had been published in the distinguished arts magazine *La Revue Blanche* in 1898.[93] Like Edvard Munch, Vallotton uses powerful imagery to suggest the disloyalty of both men and women. The daring design of this painting creates a far greater impact than expected from its small size.

Etta continued to dislike Paul Vallotton, but, like Claribel, she trusted him. Three years after acquiring *The Lie*, she bought four pieces of sculpture from the Lausanne dealer in a single day.

The year that Etta bought *The Lie*, 1927, was in fact a banner year for Paul Vallotton. In August Etta made several substantial purchases from him, and that same month Claribel bought *A Pair of Boots* by Vincent van Gogh and an ancient Egyptian bronze cat. Vallotton received twenty-five thousand Swiss francs (about $4,900 at the time) for the Van Gogh and another painting by Odilon Redon, *Peonies*.[94]

Short of money for models, Van Gogh often painted self-portraits or other readily available subjects, such as objects in his room or his own clothing. In this case, shortly after his arrival in Arles in 1887, he painted his boots. The varying degrees of brown in the background hark back to the mustier colors of Van Gogh's earlier paintings made in his native Holland.

A Pair of Boots first belonged to the Parisian dealer Julien "Père" Tanguy, who received it from the artist in exchange for paints.[95] As soon as Paul Vallotton got the painting, he sent a photograph of it to Claribel in Baltimore and offered to sell it to her.[96] By 1927 there was considerable interest in Van Gogh, and there were many fakes. When Claribel bought this painting, no catalogue raisonné of the artist's works existed. The first one, put together by J.-B. de la Faille, was not published until the following year. Claribel seems to have trusted Vallotton on that score. But when she wrote Etta four days later, she was suffering a rare moment of doubt about her purchase:

FIGURE 5.20

Vincent van Gogh. A Pair of Boots, *or* Shoes, *1887. Oil on canvas. 13 x 16 1/16 in. Baltimore Museum of Art.*
Courtesy of BMA, 1950.302

I am not so pleased with my Van Gogh—it is so unlike his <u>better</u> (more forceful more mad style perhaps) style, and the pair of shoes will not grace my living room with beauty—however—it is a Van Gogh – almost certainly—Mr. V. [Paul Vallotton] says <u>sans doute</u> [without doubt].[97]

These comments suggest that Claribel bought the Van Gogh less because it pleased her than because she thought it would be a good investment. We know from her letters that she occasionally did buy with business rather than aesthetics in mind: "This suggests to me that it may not be a bad idea for us to get a few of those old Persian ceramics which will no doubt soon be picked over and exhausted."[98]

When Etta was considering a Van Gogh for herself, Claribel advised her to follow her heart and forget what others might have to say—"Why care a darn what anybody else says of it"[99]—and encouraged her to buy what she liked. Unfortunately, Claribel's advice turned out to be prophetic. Etta bought the Van Gogh from the Reinhart Gallery in New York and hung it in her living room. But when de la Faille's catalogue raisonné came out, she was alarmed to discover that her painting was not in it. Etta got in touch with Vincent van Gogh's nephew in Amsterdam, who in turn put her in touch with Mr. de la Faille—who pronounced her painting a fake. Deeply disappointed, Etta lamented to her sister-in-law Laura, "What will I do with it?" Laura replied, "Enjoy it."[100]

Claribel and Etta's discussion of Etta's projected purchase of a Van Gogh is just a small snippet from what must have been an ongoing dialogue between the sisters. Over the years, Etta's passionate addiction to learning had gained her an almost unparalleled understanding of the history and aesthetics of art. Despite her reluctance to put her own views forward, the depth of her knowledge—which informed all of her buying decisions—was recognized by those who knew her well. In 1923, four years before her death, Claribel wrote to thank her sister for having taught her so well, saying how much she had learned from her.[101]

Claribel may have had buyer's remorse about A Pair of Boots, but she could not have been happier about her Egyptian cat, for which she paid Paul Vallotton 4,500 francs.[102] The sisters had acquired little in the way of ancient art, and this purchase was a real departure for them. At the time, Claribel thought she was buying a piece from the New Kingdom (1550–1070 B.C.), but the piece actually dates to the much later Saïtic period (664–525 B.C.).[103]

Thoroughly besotted, Claribel mentions her Egyptian cat again and again in her letters to Etta, telling her what a thrill she gets from looking at it.[104] Far from resenting the stiff price she paid to Vallotton, Claribel rather found in it new proof of his good-heartedness and generosity. And the cat loomed so large in Claribel's estimation that no other work of art could touch it. She proclaimed that nothing Matisse could do could approximate in quality the beauty of her cat.[105] She also reported to Etta that Vallotton confirmed for her that the cat was "35000" years old (though she meant to say "3500") and that it was from the time of the pharaoh Ramses II.[106] In fact it was made about six hundred years after the reign of Ramses II.

FIGURE 5.21

Ancient Egyptian cat,
circa 664–525 B.C.
Bronze. 6½ in. high.
Baltimore Museum of Art.
Courtesy of BMA, 1950.405

Not long after the adored cat was delivered to the Marlborough Apartments, a visitor—Jacob Epstein,[107] another Baltimore collector and a longtime friend of the Cone sisters—inadvertently knocked the cat to the floor, and a piece broke off. Claribel made light of the incident in front of Mr. Epstein, who was naturally quite upset. But after he left, her consternation was extreme. She took the piece to various restorers both at home and abroad, but all urged her not to have it repaired.

Claribel did not live to find out that her bronze was incorrectly dated by the sellers, and we cannot know if that would have made any difference to her. But whatever its date, Claribel was smitten with it and remained so to the end.

CLARIBEL'S LAST PURCHASE

On September 20, 1929—just nine days before she died—Claribel bought Gustave Courbet's *The Shaded Stream at Le Puits Noir,* formerly called *The Grotto,* from Paul Vallotton for twelve thousand Swiss francs. In this

inviting picture, Courbet manages to convey the wetness of the water, the warmth of the sunshine, and a deep perspective into dark shadows beyond. Far less adventurous than many of Claribel's other purchases, the peaceful painting yet fills a notable gap in her collection. She was surely conscious of this when she decided to buy the Courbet, even knowing that she had little time left to enjoy it.

For Claribel knew that she was soon to die. In July 1929 she wrote Etta what amounted to a farewell letter, but she never sent it. Claribel addressed the letter to Etta at the Lausanne Palace Hotel, where she herself was staying, although Etta was at the time in Munich. She clearly meant for the letter to be found and given to Etta should Claribel suddenly die. These, then, are Claribel's intended last words to the sister who had been her dearest friend and companion all her life:

Last night I had a pain in my heart—the first one I have ever had. This morning my pulse omitted a beat on several occasions—for that reason—and in view of the fact that I have reached the age at which the eldest members of our family die I am writing this letter to say good-by to you my dearest sister who have always been so good to me. Also to my very dear Brothers sisters Nephews and nieces.

When one begins to grow feeble one is a useless member of society—so I should say I go without regret except for the momentary pang of regret (this is ink—not a tear although it should be that!—) of regret it may be to my dear Brothers and Sisters. Give my best-love to all . . . I should like you dear Etta to select from my things—or to buy for each of them something they may like—of course for you and the collection I should wish the suitable things saved.[108]

On September 20, 1929—two months after writing the farewell letter from Lausanne and just two months shy of her sixty-fifth birthday—Claribel Cone, having contracted pneumonia, suffered a heart attack and passed away.

6

A Tribute to Claribel

Etta Cone was devastated by the loss of her sister and spent several weeks gathering herself together before returning to the United States. She cabled two of her closest friends, Nora Kaufman and Mary Nice, both trained nurses, asking them to come over to Switzerland to help her collect her sister's body. She later said she wanted both of them so that neither would suffer the trauma of coming alone. Brother Fred Cone also came from Scotland to join Etta in Lausanne.

Arrangements had to be made for the body to be brought back to Baltimore. In deference to Claribel, Etta arranged for her sister's remains to travel on the new *Statendam* of the Holland-America Line. A special train had to be hired to transport the body from Lausanne to the port in France where it would be picked up by the ship.

It was complicated to get permits to cross the various borders with a corpse, but eventually they reached the required pier in France. When the ship arrived in New York in November 1929, brother Julius Cone went along on the mail boat to meet it in the harbor. Two of Claribel and Etta's sisters-in-law, Laura and Jeanette Cone, also came to New York to meet the group, which by then consisted of Etta, Fred, and Julius Cone and Mary Nice. (Nora Kaufman had had to leave Europe earlier to take up a new position at the Union Memorial Hospital in Baltimore.)

As soon as Claribel's body had been unloaded, the entourage left New York on the train for Baltimore, where they arrived at 6:00 P.M. Having waited so long, Etta was eager to have the funeral over, and at her request it was held that very night by candlelight.[1]

Etta must have been comforted by the many beautiful letters she received praising her sister and regretting her death. Gertrude Stein was one of the first to write. Her letter reached Etta while she was still in Paris waiting for the ship to New York:

> My very dear Etta:
>
> I have just had word from Mike of the death of Claribel and it has saddened me terribly, I was awfully attached to her . . . everything she did had an extraordinary quality all her own. I had not seen much of her in recent years but she made a very important and rather wonderful part of my Baltimore past . . .[2]

Other expressive letters came from the artist Ben Silbert, who had made the lovely etching of Etta (see figure 1.2, p. 7), from Bertha Cone (the widow of Moses), from Sally Stein, and of course from Henri Matisse. In response to his condolence letter, Etta wrote, "Allow me to express myself frankly in saying that knowing you and your great work was one of the great influences of her life as well as my own."[3]

Devastated as she was by Claribel's death, Etta continued acquiring new art apace. Like Alice B. Toklas, who later took up the promotion of Gertrude Stein's writings as a kind of mission after her partner's death, Etta viewed it as a solemn duty to Claribel to nurture the Cone Collection. Claribel's death, moreover, suddenly elevated the retiring Etta to an unprecedented position of power in the world that meant most to her—the art world. She had money, three decades of contacts, and an established reputation as a connoisseur. Unused to the position of command, she began to take on something of her late sister's dominant (and domineering) personality.

Claribel's death left Fred, the youngest of the Cone children, Etta's sole resident companion in the Marlborough Apartments. In true Cone fashion, brother and sister closed ranks, with Fred taking on Etta's old role as the faithful booster offering help and encouragement from the sidelines.

THE CLARIBEL CONE MEMORIAL CATALOGUE

Following Claribel's death in 1929, Etta decided that the most fitting memorial to her sister would be a catalogue of their joint collections of art. The

FIGURE 6.1

*Etta Cone in her apartment
on Eutaw Place, circa 1930.*
Photograph by Bertram S. Berney,
Ellen B. Hirschland Archives

preparation of this volume was an important project that occupied much of her time and energy until its publication and distribution in 1934.

Many of the items then in the collection were illustrated in full-page black-and-white reproductions. (Siegfried Rosengart wrote Etta near the beginning of the project asking if she wanted color reproductions,[4] but she evidently decided against it.) The foreword was written by Dr. George Boas, professor of philosophy at Johns Hopkins University, who had once given courses attended by both Claribel and Etta. He had been their close friend for many years. Boas particularly emphasized the importance of the collection as a unique retrospective of Matisse's work.

Etta commissioned Matisse to draw a posthumous portrait of her sister for the volume.[5] The initial discussion regarding Claribel's portrait seems to have taken place on December 17, 1930, when Matisse came to visit Etta and Fred in the Marlborough Apartments. Fred, in fact, vacated his small apartment so that Matisse could use it overnight. (Matisse was in the United States at the time to discuss arrangements with Dr. Albert C. Barnes[6] for the huge murals that Barnes had commissioned for his home in Merion, Pennsylvania.)

During his visit to the Cone apartments, Matisse pointed out to Etta that one of his paintings was dirty and asked for Ivory soap, tepid water, and a soft cloth. "He then washed the painting with his own hands," Etta reported to Laura Cone.[7] The artist's visit to Baltimore did not go unnoticed. In addition to publishing a photograph of Matisse in Etta's dining room, the Baltimore *Sun* also came out with a cartoon of the artist by Edmund Duffy, a legendary cartoonist who won three Pulitzer Prizes.

FIGURE 6.2

Henri Matisse in the dining room at the Marlborough Apartments of Etta Cone, Baltimore, December 17, 1930. Over the artist's left shoulder is his painting Large Cliff, Fish *(fig. 5.10). The other painting is Matisse's* Violinist and Young Girl, *or* Divertissement *(1921). The photograph was published by the Baltimore* Sun.
Courtesy of BMA

Charles Street Evening—Or Matisse Comes To Baltimore

With Respectful Apologies

FIGURE 6.3

Edmund Duffy, "Charles Street Evening—Or Matisse Comes To Baltimore," Baltimore Sun, *December 17, 1930.*

Newspaper cartoon courtesy of Jacques Kelly and the Baltimore *Sun*

In any case, Etta and Matisse appear to have discussed the drawing of Claribel's portrait. Soon after Matisse's return to France, he told Michael and Sarah Stein about the commission, and a few weeks later Margot Duthuit, Matisse's daughter and business manager, wrote to Etta to report that her father was studying photographs of Claribel.[8]

The drawing of Claribel had to be put on hold for various reasons. Matisse was under great pressure to work on the forty-two-foot Barnes mural. He had to deal with the problem of misinformation about the exact size of the Barnes space, which necessitated his making not one version of the mural but three.[9] Matisse also had to make several illustration plates for the first Skira publication of *Poésies de Stéphane Mallarmé*, begun in 1930. (Etta subsequently bought the whole maquette for this publication, including sketches and drawings.)

It was apparently during Etta's 1933 visit with Matisse in Nice that he promised to pick up his work on the drawings of Claribel.[10] From 1933 to 1934 he made four charcoal sketches of Claribel, all based on photographs and his own recollections of her. The fourth and last one he made—a close-up of her head—is the most successful in conveying her decided nature and strength of character. This last portrait may have been modeled on the reproduction of a photograph of Claribel that appeared in the *Evening Sun* in Baltimore, on April 8, 1911.

FIGURE 6.4

Henri Matisse, Dr. Claribel Cone, *1933–34. Charcoal. 23¼ x 16 in. Baltimore Museum of Art. This is one of four drawings of Claribel Cone commissioned by Etta Cone in 1930 and drawn by Matisse from 1933 to 1934.* Courtesy of BMA, 1950.12.71

Although the original intention was that Matisse would prepare a portrait of the recently deceased Claribel for the memorial volume, somewhere along the way it was decided that he should make a portrait of each sister instead of just Claribel alone, and it seems likely that Matisse suggested the change himself. In preparation for having her portrait drawn by Matisse, Etta went to the Galeries Lafayette and had some snapshots taken. These cost the equivalent of about twenty-five cents. Her portraits by Matisse were made from these photos as well as from the artist's memory.

DR. CLARIBEL CONE A REMARKABLE WOMAN

Her Work Is Chiefly In The Laboratory, But She Finds Time, Also, To Collect Book Covers And Old Boxes.

She Unties A String With A Hairpin While She Discourses Interestingly Of The Habits Of The Wary Bacillus.

DR. CLARIBEL CONE

Dolly and I discovered yesterday that to persuade Dr. Claribel Cone to talk to us about herself was one of the most difficult feats we had ever attempted.

Did we mention her laboratory work, she proffered a book cover of the period of the De Medicis, for our admiration.

Did we inquire concerning her published volumes, she showed us a wonderful old box which came from Florence, which is two or three centuries old, and which contains the most fascinating secret compartments imaginable.

She was willing to discuss Matisse, the French artist, leader of the school of independents, at length; she brought out specimens of his work to show us, but she was as wary as one of the germs with which she is so familiar of having the light of publicity thrown upon her.

It was only when we asked her questions categorically and demanded categorical replies that we finally wrung from her some part of the story of her career.

"I studied medicine at the Woman's Medical College in this city," said she. "At that time the Johns Hopkins had not been opened, but the Woman's College had an excellent faculty. Indeed, Dr. Cordell, its president, was the man who introduced the three-year course for a medical degree into Maryland.

"Before that most of the colleges had had a two-year course; now they have a four-year one, for education is becoming more and more thorough everywhere.

"No, I am not a bachelor of any woman's college, and I am sorry," she said in answer to Dolly's question. "I approve of the broad, pyramidal growth that the Germans demand; it seems to me that sometimes in this country our education is too much like a mushroom—most of it at the top.

"After I was graduated in medicine I did special work at my Alma Mater, and then went to Philadelphia and took up post-graduate work with some of the professors of the University of Pennsylvania. At that time women were not admitted to the university, but I had a tutor, and so had a chance to go on with my studies in pathology.

"A little later there was a competitive examination for resident physicians at Blockley Hospital, which I took and was admitted. There were five physicians appointed and three out of these were women; one of the women passed at the head of the list.

"I stayed at Blockley more than a year, and then I came back to Baltimore and took the general post-graduate course in the Johns Hopkins Medical School.

"I afterward occupied the chair of pathology at the Woman's Medical College and was a trustee of that school. Since then I have been engaged in research work in the laboratory at the Hopkins, and I have studied abroad a bit too."

"Tell us about that," begged Dolly.

"Well, I spent some years under Weigert at the Senckenberg Institute in Frankfort, Germany. Senckenberg was a friend of Goethe, and the two hundredth anniverary of the Institute was celebrated a few years ago. Weigert was a wonderful man. He was a cousin of Ehrlich, who has made such wonderful discoveries of late and a great friend of our own Dr. Welch. They were both students under Cohnheim, the professor of pathology at the University of Leipsic.

"Weigert died, probably as the indirect result of a septicemia which he contracted while working in the laboratory. Albrecht, with whom I worked at the Senckenberg also, and who was a brilliant man and a very lovable one—a poet as well as a scientist—died recently of tuberculosis, also contracted by coming into contact with the germ in his work.

"I was struck," said Dr. Cone, "in my recent visit to the Japanese laboratories, with the exquisite cleanliness which they show. The Japanese study in Germany, getting the best that that country can give them, and then go back and really improve upon conditions. For instance, the Japanese isolate the workers on micro-organism of infectious disease from the other workers. And they take pains to sterilize back."

"Did you meet Ehrlich?" I asked.

"Yes, I attended a course of lectures given by him and I also spent a short time in the Pasteur Institute, too short to be important enough to mention, though."

"And have you?" asked Dolly with wide-open eyes, "and have you isolated any new little germ, on your own account. Have you made any discoveries?"

It was then that Dr. Cone spoke lightly of mediaeval missals and showed us a few. She also exhibited to us a beautiful Buddha, and an illuminated sheet of music of the Middle Ages in which the notes were represented by small black blocks.

Now all this was fascinating, but it was aside the mark, so we put the temptation from us with strong hands and spoke severely to the temptress.

"How would you like to look at a nice tuberculosis germ through the microscope?" she said, coaxingly. "Have you never seen a tuberculosis germ? Well, I have a pupil coming and I could show you one without a particle of trouble if you would like it."

I saw in this an effort to evade the point and so I demanded the name of the particular species about the habits of which she had discovered things.

"There had been other work along

FIGURE 6.5

*"Dr. Claribel Cone,"
newspaper illustration,
Baltimore* Evening
Sun, *April 8, 1911.*

Ellen B. Hirschland Archives

The challenge of making these drawings seems to have meant a great deal to Matisse, for on May 24, 1934, he wrote his lifelong friend Simon Bussy:

> I am still at my portraits from photographs of my two lady
> art lovers from Baltimore . . . a somewhat arduous job (what
> work is not), particularly arduous because the imagination,
> the memory and the exactitude must collaborate to make
> something new, nevertheless very interesting because it bears
> on two completely opposed personalities and yet of the same
> family, since they are sisters. The one beautiful, of a great
> noble and glorious beauty, beautiful hair falling in ample
> waves in the old-fashioned way, satisfied and domineering,

FIGURE 6.6

Henri Matisse, Etta Cone, *1934.*
Charcoal. 27 ¾ x 16 in. Baltimore
Museum of Art. This is one of six drawings
of Etta Cone produced by Matisse for the
memorial catalogue in honor of Claribel Cone.
Courtesy of BMA, 1950.12.69

FIGURE 6.7

Photograph of Matisse in his
studio, "Pendant le Portrait
de Miss Etta Cone," 1934.
The unknown photographer
took this picture while Matisse
was working on his portraits
of Etta Cone, one of which is
on the easel.
Courtesy of the Archives
Matisse, Paris

the other of a similar majesty of a Queen of Israel but with a less obvious beauty, smooth hair and yet falling in beautiful lines like those of her face, but with a touching depth of expression, always submissive to her glorious sister, yet attentive to everything. Limited means: paper and charcoal . . . it is nearly a month since I have worked on them every morning—it is hard but I am learning much.[11]

A photograph of Matisse in his studio in 1934 shows the artist relaxing, while one of his drawings of Etta rests on the easel at the right side of the photo and another hangs on the wall still farther to the right.

Ellen Hirschland, trying to understand the similarity of the portraits to her aunt, studied them closely:

When I first began to analyze these drawings representing my aunt, to whom I was so close, I thought that in general, they bore little resemblance to her, except superficially. In striving for likeness, I thought, Matisse lost the spontaneity which was his forte. But as the years have gone by, and the more I've studied the sixth and final charcoal drawing, the more I think it looks like Aunt Etta as I knew her.

Matisse finally finished the drawings in 1934 and must have shown them to Etta in Paris. After that he sent them to Siegfried Rosengart, who was assembling the material for the memorial catalogue. In the volume, entitled *The Cone Collection at Baltimore-Maryland: Catalogue of Paintings-Drawings-Sculpture of the Nineteenth and Twentieth Centuries*, one of Claribel's portraits serves as the frontispiece and one of Etta's follows it.

A letter from Margot Duthuit to Etta suggests that her father wanted to give Etta the ten drawings to her as a gift. There seems to be no evidence of payment, but when the drawings were shipped, the valuation for all of them was forty thousand francs.[12] Etta framed some of these drawings and hung them for a while in the small room in Claribel's apartment along with Matisse's *Blue Nude* and Vallotton's *Portrait of Gertrude Stein*, a sort of reunion of olden times.

In 1934 Siegfried Rosengart arranged for the printing of the memorial volume in Germany—surprising at a time when it was difficult to close one's eyes to the presence of the Nazis. Etta said she had used a Jewish printer in Berlin by the name of Ganymed; on the other hand, she was a romantic who somehow believed she lived in a world set apart from politics. When the long-awaited catalogue arrived, each volume had a thin cover sheet on which appeared in a tiny typeface: PRINTED IN GERMANY . . . a stratagem to avoid having to print the dreaded words in the book itself. By that time, Ellen Hirschland remembers, even Etta could not hide from herself how unwelcome among her friends those three words would be.

Most of these wrappers were removed,[13] and it was part of my mother's task to remove them.

Each week when she took her customary lunch with her Aunt Etta, she would wrap six or eight catalogs in the special packing boxes that had been made for the purpose. First the paper wrapper with PRINTED IN GERMANY was thrown away, for it was on this thin sheet that the German publisher had printed his required identification. The knots on the outside of the package had to be made in exactly the same way on each parcel; this task, like all mechanical assignments in Etta's household, had to be done precisely as instructed or there would be trouble.

Etta felt strongly that the catalogues should be distributed only to people and organizations who would appreciate them. Roland J. McKinney, at that time director of the Baltimore Museum of Art, provided her with a list of museums.[14] Upon receiving a copy, Alfred H. Barr Jr., director of the fledgling Museum of Modern Art in New York, wrote Etta:

I want to thank you for the really magnificent catalog of your collection. I think this is by far the finest catalog of a collection of modern paintings that has ever been published. The reproductions are magnificent and the notes are interesting and complete. I can't tell you how grateful I am to you.[15]

The noted art historian and author Lionello Venturi also thanked her, first raving about the catalogue, then concluding with the compliment, "Above all it is a testimony of the high level and of the courageous trend of your taste, and this is as rare as admirable."[16]

Many members of the art world who did not receive a copy of the catalogue in the first mailings wrote to ask for one. Among these people

FIGURE 6.8

The Cone–Stein Room in Claribel Cone's apartment, 1941. Portraits of Claribel and Etta by Matisse flank Vallotton's portrait of Gertrude Stein (fig. 3.11). Although the room was in Claribel's apartment, almost all the artworks in it were acquired after her death.
Ellen B. Hirschland Archives

were Macgill James, assistant director of the budding National Gallery in Washington, D.C., and Curt Valentin, a New York art dealer who offered Etta an objet d'art in return.[17]

Of the many copies Etta distributed to museums, libraries, and other collectors, only one remained unacknowledged. Ellen Hirschland later discovered why:

One night at a dinner party I happened to mention to James Johnson Sweeney, director of the Guggenheim Museum, that Dr. Albert C. Barnes had not acknowledged receiving a copy of Aunt Etta's catalogue. He knew Barnes well and suggested to me that his reason for not acknowledging the gift was the fact that he hated Gertrude Stein and probably tied the Cone sisters together in his mind, thinking they were related, as so many people did (and do). Sweeney said Barnes liked Leo but disliked Gertrude and Michael.

To the best of my knowledge, Etta never saw the Barnes Collection, although Matisse wrote to her after the installation of the large Dance *mural into the Barnes Foundation building. He indicated that he was sure she would go to see it.*

During Etta's and her family's visit to Nice in 1933, Matisse arranged for them to see a version of the nearly completed Barnes mural. The artist said he hoped that eventually one of the murals originally designed for Barnes might be installed in a specially built Cone Museum.[18]

The catalogue had great sentimental value for Etta, and she was particular in choosing to whom she gave one, guarding every copy. Most were inscribed with the recipient's name as well as the donor's, which made the gift personal. Receiving the memorial catalogue became a sort of reward for interest in art or for a special relationship with Etta. It was not enough, for instance, to be a family member and to want a copy desperately. Etta had to come to her own decision to present the book, and receiving it was a mark of high esteem. But for Ellen Hirschland, Etta reserved an even greater mark of distinction:

Since Etta was making additions to the collection continually, the catalogue was obsolete before it was distributed. She gave me a large black album with photographs of each new acquisition, assuring me that my volume was the only one besides hers that was being kept entirely up to date.

It was typical of her thoroughness and thoughtfulness that she took great pains to describe to me in full detail how she had affixed her photos into her album.

When Etta died, the several dozen catalogs left over were sold on the public market, a breach of propriety which would, I believe, have upset her tremendously.

In 1950, just after Etta's death, a copy of the catalogue fetched about forty dollars. In 1975 the museum offered remaining copies to family members first, and then to the public, for eighty-five dollars apiece. Etta had felt that this memorial was a very private affair and disdained publicity in this endeavor, as in all others.

THE RIFT WITH GERTRUDE STEIN

In the memorial volume, Etta pointedly omits Gertrude Stein's previous ownership of a number of items in her collection, thereby misleading the reader about the provenance of these pieces. And in his introduction to the catalogue, George Boas also fails to mention Gertrude's influence on the Cones, while giving full credit to Michael, Leo, and Sarah Stein as early mentors. Gertrude can hardly have failed to notice that Boas, writing the introduction at Etta's behest, claimed:

> The collection was begun now some thirty years ago by the
> late Dr. Claribel Cone and her sister, Miss Etta Cone, who
> through their friends, Mr. and Mrs. Michael Stein and Leo
> Stein, came in contact with the leaders of what Mr. Roger Fry
> first called the Post-Impressionist movement.[19]

Not only that, but in choosing which works to include in the catalogue, Etta had omitted the portrait of Gertrude by Vallotton (figure 3.11, p. 52).

Edward Cone, nephew of Claribel and Etta, recalled that by 1933, relations between Etta and Gertrude had cooled sufficiently that Etta turned down her former friend's invitation to visit her and Alice, when they were staying nearby in the south of France.[20] And then, when Gertrude came to Baltimore to deliver a lecture the following year, the one Ellen Hirschland attended, Gertrude responded to Etta's warm invitation to visit her in the Marlborough Apartments with an abrupt refusal. Though Etta continued to write to Michael and Sarah, that invitation was the last direct communication she ever had with Gertrude.

7

Etta's Acquisitions of the 1930s and 1940s

During the 1930s, it was Etta Cone's practice to acquire at least one major Matisse artwork a year. The only exception was in 1939, the last year before World War II that shipments could be made from Europe, when her major purchase was Picasso's *Mother and Child*.

YEAR	MAJOR MATISSE WORKS PURCHASED
1929	*Reclining Nude III*, bronze, 1929
1930	*Large Seated Nude*, bronze, 1923–25
1931	*Two Negresses*, bronze, 1908; *Tiari with Necklace*, bronze, 1930
1932	*The Yellow Dress*, oil on canvas, 1929–31
1933	Drawings and plates for the book *Poésies de Stéphane Mallarmé*
1934	*Portraits of Claribel and Etta*, drawings, 1931–34; *Interior with Dog*, oil on canvas, 1934
1935	*Blue Eyes*, oil on canvas, 1935
1936	*The Pink Nude*, oil on canvas, 1935
1937	*Purple Robe and Anemones*, oil on canvas, 1937
1938	Several smaller oils on canvas, including *Small Rumanian Blouse with Foliage*, 1937; *Embroidered Dark Blouse*, 1936

In the 1940s Etta's purchases of Matisse's work were more irregular, although she made several important ones, including *The Striped Robe, Fruit, and Anemones* (purchased from Pierre Matisse) in 1940 and *Seated Odalisque, Left Leg Bent* in 1942. Meanwhile, of course, she was buying works by other artists as well.

At the time of Claribel's death in 1929, the core of the Cone Collection had been established. Etta saw as her remaining task to fill out and broaden a collection that was already fine. In addition to buying her annual Matisse, therefore, she also kept a sharp eye out for the work of artists she admired but did not yet own.

Each year Etta's arrival in Paris caused a considerable stir in art circles, a fact of which she was well aware. The once-shy sister apparently enjoyed the attention and the intense activity of her life abroad. A letter Etta wrote to her great-niece Ellen in July 1937 gives a glimpse of the string of astonishing purchases she managed to acquire in roughly a month's time:

> Life is fuller even than last year. The artists and dealers have gotten hold of the fact that I am here, and sometimes it amounts to being pestered . . . I have a new Matisse, a Picasso of the pink period, an Ingres drawing, a Seurat drawing and a Derain landscape. I expect to eat very cheaply for a year, but do come for lunch Christmas & I'll give you <u>every</u> kind of cheese on the market.[1]

When the English art critic Clive Bell delivered a talk in Baltimore at the opening of the Cone memorial exhibition on January 13, 1950, he remarked that *Large Seated Nude* was "the best Matisse sculpture" he had ever encountered.[2] Etta had bought the bronze—monumental in proportions if not in size—from Matisse in 1930 for thirty thousand francs. Ellen Hirschland remembered seeing the sculpture prominently displayed during her visits to Aunt Etta's home (figure 2, p. 215):

Matisse's Large Seated Nude *was placed in the center of a large table in Claribel's apartment where it looked tremendously dramatic. Etta told me that Matisse had asked his model to sit on a chair leaning backward and then made the sculpture of her without the chair.*

The sculpture inspires tension in the viewer, who expects the figure to tumble backward. But her sharp backward lean is in fact balanced by her heavy legs. Matisse may have been recalling here the semireclining figures in Michelangelo's *Tomb of Giuliano de Medici* in the Medici Chapel in Florence or one of the *Ignudi* on the ceiling of the Sistine Chapel.[3]

FIGURE 7.1

Henri Matisse, Large
Seated Nude, *1923–25.*
Bronze. 30¾ in. high.
Baltimore Museum of Art.
Courtesy of BMA, 1950.436

In 1931, Etta further increased her holdings of Matisse bronzes with
another major purchase—*Tiari with Necklace,* which the artist had completed only the year before. Matisse had traveled to Tahiti for a few months
in the summer of 1930 and was attracted to an exotic Tahitian flower called
a *tiari,* which somewhat resembles a gardenia. On his return, he adapted
the flower to look like a woman's head. Matisse's *Tiari with Necklace* has
been compared to Constantin Brancusi's *Mlle Pogany,*[4] but the sources
of the two sculptures are very different. *Mlle Pogany* is based on a young
woman Brancusi knew, while Matisse's *Tiari* was created out of a "found
object."[5]

Ellen Hirschland recalled this story from her aunt:

Matisse told Etta that as he looked at the Tiari sculpture one day, he suddenly got the idea
of putting a necklace around its neck. He asked Margot [his daughter] to give him the
gold necklace that she was wearing and placed it around the neck of the sculptured piece.
The Cone version of the sculpture therefore differs from the other nine casts of Tiari.

Henri Matisse, Tiari
with Necklace, *1930.*
Bronze. 8½ in. high.
Baltimore Museum of Art.
The necklace was one worn
by Matisse's daughter,
Margot (Marguerite).
Courtesy of BMA, 1950.438

On September 23, 1935, Matisse sent Etta a series of nineteen black-
and-white snapshots of a large painting in progress, saying:

> I am sending you some photographs representing various
> states of . . . a painting, reclining nude . . . the dates of the
> different states are indicated on the photos—I hope that these
> different works give you a little amusement—and my goal will
> be realized.[6]

On November 16, he sent photos of the painting's three final stages. Taken together, these twenty-two photographs document the painting's journey from a fairly conventional nude to the flowing forms of the strikingly stylized masterpiece we know as the *Large Reclining Nude*, formerly *The Pink Nude*.[7] In the first stage, a young woman lies on a couch beside a vase with flowers on an ornate chair. Her lower limbs are twisted to face the wall behind, creating a tension resembling that captured in Matisse's much earlier painting *Blue Nude* (figure 5.16). Her vacant but pleasant-featured head rests at a gentle angle on her bent right arm.

After many experiments with torsion, muscles, background, and the angle and features of the head, Matisse reduced the couch in the final painting to a dark blue ground crossed with white lines to form a check pattern. The blue ground is bordered by a bright red wall, which in its turn is topped by white crossed with larger green-outlined checks, like tiles. Both flowers and chair have been reduced to accents of color and abstract

FIGURE 7.3

Henri Matisse, Large Reclining Nude *or* The Pink Nude, *1935. Oil on canvas. 26 x 36½ in. Baltimore Museum of Art.* Courtesy of BMA, 1950.258

shape, which offset the sharp verticals of the model's raised right elbow and head (now small, fully upright, and facing front) and the weighty right angle of her left arm dangling heavily below. Gone is the tension in the torso, replaced now by a flowing, flat, unmodeled, and opaquely pink form remarkable for its balance, its handsome contrast against the blue, and its feeling of total calm.

Etta's response to this extraordinary photographic record has unfortunately not survived. But her actions are clear. On her summer trip to Paris in 1936, she bought the finished *Pink Nude* for nine thousand francs (roughly two thousand dollars at the time).

I was present when Matisse first showed Etta The Pink Nude. *I believe he especially wanted it and* Blue Nude *to be shown together. When Etta bought the new painting, she hung it in Claribel's "*Blue Nude Room,*" where the two faced each other on opposite walls [figures 3–4, pp. 216–17]. Matisse would have been astonished to see that these two colossal paintings were displayed in such small quarters.*

Matisse's decision to send Etta the photographs of the work in progress shows his forethought and indicates that he hoped all along that this large, bold, and seminal work would find a home in the Cone Collection.

Etta bought Picasso's *Woman with Bangs* from Gertrude Stein in 1929 or 1930,[8] although there had apparently been some talk of Claribel buying it instead. In an undated letter from Paris, an eager Michael Stein, "working" the sisters as usual, wrote of his progress to Gertrude, "We had the Cones out to supper and the Picasso is practically sold; but not decided to which Cone as yet."[9] Once again Etta's delicacy about her transactions with the Steins has concealed how much she paid.

In the two decades between Claribel's death and her own, Etta bought three portraits of different members of the Stein family and a few pieces that had once belonged to them. But if she occasionally bought a piece as a memento of earlier days, the era of Etta's dependence on outside influences was gone for good.

Leo and Gertrude Stein, on their first visit to Picasso's studio in 1905, had bought several pictures from him: *Woman with Bangs, Two Women at the Bar, Seated Woman with Hood,* and *Dozing Absinthe Drinker,* all from the artist's so-called Blue Period; and *Boy Leading a Horse* and *Young Acrobat on a Ball* from his Rose Period. For this bounty the Steins paid the young

FIGURE 7.4

Pablo Picasso, Woman with Bangs, *1902.*
Oil on canvas.
24 ⅛ x 20¼ in.
Baltimore Museum of Art.
Courtesy of BMA, 1950.268

152

Picasso eight hundred francs—the equivalent at the time of about $150.[10] (When William Paley bought one of these pictures, *Boy Leading a Horse*, in 1936, he paid thirty-seven thousand dollars.)

Picasso's Blue Period began at the end of 1901, when his close friend Carles Casagemas committed suicide, and extended through the spring of 1904. During that time Picasso was barely earning enough to eat. And for all his confidence in his own ability and a one-man show at Vollard's Paris gallery in 1901, his ambition remained largely thwarted.

Picasso's paintings of the Blue Period reflect his somber mood during those early years, and none does so better than the tragic-looking *Woman with Bangs*. Only the black hair and black outlines and the partly red shading of the woman's blouse and pouting red lips relieve the monochromatic bleakness.[11]

It is possible that this powerfully depressing and deeply introspective painting matched Etta's mood after her sister's death, but there is no question that she also recognized it as a masterpiece from Picasso's early years. In any case, this is not a painting anyone could accuse her of buying because it was "pretty."

How different is Manet's *Lady in a Bonnet* (1881), the pastel that Etta bought in December 1930, the same year that she acquired *Woman with Bangs*. She got Manet's picture from the Thannhauser Gallery in New York for $17,500[12]—the highest price she ever paid for a work of art.

Manet drew the spirited *Lady in a Bonnet* toward the end of his life, when he was unwell and bedridden. During this period he confined himself largely to sketchy portraits and still lifes and worked in the easier-to-handle medium of pastels rather than oils. Etta particularly loved this pastel, and she hung it over the mantel in her living room (figure 6, p. 219).

Despite rising tensions in Europe during the early 1930s, Etta continued building the Cone Collection at a prodigious clip. One acquisition held a special importance for her—Picasso's portrait of Leo Stein, given by the artist to her old mentor in 1906 when they had all been together in Paris.[13] Gertrude offered it to Etta late in 1931, and Etta was eager to have it.

Gertrude and Leo had had a bitter quarrel in 1913, after which Leo decided to leave France for good. For more than three decades thereafter, the brother and sister who had been so close at the beginning of their lives never again spoke to one another.[14] Oddly, in the division of artworks between Leo and Gertrude in 1913 and 1914, Gertrude kept her brother's portrait. According to Alice B. Toklas,

Leo's portrait was a gift from Picasso to Leo. At the division
he [Leo] didnt [*sic*] want it (he was bitter even about that) so
it remained at the rue de Fleurus until Gertrude sold it to the
Cones [*sic!* Claribel was dead in 1932 when Etta bought the
portrait]. You know Gertrude's Uncle Sol in N. York offered
when she went East with Bertha to buy the photograph she had
of her grandmother (his mother)—Gertrude was outraged and
said—One does not sell one's grandmother's photograph. If later
she sold her brother's portrait she would have answered that that
was a very different matter indeed—which indeed it was. How
could she hope to forget him if he hung on the wall . . .[15]

Along with her check for Leo's portrait, Etta sent a letter asking for five copies of Gertrude's *How to Write*.[16] Nine months later she wrote again, thanking Gertrude for having sent her the typescript of "Two Women" in tribute to Claribel's memory.

> I was very much moved at your remembering my sister as you did, and I shall catalogue your manuscript among her other art books which eventually will go to a museum—no doubt the Museum of Baltimore. I thank you profoundly for this generous tribute to my sister's memory. Life continues very empty without her, but I am trying to carry on as she would have wished done . . . The Picasso picture of Leo will be an important addition to those we had and I am very glad to have it. I am also very happy to add your new books to those who collect them in Baltimore.[17]

Leo Stein said of himself, "I was both disorderly and careless and sometimes I forgot to shave. I didn't like finding myself, suddenly, unshaven, and so I grew a beard."[18] Judging by photographs from that time, his portrait was a good likeness. Toklas noted that "in the early days . . . he wore a golden reddish beard which hid his mouth and chin and brought into prominence the fine top part of his head."[19] And she, too, found the portrait "very resembling to him as he was when I first knew him."[20]

Picasso's painting shows a sensitive, thoughtful, rather introspective thirty-four-year-old man. He was highly intelligent but a procrastinator, always about to do great things. Alfred Barr, the founding director of the Museum of Modern Art, wrote that "for the two brief years between 1905 and 1907 he was possibly the most discerning connoisseur and collector of twentieth century painting in the world."[21] The purchase of this painting had great sentimental value for Etta because Leo had indeed been tremendously important to her in the early years of the twentieth century, when he was her first and most important art history teacher.

In purchasing another Picasso—a watercolor study, *Nude with Raised Arm*, that had once belonged to Leo and Gertrude Stein—Etta made a surprising departure from her usual aversion to Cubist works. Gertrude had long since sold the watercolor, along with the large oil *Nude with Drapery* (*Nu à la Draperie*),[22] for which it is almost certainly a study.

Although the close relationship between *Nude with Raised Arm* and *Demoiselles d'Avignon*—the major work that launched the Cubist revo-

FIGURE 7.6

Pablo Picasso, Leo Stein, *1906.*
Gouache on cardboard.
9 ¾ x 6 ¾ in.
Baltimore Museum of Art.
Courtesy of BMA, 1950.276

lution in art—is obvious, it is not certain whether the study was made before or after *Demoiselles*.[23] The proto-Cubist pictures from the Stein collection must have been completely shocking at the beginning of the century, and even in 1936, when she bought the watercolor from the dealer Paul Rosenberg,[24] it was an unusually daring purchase for Etta.

In another apparent departure from her more typical purchases, Etta bought a still life by Georges Braque from Siegfried Rosengart in Lucerne on August 5, 1936. Ellen Hirschland recalled an incident that may shed light on this unusual choice:

Though I usually accompanied my aunt to Siegfried's gallery—especially because I was so attached to Picasso's Boy Leading a Horse, *which he had at that time—on that day I rode the funicular up to the top of the nearby Rigi Mountain, a thrilling experience. I therefore only heard about the Braque purchase when I came down in the afternoon. A few weeks previous to Etta's purchase of the Braque, she and I had visited the home of the art dealer Paul Rosenberg in Paris and had seen the decorative marble panels, very similar to this painting, that the artist had designed in 1929.*[25] *They were to be inserted into the floor of the Rosenberg dining room. I wonder if the fact that she had seen Braque's panels might have influenced Etta, consciously or unconsciously, to buy this painting.*

Another feature that would surely have appealed to Etta was the strong influence of Cézanne, which appears in the flattening of the fruit bowl, the outline and shading, and even the composition. An interesting technique seen here is the scraping away of paint to indicate grapes and other fruit in the bowl. Although Etta's Braque was painted after the artist's strictly Cubist style had waned, its horizontal format is typical of Braque's work in the 1920s, and the organization of the plate with lemons and grapes and a leaf is strikingly modern.

During the twenty years that remained to her after Claribel's death, Etta set about to make the joint collections historically more complete. She particularly felt the lack of an important work by Camille Corot. Having finally located the picture she wanted, Etta promptly bought it for fifteen thousand dollars. *The Artist's Studio* is one of six paintings Corot made showing a female model in an Italian peasant costume sitting at the artist's easel.[26] The play of triangular and rectangular shapes and

FIGURE 7.7

Pablo Picasso, Nude with Raised Arm *(study for* Nu à la Draperie), *1907. Watercolor and pencil. 12 ⅛ x 9 ⅝ in. Baltimore Museum of Art.*
Courtesy of BMA, 1950.278

FIGURE 7.8

Georges Braque, Still
Life with Lemons,
1928. Oil on canvas.
8 ½ x 13 ¾ in.
Baltimore Museum of Art.
Courtesy of BMA, 1950.192

FIGURE 7.9

Camille Corot, The
Artist's Studio,
1865–70. Oil on canvas.
16 x 13 in. Baltimore
Museum of Art.
Courtesy of BMA, 1950.200

curved and straight lines shows Corot's carefully orchestrated, formal composition.

Etta also wanted to acquire more American art. In 1944 she bought *Rocks and Sea, Maine,* by John Marin, from the American photographer Alfred Stieglitz. The same day that she bought the painting, she went to a lecture by Stieglitz on Marin's work, then wrote to him afterward to express her thanks for the lecture, which created for her another world, where, like the paintings of Marin, "material influences disappear."[27]

All the while that Etta was conscientiously filling in the holes in the Cone Collection, she remained keenly aware of her need to maintain the collection's strength—the unparalleled series of major works by Matisse. In 1932 she bought from the artist *The Yellow Dress,* painted from 1929 to 1931, in which a seated model wearing a full-length yellow outfit with a wide-brimmed yellow hat is framed by the familiar red tile floor and lavender wallpaper of Matisse's studio. Behind the model is the half-opened window the artist had so often portrayed over the previous thirty years, since his early paintings at Collioure. Her skirt completely covers both her feet and the chair on which she sits, which is indicated rather by the shape of her dress and the folds of her skirt. According to Adelyn Breeskin,

former director of the Baltimore Museum of Art, Matisse retouched the painting after Etta bought it, lengthening the dress and filling in part of the window. Matisse himself chose the clothes worn here by the model Lisette Clarnet and often applied her makeup as well.[28]

When Etta arrived in Nice the following summer, in 1933, Matisse was unwell and bedridden, but his daughter, Margot, insisted that Etta come to visit him anyway. As it turned out, he had arranged a delightful surprise for his longtime patron and friend. As Etta sat chatting with the artist, he asked her to turn around toward the window. There, to her utter delight, was his model dressed in the yellow outfit, sitting in a chair in front of the window, just as she had posed for Matisse.[29]

When plans were under way to mount the world's fair in Paris in 1937, Gertrude Stein wrote to Etta to try to persuade her to lend some Matisse paintings for the exhibition. Matisse was extremely annoyed on learning of her intervention and promptly wrote to say that Gertrude was not authorized to ask for his paintings. Only he had this authority, he wrote Etta, and he expressly limited his contribution to the world's fair to *The Yellow Dress,* which had not been seen in Paris before.[30]

In 1934 Etta bought from Matisse his newly finished *Interior with Dog,* the largest picture in the Cone Collection. The painting incorporates many familiar features: the Queen Anne table, the blue-and-white vase (now in the collection of the Matisse Museum in Cimiez), the red hexagonal floor tiles, and the lavender wallpaper seen also in *The Yellow Dress.*

New is the little dog Rowdy, which belonged to the artist's son, Pierre. The dog is resting comfortably beneath the table on a checked cloth. Many years later, at the reopening of the Cone Wing of the Baltimore Museum of Art on June 14, 1986, Ellen Hirschland had a conversation with Pierre Matisse about the dog. She recalled:

Rowdy was a gift to Pierre from Hans Purrmann, an early admirer and student of Matisse who lived in Berlin. This contradicts the [newspaper] story that he received the dog from a Berlin butcher.[31] Pierre told me that he fed the dog hamburger meat, which established an immediate rapport. But since he lived in New York and could not easily bring the dog to America, he had given him to his father.

Henri Matisse, Interior with Dog (*formerly* The Magnolia Branch)*, 1934. Oil on canvas. 60¾ x 65¾ in. Baltimore Museum of Art.* Courtesy of BMA, 1950.257

This painting shows clearly how the artist changed his mind as he went along. The hindquarters of the dog were larger at first, but Matisse then scraped away some of the paint and defined the edge of the animal with a black line. Similarly, the tiles at the left were originally painted as vertical and horizontal lines, then altered to the diagonals that we see today. The earlier lines show through the pinkish-red color at the left. The green leaves stand out against the lavender background and the blue wall-hanging at the right. Matisse's fascination with the shapes of the leaves anticipates his use of cutouts, which he was already developing in the early 1930s.

In the 1934 photograph of Henri Matisse in his studio (figure 6.7, p. 141), taken shortly after *Interior with Dog* was completed, we see the artist sitting below the as yet unframed painting on his wall.

In 1936, two years after buying the oil painting *Interior with Dog*, Etta bought a sketch for the painting, which Matisse dedicated to her: "à Miss Etta Cone respectueusement Henri-Matisse Juin '36." In the winter of 1971, Pierre Matisse gave another sketch for the same painting to the Baltimore Museum of Art in memory of the Cones.

It was probably in 1937 that Etta bought from Henri Matisse his strongly analytical self-portrait. Like many Matisse drawings, this one fills almost the entire page, and the uppermost part of the head is cropped off at the top. As is also often the case with Matisse, the artist's first sure lines and placement of the features were changed. These old marks, left visible, form a kind of shadow offset for the final portrait.[32] The white highlights bring the near parts of the face forward, adding depth to the eye sockets and the shape of the head.

In 1937 Etta also added *Purple Robe and Anemones* to her collection. In addition to the attraction exerted by its strong colors and depiction of anemones, this picture's connection with *The Pewter Jug* (figure 5.4, p. 96), acquired by Claribel fifteen years earlier, certainly added to its significance

FIGURE 7.12

Henri Matisse, sketch for Interior with Dog, *bearing an inscription in Matisse's hand, which in English translation reads, "To Miss Etta Cone respectfully Henri-Matisse, June '36."* Baltimore Museum of Art. Courtesy of BMA, 1950.12.42

FIGURE 7.13

Henri Matisse, Self-Portrait, *1937. Charcoal on white paper. 18 ¹¹⁄₁₆ x 15 ⅜ in. Baltimore Museum of Art.*

Courtesy of BMA, 1950.12.61

FIGURE 7.14

Henri Matisse, Purple Robe and Anemones *(formerly* The Purple Robe*), 1937. Oil on canvas. 28¾ x 23¾ in. Baltimore Museum of Art. The jug here is the same one painted in* The Pewter Jug, *fig. 5.4, bought by Claribel Cone fifteen years earlier.*

Courtesy of BMA, 1950.261

for Etta. She bought it from Paul Rosenberg's gallery only a short time after it was painted.

Of many Matisse paintings owned by Etta, *Purple Robe and Anemones* is just one that portrays a woman and a vase of flowers. Yet this painting introduced a new, cheerful, and brilliantly colored style to her collection. In this painting Matisse has divided the canvas into quarters, with each area marked off by a different pattern. One has thick vertical stripes, one thinner wavy vertical lines, one much thinner slanted horizontal stripes, and one thin diagonal lines crossed to form diamond shapes. Though the perspective is only suggested, the room feels extraordinarily solid.

The large forms—the woman, the table with a plate of fruit, and the pewter vase filled with anemones—hold the design together. In the late 1930s Matisse made a few paintings similar to this one, each divided into quarters. The wavy lines of the dress and those of the vase rebound back and forth visually, just as the strong emphasis on the black dots in the centers of the anemone blossoms are echoed in the woman's necklace and the buttons of her gown.

The model was Hélène Roth-Galitzine, a member of the Russian nobility who had fled her native land five years after the start of the Russian Revolution. She was working on the French Riviera as a fashion model when Matisse asked her to pose for him, and she appears in a number of works in the Cone Collection; she is the central figure in several drawings and in *Striped Blouse and Anemones*.[33]

In addition to her other acquisitions of 1937, Etta purchased the stunning *Seated Odalisque, Left Knee Bent, Ornamental Background and Checkerboard*, in which Matisse outdoes himself at his own game of color and design. The many patterns are almost dizzying, yet so structured as to hold together beautifully. As in all Matisse paintings, the composition here is carefully crafted. The chief divisions are the horizontal yellow line just below the center of the canvas and the vertical division in background patterns in the upper half, just to the left of center and to the right of the model's head. The odalisque, seated on a yellow divan with her knee raised, cuts across the many subdivisions, linking them into a harmonious whole. Matisse may well have been inspired here by medieval manuscripts or Islamic illustrations.[34]

Again, as typical in Matisse's work, color is itself a central theme. The yellow of the curtain in the upper left is echoed in the large pot on the right; in the two lemons on the plate; in the accents on the mirror, wallpaper, and the girl's jacket; and most compellingly in the yellow top surface and border of the divan itself. The section with irregular blue dots on a white ground sets off the model's head and upper body. The wildly patterned wallpaper at the upper right is tied to the rest of the composition by the verticals of the central black mirror. Black provides a steadying effect throughout, with the upright of the mirror echoed in the model's long black hair and jacket and the horizontal of the arm support and back rail of the divan. Black is also used effectively in the wallpaper, the couch cover, and the checkerboard.

Matisse has abandoned traditional perspective here, and most of the painting is remarkably flat. Yet he manages to give a fine sense of space using the short diagonal yellow band on the cloth to the model's right and the opposing diagonal of the checkerboard to her left. With these two small elements, the eye is led back from the foreground to create the illusion of depth.

PURCHASE OF GAUGUIN'S *WOMAN WITH MANGO*

In the summer of 1937, Etta Cone went to Siegfried Rosengart's gallery in Lucerne and bought Gauguin's *Woman with Mango*. The painting arrived at the gallery from Norway late in the afternoon, and Etta was scheduled to depart from Lucerne the following morning. But upon seeing the painting as it was unwrapped from the crate, she liked it at first sight. Would she have time to complete the transaction?

Early the next morning Etta woke her traveling companion, Laura Cone, and told her she had decided to buy the Gauguin, even though it cost a hefty fifteen thousand dollars. By eight o'clock she was at the Rosengart Gallery for a second look. Delaying her departure, she remained in the gallery for an hour and did not emerge until the final arrangements had been made.

Finally, with the chauffeur, Raymond Wahl, at the helm, a triumphal party—Etta, brother Fred Cone, and sister-in-law Laura—set off for Trieste and the Dalmatian coast of Italy. Before the journey Etta had worried terribly about the trip over the Gotthard Pass, fearing that the height would cause her to have a heart attack. But during the trip, she was talking so enthusiastically about the Gauguin that she lost track of where they were. Only belatedly remembering her fear, she asked how far it was to the Gotthard Pass and was astonished to learn that they had descended it an hour before. But though the Gauguin got the party through the Gotthard Pass, they never did progress down the coast because Etta was afraid of the poor roads.[35]

When in Lucerne, Etta frequently invited her friend Siegfried Rosengart to accompany her on drives, although, as he recalled, she seldom looked out the window at the magnificent Swiss landscape. Nor did she permit him that relaxation. Instead, she insisted that he impart ever more information to her about paintings, artists, and the art market. Although he was many

FIGURE 7.16

Paul Gauguin, Woman with Mango, *or* Vahine no te Vi, *1892. Oil on canvas. 28¼ x 17½ in. Baltimore Museum of Art.* Courtesy of BMA, 1950.213

years her junior, Etta's unremitting quest for knowledge generally outlasted Siegfried's strength. He found these excursions pleasant but exhausting.

As an excited Etta left Lucerne that morning, no one could know that she would never return. She had no further meetings with her old friend Siegfried Rosengart during the twelve years remaining before her death, nor did she ever travel abroad again.

The vivid and beautiful Gauguin masterpiece Etta bought on that last trip, *Woman with Mango*, was painted in 1892, a year after Gauguin arrived in Tahiti. He had given up his position as a banker in Paris and had deserted his Danish wife and five children to seek an exotic place where he could paint. In Tahiti he found the lovely dark-skinned women, as well as the tropical landscape, decorative cloths, and "primitive" religion, all much to his liking.

Woman with Mango portrays an indigenous woman in a lavender dress with a white collar—"a Sunday missionary dress"[36]—that contrasts stunningly with the yellow background, her brown skin, and the blue-and-white patterned cloth. The colorful outfit harks back to Gauguin's earlier Breton period, while the design anticipates Matisse's decorative style. This Matisselike strength of composition and color almost certainly appealed to Etta, imbued as she was with that artist's aesthetic.

About the time that he painted *Woman with Mango*, Gauguin wrote to his wife, "I am satisfied with my last works and I feel that I am beginning to master the Oceanian character. I can assure you that what I am doing has never been done by anybody and is not known in France."[37]

The beautiful, young, serious-faced woman in the picture is Tehaurana (or Tehemana), Gauguin's mistress. She seems to be pregnant and holds a mango—a symbol of fertility. The painting may have symbolic overtones, suggesting specifically the temptation of Eve. The mango and the full body of the woman hinted at beneath the cloth may represent sexual temptation.[38] The title in Tahitian, *Vahine no te Vi*, written near the top of the painting, means literally "Woman of the Mango."[39]

Woman with Mango was first owned by Edgar Degas, who was a great admirer of Gauguin. He bought the painting on February 18, 1895,[40] three years after Gauguin had painted it in the South Seas. The artist had come back to France briefly and, deciding to return to Tahiti, held an auction of his paintings to raise enough money for the forthcoming journey, from which he never returned. After the death of Degas in 1917, his own paintings along with his other holdings, including the Gauguin, were sold at the Gallery Georges Petit in Paris.

By chance, many years after her aunt purchased this picture, Ellen Hirschland uncovered a missing link in its history:

An odd coincidence occurred when my family was in Oslo in 1958. During a casual conversation about Edvard Munch in a bookstore with a saleslady, Miss Ellen Margarete Roede, I was surprised and delighted when she invited my family and me to her home where she had some paintings by Munch, who was a relative of hers. In the course of a pleasant discussion there, Miss Roede mentioned a beautiful Gauguin that her father, Dr. Nils Roede, had once owned. He had sold it to someone in America, she said, through a Swiss dealer.

To her surprise, I was able immediately to identify the painting as Woman with Mango, *which Etta had bought from Siegfried Rosengart in Switzerland in 1937. Dr. Roede bought* Woman with Mango *in 1918 and had kept it until that year. In a book that Rosengart's daughter Angela wrote as a tribute to her late father, she said that Siegfried had bought the Gauguin from "a Scandinavian collector" who needed money for a dowry for his daughter.[41] A charming story, but in fact the Scandinavian collector's daughter, with whom we passed that delightful evening, never married. According to Miss Roede, her father needed money when he retired.*

PURCHASE OF PICASSO'S *MOTHER AND CHILD*

The last painting Etta bought from Siegfried Rosengart was Picasso's *Mother and Child*. Immediately after the dealer bought the painting from a Dr. Reber, he sent Etta a picture of it and told her he was asking $8,500. A few days later—on August 16, 1939—she cabled him to say that she would take it. Rosengart sent it to her at the last possible moment before the onset of World War II in Europe a few weeks later made transatlantic shipments impossible.[42]

In 1921, a son, Paulo, had been born to Pablo Picasso and his wife Olga, and it was always assumed that this was a portrait of Madame Picasso with Paulo on her lap. More than seventy years after the painting was completed, however, William Rubin, director of the Museum of Modern Art in New York, noted that the boy in the painting is too large to have been only a year old in 1922. Rubin goes on to try to establish that the

woman in the painting is not, after all, Picasso's wife, but rather Sara Murphy, the wife of his friend Gerald Murphy, one of whose sons would have been two years old, and that she was perhaps also a lover of Picasso.[43] At least three renditions of the same subject exist, and all may represent Sara, whose idealized face appears often in Picasso paintings during his "classical" period, with one of her sons.

Picasso's economy of line, here so brilliantly shown, is reminiscent of the control exhibited by the Greek draftsmen who created white-ground vases in the late fifth century B.C. Like those ancient artists, Picasso gives a fine sense of volume and space with almost no internal detail. He indicates the fingers of the mother's right hand moving back in space and the pudginess of the child's left leg without shading or other markings. He also captures wonderfully the warm and comfortable feeling between mother and child and the confidence of the child as he sits in his mother's lap. Ellen Hirschland related the following story concerning this painting.

An incredible coincidence occurred in the 1970s while I was teaching a course in twentieth-century art at the Museum of Modern Art in New York. My students were a group consisting of schoolteachers taking an in-service course from the Great Neck [New York] Public Schools. Picasso was the day's subject, and I naturally used the fine examples hanging in the museum to explain his development.

Since there was no painting on view of Picasso's so-called classical period, I had taken along a good-sized color reproduction of Etta's Mother and Child *to supplement the story of the artist's evolution. As I raised the reproduction, I looked up to watch the group's reaction, and there at the back of the group stood Siegfried Rosengart and his daughter Angela!*

This was an astonishing coincidence, since Siegfried had sold this very painting to Etta over thirty years previously. It was even more startling because Mrs. Sibyl Rosengart had been chronically ill and the family had never before been to America. It turned out that Sibyl had died, and, free of concern for her health, Siegfried and Angela had finally come to New York and headed straight for the Museum of Modern Art.

Pablo Picasso, Portrait
of Allan Stein, *1906.*
Gouache on cardboard.
29 ⅛ x 23 ½ in.
Baltimore Museum of Art.
Courtesy of BMA, 1950.275

Because of the war, Etta ceased traveling abroad and instead spent at least part of each summer visiting her favorite sister-in-law, Laura Cone, at Laura's beautiful summer home in Blowing Rock, North Carolina. Laura always enjoyed Etta's visits but could not abide her piano teacher and companion, Lilly Schwarz, who complained constantly. According to Laura, for instance, Lilly insisted that "presperation" caused by the summer heat damaged her eyes.[44]

Etta's visit to Blowing Rock in 1948 was cut short by Lilly's fussiness. Laura then decided to take matters into her own hands. When, the following year, Etta's physician in Baltimore announced that Etta had a bad heart and recommended portentously that she spend the coming summer "wherever she was happiest," Laura immediately invited her to Blowing Rock and started making arrangements for a nurse.[45]

Photograph of young Allan Stein, 1905.
Courtesy of BMA.

176

When Lilly flatly refused this proposition, Laura brokered a compromise. Nora Kaufman, another of Etta's old friends who was also a nurse, would deliver Etta to Laura's summer home in July. Lilly could go wherever she wished during that month and then join Etta there in August. This arrangement was agreed to by all parties.[46]

Blowing Rock is a very small town, and when an overseas call for Etta came in to the tiny local telephone office (located in a trailer), it caused considerable consternation. Etta was by then hard of hearing, and Laura took the call. Allan Stein was phoning from his bed in the American Hospital in Paris, saying he needed money and wanted to sell his own portrait by Picasso.[47]

Allan knew that Etta loved the picture and correctly surmised that she would jump at the chance. For it was not only beautiful in itself but also a memento of those happy times Etta had spent in Paris forty-three years before. Etta also loved children and had frequently taken the young Allan for walks. Etta's account book for 1906 contains repeated entries for "candy for Allan" and "Allan's treat."[48]

In the spring of 1906, Sarah Stein had commissioned the portrait from Picasso as a birthday present for her husband, Michael.[49] Much later, Alice B. Toklas, who had little use for Allan, remarked that "both Matisse and Picasso had painted portraits of him, the greatest distinction he was to know."[50] But Etta had always liked the painting of the boy and was delighted to have even so belated an opportunity to acquire the portrait.

Yet, eager as both purchaser and seller were, completing the transaction proved to be a complicated process. When Laura reported Allan's request to Etta, she responded that she didn't even know if the painting belonged to Allan anymore. They then checked with Allan's mother, Sally Stein (then living in Palo Alto, California), who confirmed that the painting did in fact belong to Allan, although it was hanging in Sally's house at the time.[51]

Etta and Laura then discussed what price to offer. Etta reasoned that a dealer would pay ten thousand dollars and a collector probably twenty thousand. She then concluded, "Let's offer him fifteen and he'll take it." Etta cabled Allan, telling him she would pay fifteen thousand dollars through American Express after receipt of the painting, which was to be sent directly to Etta's bank, the Safe Deposit and Trust Company of Baltimore. Allan replied that the price was acceptable but insisted that Etta also buy from him some linens. He also asked Etta to deposit the money at American Express in Baltimore, which Etta flatly refused, explaining, "I don't use branch offices. I'll deposit the money in the main office in New York City."[52]

After receiving his response, Etta worried about whether Allan would send the right painting. He did, but Etta never had the opportunity to confirm what became her final purchase. The painting arrived in Baltimore, correct and in good condition, on September 1, 1949—the day after she passed away.

8

Etta and Ellen

Etta Cone had no children of her own, but she enjoyed a number of warm relationships with the offspring of her relatives. One member of those younger generations with whom she developed a special bond was her great-niece Ellen Berney Hirschland. Ellen's mother, Dorothy Long Berney, whom Etta adored, was the daughter of Etta's oldest sister, Carrie Cone Long. Etta's relationship with Ellen, however, went beyond the bounds of familial love to include a shared appreciation of art and art history—an appreciation that would also be acquired later by Ellen's daughter, Nancy Hirschland Ramage.

ELLEN'S CHILDHOOD VISITS

During the culturally lean years of the 1920s—and even more so in the 1930s and 1940s, when the world's taste was beginning to catch up—the eighth floor of the Marlborough Apartments served as a kind of secret haven for Baltimore's sophisticated set. Ellen recalled with delight the hours she passed at Aunt Etta's table:

Meals in the Cone apartments were exquisite, and served by a staff of efficient and friendly servants. When I was Etta's sole guest at luncheon, which occurred frequently, she always served my favorite dishes, including cheese soufflé and artichokes.

At formal parties, fellow guests were likely to be painters and sculptors, museum directors and curators, professors, architects, writers, historians, publishers, and musicians, representing many nationalities. Etta seldom invited more than eight or ten at a time, which gave an opportunity for the guests to talk intimately with one another.

The conversation was generally enlightening, but occasionally the hostess would get involved in telling a long petty story about social gossip or charity donations that would be out of place and embarrassing to everyone. The surroundings and the company, however, were so conducive to good conversation that any awkwardness was soon overcome.

ETTA TAKES ELLEN ABROAD

In 1935 and again in 1936, Etta offered to take Ellen, who was then a teenager, on her annual summer pilgrimage to Europe. Ellen declined the first offer so as to return once more to her beloved summer camp, but she accepted the second offer with alacrity.

Intensely aware of her role as chaperone, Etta kept Ellen away from Pablo Picasso but had no qualms about introducing her to Henri Matisse and his family. Ellen kept a diary of that remarkable summer when she traveled with her great-aunt and had the following reminiscences.

At the age of 17, at the invitation of Aunt Etta, I went on a European journey with her—which was one of the great experiences of my life. Etta was the indefatigable teacher when we rode day after day through France and Switzerland together.

She had engaged the same chauffeur, Raymond Wahl, each summer for several decades and he naturally knew her idiosyncrasies well. In Paris, where she generally spent at least a month each summer, he would call for us in his Renault each morning at the Hotel Lutetia. We would drive first to the Chase Bank on the rue Cambon where she picked up her mail and then went either to visit Henri Matisse, her constant friend from 1905 until her death 44 years later, or to an art gallery where she never tired of looking at art until the dealer's supply was exhausted. Very likely the dealer was exhausted too, but Etta would be thoroughly refreshed!

FIGURE 8.1

Snapshot of Raymond Wahl, Etta's faithful driver in France, with Etta, in his Renault, 1936. Etta liked cars she could essentially walk into.

Photograph by Ellen Cone Berney [Hirschland], Ellen B. Hirschland Archives

Then came lunch, often at the Perigourdine, looking out toward Nôtre Dame, or at the Brasserie of the Lutetia. A nap at the hotel followed, after which, with assorted visitors—artists, dealers or art historians—we would all ride with Raymond out to some lovely country spot. The group would eventually dine at a fine restaurant and talk in a leisurely way about art and aesthetics.

One afternoon, we drove out to Garches to see the house that Le Corbusier had built for Michael and Sally Stein in 1927. Etta knew it well from inside, but the family had recently moved to Palo Alto so we could only look from the outside. It was extremely modern for its time, and it made a lasting impression on me.

The Paris schedule included frequent trips to the Louvre, and visits from various merchants of laces,[1] textiles, and jewelry. Fittings with dressmakers and seamstresses who came to the Lutetia to make almost every article of Aunt Etta's clothing by hand were also time-consuming.

Even the undergarments had embroidered monograms, as did handkerchiefs, bed linens, and table linens.

Though Aunt Etta seemed to me to be physically quite old when we traveled together, she was actually a few months short of 66—not really so old. Thinking back to my attitude then, I pictured Aunt Etta as a rather elderly lady who tired easily. A typical day's schedule will show, however, that she was incredibly hardy.

We would sometimes spend the whole morning at the Louvre. After lunch, we would typically take a stroll through the streets of Paris. On one day, for example, we went to explore the Cathedral at St. Denis and subsequently the Chantilly Castle, where we watched people feeding the ancient carp. Eventually we took a ride to Versailles and stayed in the country for a grand dinner.

Aunt Etta was a really wonderful guide, opening my eager eyes to art, architecture, and nature in a very positive way. The first day after my arrival in Paris, she took me to the Louvre. I remember wanting to concentrate on the Impressionists, but she knew better and wanted to show me other things. We looked at the well-known icons of the Louvre, such as the Winged Victory and the Mona Lisa, but also at the early Italian artists (especially Giotto and Fra Angelico) and Dutch paintings as well as Rubens and many others.

FIGURE 8.2

Etta and Ellen in Lucerne, 1936. The child at left is Angela Rosengart, Siegfried Rosengart's daughter.
Ellen B. Hirschland Archives

THE CONE SISTERS OF BALTIMORE

Mealtimes were pleasant except for my resistance to Vichy water. Etta felt responsible for my health and refused to indulge my preference for "eau naturel." Yet she often gave me great freedom in other ways.

During our long car rides through Normandy and Switzerland, Etta and I would talk earnestly about painters and art works and philosophy throughout the mornings. After a good lunch en route, she would doze for an hour or two, sitting straight up in the back seat, while I took my daily French lesson from Raymond, joining him in the front. We never covered great distances in a single day, so there was ample time to dress and look about the town before dinner at an endless series of Hôtels de la Poste.

On our journeys Aunt Etta would go a whole day's travel off the route just to show me a special church, château, or wonder of nature. An example is Étretat, the town on the Normandy coast with a strange rock formation, which was painted so frequently by Courbet, Monet, Matisse, and others. She simply wanted me to see it, to share it with me, so we rode there, disembarked and walked on the boardwalk along the beach.

Another special treat was the Forest of Fontainebleau, made familiar to me by the Barbizon painters and Cézanne. We rode to Moret to find Sisley's views and to Mount St. Michel. The Grand Rue up the hill to the abbey church was too steep for Etta to climb, so she waited for Miss Mary Nice,[2] Aunt Etta's old friend, and me at the bottom. Later in the summer, at some of the châteaux along the Loire, Etta sat patiently in the car, sending Raymond along to chaperone me. Another day, she changed the itinerary so I could see the beautiful façade of the cathedral at Bourges. Her forbearance in this generous pursuit was boundless. Over the years, I have had reason to appreciate profoundly these trips arranged especially for my edification.

Another remarkable aspect of Etta's travels was her contact with many of the foremost collectors of the day. She took me to see the private collections of Dr. Oskar Reinhart, the Hahnlosers, and Mr. and Mrs. Sidney Brown (the first two in Winterthur, the last in Baden) that for the next decades most people hadn't heard of, but all of which have since become major public collections.

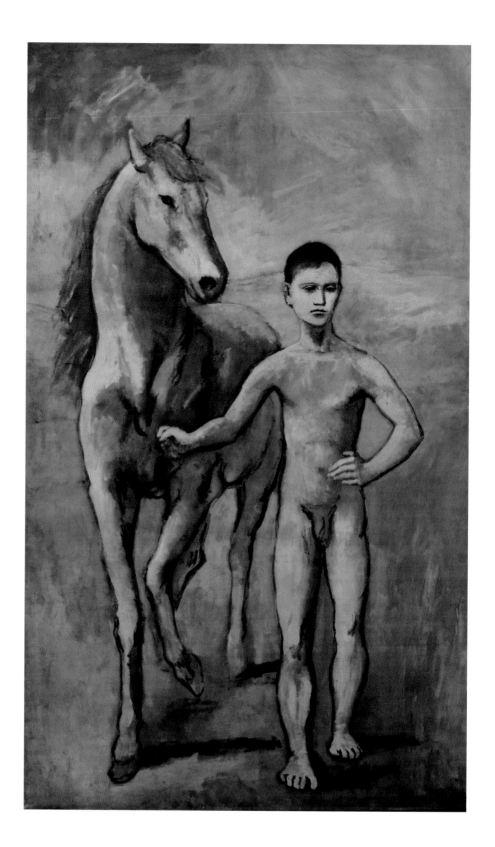

FIGURE 8.3

Pablo Picasso, Boy
Leading a
Horse, *1906.*
Oil on canvas.
7 ft. 3¼ in. x
4 ft. 3 in.
Museum of Modern
Art, New York.

Reproduced by
permission from the
Museum of Modern Art,
the William S. Paley
Collection (575.1964).
Digital image copyright
© the Museum of
Modern Art, licensed
by SCALA/Art
Resource, New York

In Switzerland, Ellen fell in love—not with a living boy but with a painted one. The object of her affection was Picasso's *Boy Leading a Horse*.

When Etta and I were in Lucerne in 1936, we visited Siegfried Rosengart's art gallery, located directly across the street from our hotel, almost every day for about a month. And each time we went we contemplated the magnificent Boy Leading a Horse *that Picasso had painted in 1906. Etta already owned two sketches for this painting, one a sepia drawing and the other an etching with the same subject called "The Watering Place" (1905).*

Etta badly wanted to buy the painting but was worried about its enormous size. Her apartments at the Marlborough did not have very high ceilings. In the end, with great reluctance, she turned down the opportunity to purchase this outstanding painting. Almost immediately, William S. Paley, president of CBS in New York, made the acquisition that both Etta and I had wanted her to make. Fifty-four years later, several weeks after Mr. Paley's death (on October 26, 1990), he was pictured on the front page of the New York Times *(November 3, 1990) standing in front of* Boy Leading a Horse, *which he had bequeathed to the Museum of Modern Art in New York.[3]*

During her time in Paris, Ellen went frequently to the Matisse residence with her great-aunt. Although Ellen spoke French somewhat haltingly and Matisse did not know English, the elderly master was evidently beguiled by the beautiful teenage girl.[4] Toward the end of June he prepared a magnificent surprise:

One day in his studio,[5] M. Matisse suddenly took me aside and indicated that he wanted to give me a drawing. He had placed three of these out flat on a table, and asked me to choose one. Two were ink drawings—each of a girl with a Romanian-type blouse, as I recall—and the third was a somewhat smaller simple pencil drawing of a woman's head.

After a bit of thought, I chose the pencil drawing. Immediately, he began nodding energetically in approval, saying that I had chosen the right one. He then wrote an inscription in the bottom right corner:

> *à Mademoiselle Ellen Berney*
>
> *hommage respectueuse Juin 36*

Henri. matisse 34   « Mademoiselle Ellen Bierney »
                           hommage respectueux juin 36

and then he signed it. It was already signed "Henri-Matisse 34" on the lower left. After that, he asked me something else, and to this day I am wondering what the question was. He spoke no English and my French was a bit weak. Since so many happy events had already taken place, I thought it safe to answer in the affirmative—whereupon he started to erase the inscription!

I quickly indicated how upset I was at this new development, and he promptly wrote my name and his message again on the same spot. I daresay that this is probably the only picture that he inscribed twice (and signed three times). As we got ready to leave, I thought M. Matisse would give me my drawing, but no, he said he would like to keep it and have it framed for me. His daughter Marguerite designed the frame. It is cleverly and attractively made of wood with a projection of an inverted V-shape which prevents a shadow from falling on the drawing. The frame is painted silver.[6]

I kept the drawing for a while in my dormitory room at college so that I would have the pleasure of looking at it.[7]

Delighted that two of her favorite people in the world were getting along so well, Etta wrote a description of the incident to Ellen's mother, Dorothy Berney, back home:

> Mme Matisse said in French, "She is exquisite," meaning a more profound thing than mere beauty. Mons. Matisse did an unheard of thing—he took Ellen aside & let her choose as a present between 3 drawings & was delighted when she selected the best. He was very attracted to Ellen & I know why. It is her quiet charm and evident intelligence plus extreme good looks—a rare combination. Where did she get it? I can answer—"From both parents directly . . ."
>
> I could write a book on Ellen, for as you both know she is a lovely human. I sometimes am not sure of what she thinks, but that makes her interesting. No doubt she could, or I should say, will be able to write a book on me & I am sure it will be an easier task . . .[8]

Head of a Woman displays the economy of line that was one of Matisse's greatest strengths. For in the deceptively simple drawing, the artist portrays a face in the round with one sure line. Barely lifting his pencil, Matisse has indicated the shape of the head and also the profile. A perfectly placed left eye implies the cheekbone, and while the right eye would hardly be visible from the angle chosen, by including the eyeball Matisse successfully conveys a three-dimensional sense of volume. Ellen continues,

Who was the model? In 1986 I asked Pierre Matisse if he knew who had been the model for the woman in this drawing. He thought it was Madame Lydia Delektorskaya, Matisse's model and assistant for many years, whom I had met in his studio in 1936. Still, Pierre wasn't sure and wondered if it might possibly be Mme. Hélène Roth-Galitzine, another of his father's models. He wrote to Lydia to ask what she knew about this. Madame Delektorskaya responded,

"Le dessin de M./Mme. Hirschland n'est ni de moi ni de Galitzine! Nous avons passées plus tard—moi, de 1935, Galitzine de 1936. C'est une modèle de 1934, je crois Odette."[9]

["Mr./Mrs. Hirschland's drawing is neither of me nor of Galitzine! We came along later—myself in 1935, Galitzine in 1936. It is a model of 1934, I think Odette."]

Later Dr. Margrit Hahnloser-Ingold, a Matisse scholar in Switzerland, looked in the Matisse archives in Paris on our behalf to find more conclusive information. After this research Dr. Hahnloser-Ingold was sure the model was indeed Odette, who had won a beauty competition in 1933 and posed for Matisse only in 1933 to 1934. She wrote, too, that Odette also appears as the model in some of Matisse's drawings for his first illustrated book, Les Poèmes de Stephane Mallarmé, *published in 1932.[10]*

I wrote in my diary the evening of June 30, 1936, "Aunt Etta and I went to Matisse's home again, where the most wonderful, most remarkable and very most thrilling thing happened— He gave <u>me</u> *a drawing . . . That was an experience of a lifetime. Madame Matisse is awfully nice, too. She showed me his very first oil painting (some books on a table) . . ."*

A friend once said to me, "You are just impressed because the picture is signed by a famous artist. It took him only a few moments to make it." I replied, "You are right; it took a few moments, plus forty years of preparation." As one sees so often with Matisse, he knew what major lines to include and what extraneous details to leave out.

When other skeptics wondered what was so special about the simplicity of the drawing, I urged them to try to copy it. This should have been an easy exercise because Matisse had designed it; the hard part was done. But the results of the sketches were appalling. It turns out that the surety of Matisse's line is virtually impossible to reproduce by another hand.

Etta remained resolutely oblivious to the horrors taking place all across Europe at that time. In one instance, this willful ignorance even brought up the possibility of entering Germany at a time when it was not only ill-advised but even dangerous to do so, particularly for anyone who was Jewish, regardless of nationality. Even the teenage Ellen could sense the danger. She later recalled:

Aunt Etta offered to let me accompany Mr. Rosengart to Germany in the summer of 1936, though she had been so overprotective in other ways. She liked and trusted Mr. Rosengart and thought I would enjoy seeing Freiburg, which he had to visit on business for a few days. It was I who declined the invitation because of the political situation. I did not want to support the German government even by my presence there.

The following year, careful to avoid the most troubled areas of Europe, Ellen's parents took her and her brother to Switzerland and France. Ellen recalled her subsequent visit to Matisse:

In the summer of 1937 I wrote Matisse from Lucerne to tell him that I was intending to visit Paris for a week. He wrote to me at my hotel, suggesting that I visit him the following Saturday. Quoting from my diary,

> **August 21, 1937.** *"The family's left me all alone" [quotation from a play by Maeterlinck], but this time it was voluntary, for I didn't want to spend my precious time seeing Versailles again. Therefore, I stayed in Paris with the "drudgery" of visiting M. Matisse. Tremblingly I walked into the place, expecting at least the comparatively calm atmosphere that prevailed there before.*
>
> *But no, it was like a madhouse. Dogs barked and yelped and hopped around, his birds (about 50)*[11] *chirped their hardest from their enormous cage that takes up almost all the space, he, himself, hardly said anything but only clucked instead, and I kept on trembling and thinking how I'd tell all my descendants, if any, about that trip.*

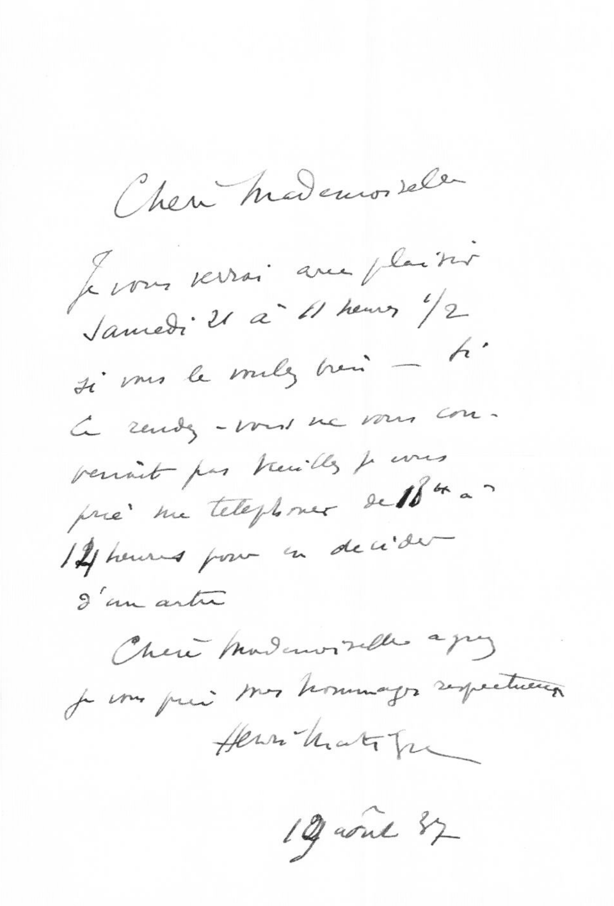

Chère Mademoiselle

Je vous verrai avec plaisir Samedi 21 à 11 heures 1/2 si vous le voulez bien — si ce rendez-vous ne vous convenait pas veuillez je vous prie me telephoner de 13h à 14 heures pour en decider d'un autre

Chère Mademoiselle agréez je vous prie mes hommages respectueux

Henri Matisse

19 août 37

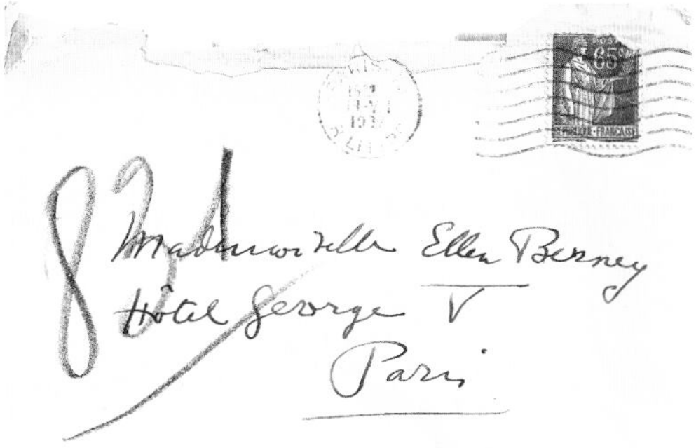

831

Mademoiselle Ellen Berney
Hôtel George V
Paris

FIGURE 8.5A *(above)*

Envelope that contained letter from Henri Matisse to Ellen Berney, August 19, 1937.
Edward C. Hirschland Collection

FIGURE 8.5B *(left)*

Letter from Henri Matisse to Ellen Berney, August 19, 1937.
Edward C. Hirschland Collection

He signed a book I have—a brand-new one at the time entitled Henri Matisse, *by Raymond Escholier, published in 1937. On the cover is a reproduction of a charcoal self-portrait which Etta purchased from the artist (for $350).*[12] *Matisse inscribed the book 'à Mademoiselle Ellen Berney respectueusement Henri Matisse août 37' . . . Matisse also gave me a poster reproduction of one of his pictures—then on exhibit at the Petit Palais. The poster was* Blue Eyes (1935), *a woman resting on her arm. Unfortunately I neglected to ask him to sign it. Pierre Matisse owned the painting for a long time but must have sold it, since I found it in the Pompidou Center in 1983.*

The Zorach Sculptures

In 1941 Etta paid her twenty-two-year-old great-niece the ultimate compliment by commissioning the American sculptor William Zorach to sculpt her portrait. The result was a bronze head particularly treasured by the Hirschland family, *Portrait of Ellen*. As Ellen Hirschland recalled:

Soon after our marriage in 1940, I was attending a lecture at the Metropolitan Museum in New York when I happened to meet an old camp friend, Dora Jane Janson. It turned out that both of us were interested in art. (She subsequently coauthored with her husband, H. W. Janson, the widely read survey book, History of Art.*) Dora was friendly with one of the children of the sculptor William Zorach and asked if I would like to meet him.*

I had admired Zorach's work ever since seeing a large sculpture of a child hugging a dog, called Affection, *at the Century of Progress world's fair in Chicago in 1933,*[13] *and was delighted at the prospect. When we contacted him, Zorach graciously asked me to bring my husband as well. Paul and I wasted no time and went over the following weekend. Thus began a friendship with Bill and Marguerite Zorach that lasted until his death.*

Knowing of our friendship, Etta commissioned Zorach to make a sculpture of my head in 1941. She had already bought Hilda, *another of Zorach's heads, some years before.*[14]

FIGURE 8.6

William Zorach, Portrait of Ellen, *1941.*
Bronze. 14¼ in. high. Baltimore Museum of
Art. Zorach wanted to make Ellen Hirschland
look heroic, in the style of the Works Progress
Administration (WPA) art of the period.
Courtesy of BMA, 1950.403

In 1941 I drove across the Brooklyn Bridge once or twice a week from our
apartment in Manhattan to the converted carriage house that was the Zorach
home on Hicks Street in Brooklyn. The ground floor, which Bill used as a
studio, was spacious and flat—good for moving the large raw material in and
the finished sculpture out. He and Marguerite lived on the floor above.
Marguerite was a distinguished artist in her own right and specialized both in
painting and in weaving.

Bill had estimated that just a couple of weeks would be required to make the
bust, but he took a lot longer. He did not want me to sit stiffly; but instead, I
moved about or sat on a stool just chatting with him, asking him to relate stories
of his life in Paris so many years earlier. Sometimes he stopped working to dance
around the studio, acting out some event that he recalled. Marguerite often joined
us, adding stories of her own and also teaching me to cook!

From time to time, Zorach would take out a gadget for measuring my face, and would then proceed with his job of molding the clay. I was careful not to comment on his progress, to say I liked or didn't like any part of the modeling. Only once, as I recall, I said shyly that I didn't realize that my hair looked the way he had formed it. He smiled and said that he wanted the head to look "heroic." It was remarkable to watch the development of the clay into a portrait. This was a wonderful time for me; it was so pleasant and instructive.

The bust took months to complete. When my head was finally modeled and about to be cast in bronze, Etta decided to increase the order from one to three casts: one for herself, one for my parents, and one for Paul and me.[15] Each time my aunt passed the bronze on the bookcase in the little entrance foyer of her apartment en route to her living room, she patted the cheek of the sculpture. She told me she did this, and I often observed her doing it.

In Zorach's book *Zorach Explains Sculpture* (1960), several of the illustrations are modeled on *Portrait of Ellen*, showing the same head shape and hair as seen in Ellen's portrait.[16]

Etta was extremely fond of Ellen's new husband, Paul Hirschland, a handsome young immigrant from Germany. When the young couple considered buying art for themselves, they naturally turned to Etta for advice. As Ellen recalled:

When it came to talking about or buying art, there was no better companion than Aunt Etta. In the 1940s when Paul and I were buying Impressionist paintings, we often spoke with her about the pieces we were contemplating acquiring—or sometimes we told her afterwards what we had already chosen.

Often when we were chatting about Cézanne or Renoir in Baltimore, she would reach into one of her petticoat-buried pockets for a key, go into the next apartment with me, put her hand right on the book she wanted and present it to me. Usually these were limited numbered editions. It was a habit of both Etta and Claribel to purchase multiple copies of the same book; one never knew when an extra copy might be needed. Most of Etta's duplicate copies were housed in the pantry of Claribel's apartment, though great quantities of books were spread about the home.

194

FIGURE 8.7

Ellen Hirschland near Blowing Rock, 1941 (age 22), around the time that Zorach sculpted her portrait in bronze.

Photograph by Paul M. Hirschland, Ellen B. Hirschland Archives

Aunt Etta knew quality and she knew the art market, keeping up with its fluctuations even after her traveling days were over. On another occasion, we told her over the long-distance phone that we had been offered the portrait of Clovis Sagot, the ex-clown art dealer who introduced Leo Stein to Picasso, which Picasso painted in 1909. "Oh," she said, "I remember M. Sagot very well. When Picasso had financial problems, Sagot gave him paints, brushes, and the other supplies that he needed. I would guess that the picture costs so-and-so much." She was right to the penny! She encouraged us to make the plunge and buy it, which indeed we did.

In 1943 Paul began using his considerable charm to convince Etta to let Zorach make a portrait of her as well. Ellen describes his efforts thus:

Over many months in 1943, my husband, overcoming great resistance on her part, persuaded Etta to ask Zorach to make a sculpture of her head too. She was reluctant then, just as she had been when there was a chance to have Picasso make her likeness early in the century. But Etta eventually yielded and invited Zorach to come to Baltimore for the purpose of making the piece. He made the bust in plaster first and then in stone, because during the war he could not get the metal to cast it in bronze the way mine had been done. In the end, the stone piece lacked the soft, kind look that Etta had. The bust was subsequently cast in bronze but again did not capture Etta's personality.

FIGURE 8.8

William Zorach, Portrait of Etta Cone, *1943. Marble. 14¼ in. high. Baltimore Museum of Art.*
Courtesy of BMA, 1950.400

Of Etta's portrait Zorach himself wrote:

> I have done a few portraits of friends in bronze either because
> of friendship or because the abstract forms of the head
> interested me. And I have done certain heads as commissions.
>
> I did one of Etta Cone of Baltimore. I did a marvelous
> factual likeness. She was a Martha Washington type. But
> Matisse had made drawings of her and she was convinced
> she looked like these drawings [see figure 6.6, p. 140]. They
> too were a likeness but I couldn't see her through the eyes of
> Matisse. The head I did is in the Baltimore Museum with the
> Cone collection. I don't think Etta ever liked it; it was a new
> way of seeing herself.
>
> I had a miserable time making this portrait. It was during
> the war and Etta had arranged for me to stay at a hotel in the
> neighborhood. It was the worst hotel in the world. I was really
> shocked. The bed sagged horribly, the towels were rags, and
> everything was filthy. I got the room cleaned up and spread
> newspapers to walk on but I was miserable there.
>
> I remember Etta saying, "I hope you like the hotel. I really
> don't know what it's like now but I remember forty years ago
> it was a very nice place to stay." I didn't like to disillusion the
> old lady, but if there had been another place to stay in the
> vicinity I would never have stayed there.[17]

Etta's and Ellen's deep affection for each other lasted until Etta's death
in 1949. It was shortly afterward that Ellen decided to write about her
great-aunts and their remarkable collection. This, then, is the book that
has eventually come to fruition, the result of Ellen's life's work on Claribel
and Etta Cone.

9

Legacy

To the end of Etta Cone's life, her mind remained lucid and her days busy. Yet hers was not a happy and buoyant nature, and she worried a great deal. A congratulatory note to Dorothy and Sidney Berney in 1942 on the birth of their granddaughter Nancy Hirschland (now Ramage; daughter of Paul and Ellen Hirschland) from the family rabbi, Morris Lazaron, mentions Etta's subdued, even depressive, nature:

> It is hard to think of you as grandparents. I share your joy in the birth of Nancy Louise.
>
> Dorothy, I cannot help recall the years ago when your dear mother [Carrie Cone Long, sister of Etta and Claribel] became a grandmother. You remind me so much of your mother in many ways . . . I can see her now moving with such wonderful grace and dignity, for all the bigness of her body, around the porches and through the gracious rooms on the hill at Park Avenue overlooking the French Broad river [in Asheville, N.C.].
>
> Miss Etta reminds me somewhat physically of her but, of course, your dear mother's eyes were blue and there was a merry twinkle in them that poor dear Miss Etta's do not possess. Perhaps it is the difference between the fulfillment of life and the unfulfillment of life.[1]

The rabbi may have seen her life as unfulfilled, but it is highly questionable whether Etta herself felt the lack. Particularly in the later years of Etta's life, art filled her so completely that it excluded almost all other thoughts.

In her later years, moreover, Etta became obsessively secretive about her wealth. Etta's sister-in-law Laura Cone told the story that when the two of them were traveling together in Europe before World War II, Etta learned she would have to declare the amount of money she was carrying at the Austrian border and promptly called off the trip—according to Laura, for fear that her chauffeur would find out and ask for a raise.[2]

While other American Jews worked feverishly to save their people from extinction by the Nazis, Etta consistently refused to help Jewish charities on the grounds that she did not want to give out the financial information required. Charity for Etta was always personal, and she did sponsor at least one young man who came to Baltimore from Germany. But fearing an opening of the floodgates should it become known how well-off she then was, she limited her involvement to helping the occasional refugee.

WOOING THE COLLECTOR

In addition to filling out the Cone Collection, Claribel had left Etta with another monumental task—deciding where the collection would finally reside. Both sisters were agreed that this remarkable assembly should never be sold or given away piecemeal. Both intended it to be left to a public institution, preferably in their hometown of Baltimore. But when Claribel passed away, her will left the final disposition to Etta:

> It is my desire in respect to the above Art Collection that in
> so far as is possible, or practicable, the same be kept intact
> as one individual collection. It is my suggestion, but not a
> direction or obligation upon my said Sister, Etta Cone, that
> in the event the spirit of appreciation for modern art in
> Baltimore becomes improved, and if the Baltimore Museum
> of Art should be interested in my said Collection and desire
> to be named as appointee hereunder to receive the collection
> after the death of my said sister, Etta Cone, that said
> Baltimore Museum of Art be favorably considered by her as
> the institution to ultimately receive said Collection.

My second preference for an appointee would be the Metropolitan Museum of Art, of the City of New York.

But I name these two names as suggestions merely and leave it in the absolute judgment and discretion of my sister, Etta Cone, to be exercised by her in accordance with conditions that may arise hereafter as to whom she shall appoint to receive this collection under the power herein granted.[3]

Indeed, when Claribel died in 1929, Baltimore's "spirit of appreciation for modern art" was in considerable need of improvement. The eloquent recollections of Shelby Shackelford Cox, a young artist living in Baltimore in 1928 (and much later a trustee of the Baltimore Museum of Art), give a good idea of what it meant to be a devotee of modern art in those unsophisticated times in the city (see appendix E).

During those days an invitation to Etta's crowded, cultured home was coveted by many in the art world, as proven by the many thank-you letters she received from the art luminaries, including Alfred Barr, Lionello Venturi, Gerstle Mack, Paul Sachs, Duncan Phillips, Chandler R. Post, and Jakob Rosenberg, who came from far and wide to visit her at the Marlborough Apartments. After a visit in 1929, the eminent art collector Stephen Clark wrote that

> it is always refreshing to find someone who quietly and unostentatiously and with perfect taste gathers some pictures together merely for the pleasure which they give. It has been my observation that most of the so-called connoisseurship in art is a sham and merely the reflection of somebody else's taste combined with a knowledge of commercial values. The real test comes when a collection is formed like yours, which calls for a spirit of adventure. Your Matisses are by long odds the finest that I have ever seen . . . to me he is the greatest living artist.[4]

In later years, moreover, the feeding frenzy of museum directors eager to secure the Cone Collection for their institution rose to a fever pitch. As early as 1934, Etta wrote to Gertrude Stein, "Many museum directors have been here this winter,"[5] and according to a list compiled by the past director of the Baltimore Museum of Art Arnold Lehman, those wooing Etta included director of the Museum of Modern Art Alfred H. Barr Jr.; curator at the Philadelphia Museum of Art Henry Clifford; and a host of directors and curators from the San Francisco Museum of Art, the Boston Museum of Fine Arts, the Brooklyn Museum, the Phillips Gallery, and the National Gallery of Art.[6] Barr in particular, who was fascinated by Matisse, was pushing Etta hard to choose the Museum of Modern Art. Yet Claribel's will had specified New York's Metropolitan Museum of Art, and not the Modern, as the first alternative to Baltimore.

Even Alice B. Toklas weighed in on the subject. In 1947, an Alice eager to improve the Gertrude Stein collection at Yale advised curator Donald Gallup that Allan Stein would "definitely refuse" to give anything to the Gertrude Stein collection and mentioned Etta as another possible source. But even when seeking Etta's help, Alice could not resist making catty remarks about her to others. She told Gallup:

> "I dont [sic] think Etta Cone would give any picture away—
> particularly if she thought it was important enough for
> Y.U.L. [Yale University Library] to want it—but if you could
> flatter her (and she accepts what would be for anyone else
> an enormously indigestible quantity) she might bequeathe
> [sic] the letters if she has kept them. Could you say that they
> would become part of the correspondence but known as the
> Etta Cone bequest or something equally grossly publicising
> herself you'd have a fair chance of getting them.[7]

Although Etta certainly enjoyed the attention, she was more than conscientious about her role as trustee, both for her own collection and that of her sister. As Ellen Hirschland recalled:

Etta frequently discussed the problems of her bequest with me, and it was clear that the responsibility of choosing the best location for the Cone Collection entailed much soul-searching on her part. Museums in other cities, knowing of the proviso in Claribel's will, were constantly cajoling her and suggesting subtly that their institutions were the best possible final repository for the Cone art treasures.

This was no easy decision. Like Claribel, Etta leaned heavily toward making her native city the recipient. But would Baltimore ever be ready?

It was the task of Adelyn Breeskin, first curator of prints and drawings and later director (1942–62) of the Baltimore Museum of Art, to convince Etta that Baltimore was indeed ready and would appreciate and benefit from the gift. Breeskin herself is quoted as saying, "In 1942 when I was made acting director, I knew it was my main job to see that it [the Cone Collection] came to us."[8] A 1977 interview preserves Breeskin's own account of that victorious campaign:

Q: *What sort of handholding was involved?*

AB: I was very friendly with Etta. I kept her acquainted with what we were doing, with what contemporary exhibitions we had, and asked her to be on the museum board. She preferred that her brother Frederic be on the board. She wanted no publicity. She was quite different from her sister, who was only too eager to be a public figure . . .[9] There was a telling anecdote about someone going to see the Cones and taking a bouquet of bright orange nasturtiums to Dr. Claribel and a little bunch of violets to Miss Etta. That was the difference between the two personalities.

Q: *Was Frederic Cone on your side in securing the collection for the museum?*

AB: Yes, but he was not very interested in art. He had the apartment next to Etta's, and one could enter it from her back living room. Etta would prepare meals for both Claribel and Fred. Claribel would ring the front doorbell and enter as if she were a guest, and for the most part, I think Fred did too.

Q: *Alfred Barr (formerly of the Museum of Modern Art) was one of the competitors for the collection. Who were some of the others?*

AB: He's the one I remember most, because he was so outspoken. He pronounced the collection to be "far too good for Baltimore," especially the *Blue Nude*. He came to Baltimore quite often to see Etta. The quality of the collection was much better known outside of Baltimore, especially by most museum directors. They also knew that Claribel had left her share to Etta, with the understanding that Etta would determine where it would go.

Q: *How did you handle it when you knew that someone like Barr was paying visits to the Marlborough Apartments?*

AB: I could only hope that I would prevail . . . Philip Perlman, a wonderful friend to the museum, also had a great deal to do with Etta Cone's determination to leave the collection to us, because he made out her will.[10]

During the last decade of Etta's life, Breeskin was a frequent guest at the Cone apartments. Her methods were not subtle. Apparently, in the pursuit of her objective, the museum director deemed no excess of flattery too much.

Past director of the Baltimore Museum Arnold Lehman cites Breeskin's "extraordinary skill, grace, and professionalism,"[11] and her obituary in the *New York Times* credits her "diplomatic skills" as the deciding factor in getting Etta to leave the Cone Collection to Baltimore—a gift, the obituary goes on to say, "that raised the Baltimore Museum to national rank in modern art."[12]

Ellen Hirschland, who was present during a number of Breeskin's visits, recalls being astonished at the transformation that came over the otherwise dignified woman:

She became obsequious, almost slavishly adoring of Etta, which was not her usual way of behaving, but it was an understandable position in view of the fact that it was her job to try to get the collection for Baltimore. I knew Mrs. Breeskin well, having worked as her volunteer assistant for two summers, and I never otherwise saw her act in this manner. To her credit, her policy worked.

ETTA PASSES ON

On the evening of August 31, 1949, in Blowing Rock, still consumed with her final purchase—Picasso's *Portrait of Allan Stein*—Etta Cone had a coronary occlusion and died peacefully in the arms of her companion, Lilly Schwarz. Etta's body was taken back to Baltimore. On September 2, she was laid to rest in the Cone family mausoleum at Druid Ridge Cemetery just outside the city limits of Baltimore, where Claribel and Fred were already interred. Ellen Hirschland noted that both Etta and Claribel

FIGURE 9.1

*The Cone family mausoleum
in Druid Ridge Cemetery
outside Baltimore, where
Claribel, Etta, and Fred Cone
were laid to rest.*
Photograph by Nancy H. Ramage,
1992

*tried to ignore death altogether and both disliked the idea of being buried underground
. . . which is undoubtedly why they wanted to be buried in a mausoleum. When Etta's
nephew Irving Long died suddenly at an early age, Aunt Etta did not attend the funeral
because, as she later explained, "It would have upset me too much."*

At Etta's service, Rabbi Morris S. Lazaron delivered the following eloquent eulogy, aptly capturing the tenor of Etta Cone's life:

> How sensitive she was! How exact, discriminating, and exquisite her taste. Her sensitivity was a native endowment. Her taste was her own achievement, won through long, earnest study and the most rigid, self-imposed disciplines. She not only appreciated beauty and the arts; she knew and understood them—though she would have been the first to disavow any claim to speak with authority. For she was both modest and humble.
>
> Men gather to themselves many things and for various reasons: the sheer frenzy to accumulate or to feed their pride of power or to impress others. She loved her pictures. Each acquisition was a source of excitement. And she bashfully told how from time to time she placed one or another at the foot of her bed where she could study it.
>
> It is not as a patron of art or even as generous-hearted and devoted friend that we think of her at this moment. This city through the Cone Collection will enjoy a treasure of beauty and inspiration beyond compare. We rather think of her as a human being.
>
> There was a childlike naïveté about her for all her sophistication. How often we heard her say, "Do you really think so?" As if uncertain of her own opinion, she happily welcomed confirmation of it from another, though he was not so well equipped as she to offer it. She was born in another era, a sweeter, kindlier, and more gracious time, and she never tried to catch up with the mad temper of our day.
>
> Sweet friend, when you died you took with you and out of our life a rare charm. For many of us you linked us with the precious past. Your genuineness and simplicity were an ever-present reminder to us that we can make our lives sweeter and lovelier. You called us to tender things that never grow old and to fine things that are ever young.[13]

The morning after Etta died, a letter arrived in Blowing Rock from the Safe Deposit and Trust Company of Baltimore reporting that Picasso's *Portrait of Allan Stein* had arrived safely at the bank. However, the crate containing the painting shipped from Allan Stein was not opened until after the funeral. It appears that Etta's fears had not been unfounded. The crate was opened in the presence of Laura Cone, Etta's sister-in-law; Philip B. Perlman, Etta's lawyer, who was also solicitor general of the United States; and Mr. J. K. Brigstocke, vice president of the bank. To Laura's relief, the painting looked in good condition, and she approved it. The crate also contained an invoice for $1,500 for the linens, which they all agreed should be honored as part of the original deal. But Etta had also bargained for two preliminary sketches for the Picasso portrait, which were not there. Instead the package contained two Matisse drawings of an entirely different subject.

Shortly thereafter, Allan's second wife phoned from New York to declare that she was the owner of the Matisse drawings. But when she asked permission to visit, Laura declined, informing Mrs. Stein that this was strictly a bank matter. Mrs. Stein persisted, saying she had other paintings, until Laura told her flatly, "The last Cone to buy paintings has just died."[14]

The next morning, Mr. Brigstocke phoned from the bank to say that Mrs. Stein was in Baltimore claiming the Matisses. In the end, one Matisse drawing went to Mrs. Allan Stein and the other to Etta's estate.

Allan's son by his first wife, Danny, was largely raised by the boy's grandparents, Sally and Michael Stein. Unfortunately, Danny had the habit of betting on horses, and the Steins were forced to sell most of their paintings to settle his debts.[15]

THE BEQUEST

Unlike the Stein family, the Cone sisters had always made one of their first priorities keeping their collection intact. Etta's will therefore contained a bequest to the City of Baltimore of four hundred thousand dollars to build a wing to house the collection. While this sum was probably adequate in 1949 at the time of Etta's death, by the time the city actually received the Cone Collection, building costs had skyrocketed.

For when it came to money, Etta had another priority—her brother Moses—which trumped even the need to house her precious collection. Upon the death of Bertha Cone, the widow of Moses Cone, in 1948, Flat Top Manor—the mansion that Moses Cone had built—passed to the trustees of the still-to-be-built Moses H. Cone Memorial Hospital,[16] and Etta's death contributed several millions more. Claribel, Ceasar, and Frederic Cone had all contributed as well, and on May 2, 1951—nearly three years after Bertha's death and two years after Etta's—the cornerstone was finally laid. Bernard M. Cone, the eighth of the Cone children, gave the dedicating address, which included the following story:

> One day I was accosted by an elderly man who used to run a crossroads country store in a small town in North Carolina. "I'll never forget your Brother Moses," he said. "I used to buy groceries from him. But one time I had a fire in my store and was burned out completely. A few days later I got a letter, postmarked Baltimore, and with the name H. Cone & Sons on the envelope. 'Ah! Ah!' I said. 'There it is. They want their money.' I opened the letter. It read like this.
>
>> Sorry to hear about your bad luck. When you get straightened out let me know what goods you need and I will ship them. Don't worry about the old account. You can pay when you are able.
>>   —Moses H. Cone
>
> Mr. Cone, when I read that letter, I just sat down and cried. But I want to tell you I paid the old account and also for the new goods he shipped me."[17]

Etta certainly felt that a hospital named in memory of her favorite brother—whose incredible energy and business acumen had helped build the fortune that allowed her to amass her remarkable collection of art—deserved her support. But Etta's devotion to Moses left the as yet unbuilt Cone Wing of the Baltimore Museum of Art in the lurch.

Luckily her lawyer, Philip Perlman, was able to convince the city officials to approve another $175,000 for the Cone Wing building project. On February 23, 1957, almost eight years after Etta's death, the three-story Cone Wing was opened, but since the city had paid part of the tab, its contents were not restricted to the Cone Collection. The Cone paintings, some drawings, and most of the sculptures were displayed on the main floor. The ground floor was used for offices. Only a small portion of the Cones' vast collection of furniture and decorative arts found their way, as originally intended, to the top floor, and during the half century since Etta's bequest was made, most of these objects have remained in storage.

Prepared with Perlman's expert help, Etta's will was quite specific about which art objects the City of Baltimore was to receive:

> sundry pictures, oil paintings, water colors, lithographs, colored aquatints, etchings, prints, drawings, engravings, photographs, Piper prints . . . also all of my laces, jewelry, shawls, fabrics, rugs, draperies, portiers, embroideries and other textiles, bric-a-brac, bronzes, antique furniture, marbles, sculptures, curios and other objets d'art . . . and also all of my art library.[18]

According to the terms of the will, the museum was given the right to make its selections and was then to turn over the remaining items to the Women's College of the University of North Carolina.[19] Because of Etta's generosity, the Women's College Weatherspoon Gallery today has a sizable collection of items not kept by Baltimore, including Matisse bronzes and prints, many of which were duplicates.

Before the wing was completed, parts of the Cone Collection were shown in New York, Minneapolis, Cincinnati, and Richmond. But once housed in the Baltimore Museum wing, the collection did not travel for many years. In recent years, however, a number of pieces have traveled to museums in Houston, Boston, Denver, Birmingham, Toronto, and elsewhere, as well as to the Isetan Museum of Art in Tokyo. A completely renovated Cone Wing at the museum was opened in April 2001.

THE MUSEUM AND THE FAMILY

After Etta's death, the Cone family's relations with the staff of the Baltimore Museum—and with museum director Adelyn Breeskin in particular—became strained. In 1957, when the Cone Wing was finally finished, Breeskin sent out five thousand invitations to the opening, but she failed to send one to Paul and Ellen Hirschland. On another occasion, recalled Ellen Hirschland:

Tom Freudenheim, former director of the museum, read the piece I wrote about the Cone sisters in the Dictionary of American Biography *[published in 1974]. Saying that it was the best writing he had ever read about the sisters, he asked my permission to use it, in abridged form, on panels in the Cone galleries. I said I would be flattered. He accordingly requested that the curator prepare the panels but she never did.*

Although Ellen brought up her family outside New York City, the Hirschland family made frequent trips to Baltimore to visit the Cone Collection. During the 1960s and 1970s when the Zorach head of Ellen was displayed (see figures 8.6, 2.3), a couple of amusing incidents occurred.

Once, my son Roger took a young lady to the museum, and as she went past the Zorach, she stroked the bust of my head. To her undoubted astonishment Roger shot out, "Don't touch her. That's my mother."

Another time, when Paul and I were visiting the museum we happened on a class being given in the gallery. The pupils were a mixed group of very young children. Paul quietly told the teacher about my portrait on view there. She led the children near the bust and then asked them if they thought the head looked like anybody in the room. They looked and looked for a long time, and finally one of the children discovered the resemblance to me.

Zorach's stone head of Etta has been broken at the nose and repaired. The head of Ellen disappeared into the cellar for years but by 1999 was on display once again, installed in a reconstruction of the Cone apartments in the renovated Cone Wing. In recent years, too, the museum staff's attitude toward the Cone family has changed so that today the Baltimore Museum of Art is open and welcoming not only to members of the Cone family but to all researchers and visitors to the Cone Collection.

REFRAMING

This change in attitude has coincided with a reassessment of Etta and Claribel as collectors and, literally, with a change in how the collection has been framed. In 1986, the curatorial staff decided to remove the Matisse paintings from the frames chosen by the Cone sisters and to replace them with strip frames, which reveal the entire canvas to the edge of the stretcher. In a museum brochure entitled "What's in a Frame?" the curator, Brenda Richardson, argued that the museum had done the right thing in removing the Cone frames, which she considered of a different "time and place" than the radical pictures they bordered. Richardson went on to suggest that the sisters' choice in frames was indicative of their essential ignorance of modern art:

> Dr. Claribel Cone and Miss Etta Cone were of a time and a place; the frames they selected for the paintings they purchased primarily in the 1920s and 1930s reveal their fundamentally Victorian family traditions as well as the conservative domestic ambience of their Baltimore apartments. Reflecting their time and place—and *revealing perhaps how tenuous their real understanding may have been of the radical paintings they acquired*—they chose frames that . . . domesticated the art, adapted it to their ambience, subjected it to their own taste.[20]

Richardson's strip frames displayed the edge of the painting, which is frequently unpainted, creating a white line at the border. Under the new directorship of Doreen Bolger, however—and after many visitors to the museum objected to the new framing—the Baltimore Museum reversed its framing policy. The Cones' original frames were reinstated, restoring much of the warmth and personal charm of the collection.

The Baltimore Museum of Art and the City of Baltimore now recognize the collection formed by Claribel and Etta Cone as a core contribution to the cultural life of the people who live in the city and of people the world over who come to see it. The sisters would rejoice in the public acceptance of their wide-ranging taste, especially in art of the avant-garde. The renovation of the Cone Wing of the museum is only the latest testimony to the ongoing recognition of the remarkable accomplishments of these two unconventional, doggedly determined, and far-seeing women. Claribel's letters bear witness to their innermost musings, not always generous or kind, yet often insightful and sentimental; and the recollections here recorded give a rounded picture of their multifaceted personalities. Above all, the artworks they acquired stand as the irrefutable proof of the wisdom, sensitivity, and aesthetic taste of Claribel and Etta Cone.

The Marlborough Apartments

The blaze of vibrant color upon entering the Cone apartments took the visitor's breath away. Crowded into the triple suites' many small rooms were great quantities of fine old furniture in a variety of styles. Every surface was covered with scarves of various hues and cluttered with sculpture.

The most striking feature was of course the paintings, which were hung close together, often one above another. Matisse's oils, with their warm Moroccan colors, shone like a guiding theme throughout the apartments. A sense of Eastern splendor emanated from the Oriental rugs covering the floors, the red damask draperies that framed the tall windows, and the antique furniture that filled each of the small rooms. Even some of the doors were covered with colorful brocades.

Dishes of fruit and enormous Normandy milk jars filled with brightly colored flowers abounded throughout the year in the occupied and unoccupied apartments alike. These copiously filled urns of copper or brass added life and warmth. The flowers seemed haphazardly arranged yet gave an entirely artistic effect, while the frequently chosen anemones echoed Matisse's vibrant hues.

The narrow halls were barely passable, with bookcases, chairs, and tables reducing the actual width by half. A disadvantage of the intimate, personal atmosphere was the extreme difficulty of viewing the works of art. It was impossible to step back far enough to achieve an adequate vista.

Crammed into the rooms were endless boxes, drawers and chests, tables, desks, bookcases, chairs, and armoires, often topped with candlesticks, in addition to sculpture and the gaily colored flowers. The taste in furniture

FIGURE 1

A hallway in Etta Cone's apartment, 1941.
Ellen B. Hirschland Archives

213

was eclectic. Interspersed among the Hispano-Moresque desks were colonial American cabinets and bookcases with the traditional thirteen glass panes on their hinged doors. The furniture ran the gamut from hard, stiff Renaissance chairs to a few contemporary couches. (It was the hard chairs to which young visitors were assigned.)

The couches overflowed with pillows covered in multicolored fabrics, some cut velvet, some patterned, the majority stitched in petit point. Strangely enough, the effect of all this seeming clutter was one not of restlessness but rather of warmth. Some of the Victorian crowdedness of the old family homestead remained, but the overwhelming atmosphere was avant-garde rather than old-fashioned.

The Cone sisters' collection of the decorative arts, although less publicized than the paintings and sculpture, included many rare and valuable treasures. Their drawers and antique chests, which smelled of camphor when opened, abounded with fabrics from around the world and precious lace collected from many places and dating from the Renaissance to the nineteenth century. One large highboy housed the sisters' jewelry in shallow drawers—much of it colorful stones and eighteenth-century jewelry in exotic gold and silver settings seen against contrasting colored velvet linings.

In 1941 Etta had a fine set of photographs made of the Cone apartments. Keeping one set for herself, she gave the other to her great-niece Ellen Hirschland in New York. In typically meticulous fashion, the photographs arrived with detailed instructions from Baltimore on how to mount them (dated July 30, 1941).

FIGURE 2

Claribel Cone's living room, 1941. Matisse's Large Seated Nude *(fig. 7.1), a bronze sculpture of a woman leaning back daringly, is placed alone on a large table in the center of the room. On the far wall above the mantel is Matisse's* The Pewter Jug *(fig. 5.4).*
Ellen B. Hirschland Archives

Claribel Cone's Blue Nude Room *(now called the Cone-Stein Room), 1941.*
In this tiny room, where it had an overpowering impact, hung Matisse's huge
Blue Nude *(fig. 5.16)—three feet high and nearly five feet long. In addition,*
large furniture, a table covered with oversize boxes, and a standing rack of portfolios
containing almost all of the early Picasso drawings made it hard to maneuver.
Ellen B. Hirschland Archives

FIGURE 4

Claribel Cone's Blue Nude *Room (opposite side of room), 1941. When Etta purchased Matisse's* Large Reclining Nude, *or* The Pink Nude, *of 1935 (fig. 7.3), she placed the two large paintings facing each other on opposite walls. Next to* Large Reclining Nude *is Braque's* Still Life with Lemons *(fig. 7.8), and beyond it to the right the earliest Matisse in the collection,* Yellow Pottery from Provence *(fig. 3.14).*

Ellen B. Hirschland Archives

FIGURE 5

Entryway to Etta Cone's living room, 1941. In later years the foyer to Etta's apartment contained Matisse's large Interior with Dog *(fig. 7.11), barely visible through the doorway. To the left of the doorway is a painting especially dear to Etta, Gauguin's* Woman with Mango *(fig. 7.16). Beneath it is Renoir's bronze sculpture* Mother and Child, *whose angle mirrors that of the woman in the Gauguin painting. To the right of the doorway, Matisse's brightly colored* Seated Odalisque, Left Knee Bent, Ornamental Background and Checkerboard *(fig. 7.15) hangs over a Hispano–Moresque desk on which sit three Matisse bronzes.*

Ellen B. Hirschland Archives

FIGURE 6

Etta Cone's living room, 1941. Most used of all, Etta's living room was small but warm in feeling,
with bright paintings all around and colorful rugs and fabrics on the furniture. To the left, in an area
facing an incoming visitor, are Matisse's Interior, Flowers and Parakeets *(fig. 5.11)*
and Maillol's small bronze figure of a woman. Manet's Lady in a Bonnet *(fig. 7.5) hangs over*
the mantel, with Renoir's small La Lecture *(c. 1895) to the left, and Matisse's* Blue Eyes, *a*
favorite of Etta's, hangs in the niche to the left of the mantel. On the mantel beneath the Manet
are several Matisse sculptures on a red scarf. Flowers are, as usual, displayed in abundance.
Ellen B. Hirschland Archives

Etta's dining room, 1941. On the short wall to the left is Cézanne's small but powerful Bathers *(fig. 5.13). On the far wall are Matisse's* Large Cliff, Fish *(fig. 5.10) in the center, flanked by equal-size Matisse oils from the twenties:* Divertissement *(1922), showing two girls with a violin, and* Girl at the Window, Sunset *(1921). Under the latter sits the wooden sculpture* Cérès *(1926) by Simone Brangier Boas, a French-born artist and the wife of the Cones' teacher and friend Professor George Boas. The Hepplewhite chairs around the table—on which sat many an artist, art historian, and collector—were later used by Professor Edward Cone in his dining room in Princeton. The rug under the table is a fine Bokhara.*

Ellen B. Hirschland Archives

FIGURE 8

Etta's back sitting room, 1941. Brother Fred's apartment opened off to the left of this cozy second sitting room. Picasso's Woman with Bangs *(fig. 7.4) hangs in the center over a Hispano–Moresque desk near the door. To the right of that painting, his* Family of Saltimbanques *(1905) hangs above the light fixture and* The Monkey *(fig. 3.8) below it. Continuing to the right, Picasso's* La Coiffure *(1905), a fairly late acquisition, hangs above two Degas bronze dancers on a chest. No one spent much time in this room.*

Ellen B. Hirschland Archives

FIGURE 9

Art in the bathroom, 1941. Pressed for space, the Cones hung precious paintings in some of their bathrooms, confirming their reputation for eccentricity. Actually, these rooms were no longer used as bathrooms, but no one had bothered to remove the plumbing. Similarly, the Cones used a former pantry as a library.

Photograph courtesy of BMA

APPENDIXES

Appendix A

Letter from Joseph Rosengart to Herman Cone, April 16, 1846

Place your full trust and confidence in God who will send his angel to guard you. So do not be discouraged and do not be afraid of leaving or of the voyage but consider your fate a good fortune, designed for you by God.

You may shed tears because you are leaving your parents' house, your Father, Brothers and Sisters, relatives, friends and your native land, but dry your tears, because you may have the sweet hope of finding a second home abroad and a new country where you will not be deprived of all political and civil rights and where the Jew is not excluded from the society of all other men and subject to the severest restriction, but you will find a real homeland where you as a human being may claim all human rights and human dignity.

Be careful of your voyage and pay attention to your health as well as your belongings. Avoid the company of all but respectable and educated people. Be modest and polite to everybody. Thus you may surely expect good treatment for yourself.

Every evening and every morning turn to God with sincere prayers; do not be afraid of anybody and do not let anybody disturb your devotions. Even if some people should make fun of you at first, they will understand later and show their respect.

I recommend to you the faith of your fathers as the most sacred and the most noble. Try to follow all the Commandments most painstakingly and thereby attain actual happiness. Do not sacrifice your faith for worldly goods. They will disappear like dust and must be left behind in due time.

Remember particularly the Sabbath day, to keep it holy, for it is one of the most

important pillars on which our Faith is established. Do not disregard this day and do not let gold or silver make you blind and do not let any business however tempting induce you to violate the Sabbath, but at least on this day think seriously about your existence and your work.

It is not man's destiny to accumulate worldly goods just to be wealthy, but to acquire them to be used as means for the attainment of eternal happiness. I am, therefore, giving you as a keepsake an excellent religious book for your instruction. Make it your sacred duty to read one chapter on each Sabbath and holy day with serious devotion and meditation. Do not lay it aside when you have read it through, but keep it and read it again from time to time.

You will thereby learn your religion thoroughly, act accordingly, and thus be honored by GOD and men. It will be your counsel in good times and bad, and will preserve you from all evil.

Honor your Father and your Mother, that your days may be prolonged. Even in that distant country you can show your respect and love towards your Father by always remembering his good advice and by frequently writing him loving letters, thus giving expression to your devotion to him and your Brothers and Sisters.

Although your sainted Mother is now in Heaven and although you never knew her, you can show her your greatest respect and love by following the Faith as she did. You will thus be able to know her and be with her in Heaven.

Your Sister and Brother-in-law in America will surely receive you in their home with loving care. Consider their home as your Father's house and be respectful and modest toward them, show them your filial devotion and be attached and faithful to them, as you have always been toward us. Follow their advice and their suggestions and, whatever you may undertake, first ask them for their counsel. They will always give you the best advice and you will derive benefit therefrom, I am sure.

If you should be lucky enough to become wealthy in that distant land, do not let it make you proud and overbearing. Do not think that your energy and knowledge accumulated that wealth, but that GOD gave it to you to use it for the best purpose and for charity. Do not forget that you are also under obligation to assist your relatives and to help them to get ahead.

However, if you should not become wealthy, be satisfied with what you do have and try to be as comfortable and happy as if you had the greatest treasures.

Follow the middle way between avarice and waste. Do not be stingy, but live according to your position and your finances and be particularly liberal toward the poor, and charitable to the needy. Be glad to help and give part of your bread and give assistance to the distressed.

Do not let anybody call you a miser, but be known as a philanthropist. On the other hand, do not be extravagant or a spendthrift. Even if the necessity should occasionally arise to spend more than usual, never feel obliged to squander. It is of utmost importance that you keep account of your expenditures and live within your income.

I am closing with the quotation:

"Do right, trust in God, and fear no man."

Joseph Rosengart
Buttenhausen, April 16, 1846

In Jacob Rader Marcus, *This I Believe: Documents of American Jewish Life* (Northvale, N.J.: Jason Aronson, 1990), 79–81.

APPENDIX B

Claribel Cone's "Introductory Address to the Medical Class of the Woman's Medical College," 1896

We are assembled here to-day to celebrate the opening of the thirteenth year of the Woman's Medical College. In the name of the faculty I welcome you—Ladies of the Medical Class—to its privileges and its trials—and trials are privileges when well used. We welcome you to the sheltering care of your chosen Alma Mater.

. . . Who would not pause on the threshold of a new life, and ask: "Am I fit to enter here?" And how are we to measure the qualities of fitness? It may be by intuition—one simply feels this to be her vocation (they say a woman arrives at all conclusions by intuition; that is a large measure, but a very inaccurate one). It may be, by a just estimate of one's powers:

Of perseverance;
Of energy;
Of sympathy;
Of self-sacrifice;
Of observation;
Of presence of mind;
Of ability to inspire confidence;
Of tact.

In fact by an intelligent estimate of all one's faculties, in addition to a healthy body and a vigorous mind. And feeling that one possesses these, is she prepared to take up as a life work so great a task? Can she feel its responsibilities? Has she the courage to combat its many annoyances? Does she realize that it often means to her the saving of a human life? And death, when death must come, having done her level best, the level best, can she let death pass without making too deep an impress on her nature? Only the affirmative to such questions can place one on the list of eligibles to the degree of doctor of medicine . . .

Sympathy belongs to woman by inheritance. Why should she, too, in dealing with human suffering, not be refined and ennobled by the constant exercise of this quality? Only in coarser natures are influences of this kind overpowered by a more material view of things . . .

Seldom does one take up the study of medicine without being reminded by a host of solicitous friends that the life involves constant *self-sacrifice*. What egotists they would make of us! Do they not know that the life which radiates outward, is more apt to bring us happiness? No less a man than Goethe has said: "We are, and ought to be obscure to ourselves; turned outwards and working upon the world which surrounds us." Nor are we to be praised for this eternal sacrifice of self. The physician who sits up all night with his dying patient, trying to fan into life the flickering spark, yet conscious of the utter hopelessness of the case—could such a one sleep well if he felt his presence might make a death easier?

If we follow right for the sake of duty, it brings us content. If we do well because it is pleasant to do so, it brings us happiness.

And should one's work lead him into a more contracted (perhaps a more selfish) sphere—the laboratory—here too, is he able to add to the relief of suffering, by discovering the relation of cause and effect, or by providing the means for the removal of these.

Confidence and encouragement are among the mental placebos which a physician is constantly called upon to administer; and yet, who would scorn to acknowledge faith cures! . . .

Perseverance and energy reward themselves. One should be satisfied with nothing short of the best. Success means long-continued perseverance; effort which allows no failure—for even our mistakes may bring us gain. The great men and women of the world are not those who stopped short with each discouragement . . .

There is a galaxy of noble women to whom especially belong our admiration and respect: those who, independent of aid, with a mighty purpose, and the courage of their convictions, grappled with difficulties and overcame obstacles. I refer to the pioneers in medicine among the women of this country: to Ann Moore, to Elizabeth Blackwell, to Emily Blackwell[1] and others . . .

But this is a digression. We were speaking of the attributes of a successful physician.

The *habit of observation* is not the least of these . . .

And *presence of mind* is an instinct which must be acquired. It may be considered the power of observation put to its best uses. Emergency will not tolerate indecision. It will not wait for the answer which comes "just three hours too late." It has been said that in the dynamics of human affairs two qualities are essential to greatness—power and promptitude; every physician and surgeon knows this.

Tact is a quality which cannot be taught. It is the harmonious adjustment of all our other faculties. If we use these rightly we have tact. He has tact who knows when and how to enter a sick room and how to leave it, who can use language to conceal his thoughts; who knows what questions not to hear. Indeed, the tactful man is he, who recognizes the eternal fitness of things and tempers all "with brains sir.". . .

Of *punctuality*—there is not time to talk, or it may lead us into curious inconsistencies . . .

It has been objected that the woman doctor becomes unbearably dogmatic and mannish. Unfortunately of some, this is too true. Assuming the appearance of self-confidence, they acquire an unbecoming masculinity. I have seen fine women spoiled by such affectation. It is an admission of inferiority that puts the sex to shame. Let woman remember that she is woman—woman before doctor—and if either calling must be sacrificed, let her not hesitate in the choice!

Again—it is claimed that the profession unfits one for social duties. And why need it affect woman in this way more than man? "Because"—is one answer—"she is too conscientious, and must give all of her time to work." Even so, if it make her and her patients happier, why object? But does it unfit a woman for social duties? There is no profession which so broadens one's views of humanity and makes her so tolerant of its faults, none which so helps her, by a knowledge of these faults, to correct them or which prepares her better to mix with the world . . .

As to *dress*—the average woman doctor is no disciple of Worth.[2] But her common sense is being copied by the fashion plates, and soon, with a little yielding on both sides, all inharmonious contrasts will be obliterated. Why should a woman doctor not dress well? There is no necessity to label herself "woman doctor" by eccentricity of style. And, indeed, upon the sensitive sick, a quiet unobtrusiveness and graceful daintiness of costume may make more favorable impression than we know. A very serious question now opens itself to us.

The woman-doctor may marry?[3] Yes, she may. And, if she marry, what becomes of the noble cause she has espoused? The cause can take care of itself, let the woman-doctor do the same! If she is sufficiently well-balanced and cares to do so, she can continue her practice. This is especially true if it be office work or a specialty. The success of some who have done so, is proof . . .

Or, if she elect to give up her profession for another work—for that which has been considered woman's sphere at all times and in all places—she is but the stronger for her work in the garrets of the poor, and but the better for a touch of the ineffable, gained by her glimpse into the mysteries of the human soul . . .

Claribel Cone, "Introductory Address to the Medical Class of the Woman's Medical College," *Bulletin of the Medical Society of Woman's Medical College of Baltimore* 11, no. 1 (February 1, 1896): 1–3.

APPENDIX C

Regarding the Situation of Female Doctors at the Turn of the Twentieth Century

While Claribel Cone had to cope with remarkably little interference from the domination of male doctors, several other women of her day have described what it was like to be a female physician.[1] About ten years after graduating from Woman's Medical College of Baltimore in 1897, for instance, Dr. May Farinholt-Jones, who was then a resident physician at the Mississippi State Industrial College that housed more than seven hundred young women annually, wrote in a letter:

> In thinking it over I find your question, "How are women physicians received by the laity?" a difficult one to answer. My position as resident physician

in the State College, which is supported by the Legislature, makes one, as
a physician, somewhat independent of the opinion of that great majority
which we term the laity. The physician here is approved and signed with the
seal of the Governor, the board of trustees and the president of the college.
The institution draws its patronage from rich and poor, from the homes
of plebeian and aristocrat alike. The college uniform levels all ranks. The
daughter of a town policeman has the same attention and privileges as the
daughter of the United States Senator and ex-Governor. I was fortunate in
having no predecessor. In the first few years of my residence here some of the
parents felt some anxiety and lack of confidence in the "lady doctor," as they
would persist in calling me. That feeling has been entirely overcome, and
parents frequently tell us that they send their daughters here that they, in
case of illness, may have a woman physician.

Among some classes I can give you the opinion of the woman physician in
one brief sentence, a comment made by an old countryman when he heard
a gentleman here speak to me as "Dr. Jones." "Sir, what did you call her?"
And when told, he thought his ears had played him false. "Well, sir, I would
as soon call a niggar mistah as to call a woman a doctor." That was the worst
thing that a Mississippian could ever have to do.

Quoted in a published paper, W. Milton Lewis, "The Graduates of the Woman's Medical College of
Baltimore and Their Work" (Baltimore, 1907), 4–5. The letter was written on October 2, 1905.

Appendix D

List of Claribel Cone's Published Papers, in Chronological Order

"Encysted Dropsy of the Peritoneum Secondary to Utero-Tubal Tuberculosis and Associated with Tubercular Pleurisy, Generalized Tuberculosis and Pyococcal Infection." *Johns
Hopkins Hospital Bulletin*, May 1897, 91–101.

"On Tuberculosis of the Oesophagus with the Report of a Case of Unusual Infection."
Johns Hopkins Hospital Bulletin, November 1897, 229–33.

"On a Polymorphous Cerebral Tumor (Alveolar Glioma?), Containing Tubercles and
Tubercle Bacilli." *New York Medical Journal*, March 11, 18, 25, 1899, 1–27.

"Multiple Hyperplastic Gastric Nodules Associated with Nodular Gastric Tuberculosis."
In *Contributions to the Science of Medicine Dedicated by His Pupils to William Henry Welch,
on the Twenty-Fifth Anniversary of His Doctorate*, 877–90. Baltimore: Johns Hopkins
University Press, 1900.

"Zur Kenntnis der Zellveränderungen in der normalen und pathologischen Epidermis des Menschen." *Frankfurter Zeitschrift für Pathologie*, February 28, 1907, 37–87.

"Making Ward-Rounds with Dr. Osler." *Sir William Osler Memorial Volume* (*Bulletin* no. 9, International Association of Medical Museum), 1927.

Appendix E

Shelby Shackelford Cox's Recollections

In 1975, the American artist Shelby Shackelford Cox (1899–1987) offered her recollections of how it was in 1928 when modern art was frowned upon by most of Baltimore society.

To look back 50 years and recall a particular episode would ordinarily be difficult. However, the one I have recently been asked about was a one-of-a-kind in my life, so I remember it well. It deals with art in Baltimore in 1925, and this is how matters then stood:

The splendid private art collection of the Walters family was open only on special days. The Baltimore Museum of Art, then on Monument Street, a block west of Mount Vernon Place, showed "accepted" art. There were no local art galleries handling anything experimental. The Maryland Institute was under the direction of Hans Schuler, a well-known Baltimore sculptor, who had declared that "the purpose of the Maryland Institute is to teach pure art . . . I am not going to allow modernists to display their meaningless stuff in the galleries of the school and counteract the true art education we are giving . . ."

A few years before I had graduated from the institute, and, with a scholarship was sent by Alon Bement, then the director, to study with Marguerite Zorach in Provincetown, Mass. She opened to me a new world so different from what I had been part of I was bewildered, excited, and helpless. Gradually I became aware of the infinite possibilities of material for paintings used by the group of Parisian artists then venturing into new forms of expression. Of course Cézanne, "the father," had been dead since 1906 but in Baltimore there was only a handful of people who knew he had ever existed.

I was eager to see this new art, and so the following year I went to Paris and worked in the studio of Fernand Léger.

On my return to Baltimore I looked for a place to paint. I finally found a room with two large north windows over a grocery store across from the then flourishing Richmond Market. It had a fireplace with a grate and the rent was $5.00 a month. The building was otherwise occupied by retired servants and odd-job men. Here I worked for a year.

There were no local galleries to which I could apply for a showing so I approached the Maryland Institute, a request usually granted graduates of that institution. Mr. Schuler looked at my work with shocked disapproval and gave me an emphatic "No." "The modernists' canvases are the cripples of the art world," he said. I was indeed chagrined! This was to have been my first one-man show with all the hopes surrounding it.

There was at that time a young Englishman, H. K. Fleming, on the staff of the *Sun* papers, and I told him of my rejection. A few days later an article appeared in the *Sun*, stating my case. To my surprise and trepidation, letters began to pour into the *Sun*, pro and con "modern Art." Photographs of my work appeared. A poem was written about one of my paintings, *Lines to the Portrait of a Russian Lady,* which began:

> So this is modern art
> Great gobs of tar
> How came it so?
> Are beauty, taste,
> And color
> Symmetry of line
> And loveliness of form
> No longer elements of art?

There was also a cartoon by Edmund Duffy showing the hand of Schuler marching a student away from a picture of a nude sitting in a tree; the caption saying "Forbidden Fruit."

As the arguments continued in the newspaper, I was offered several places in which to show. With appreciation, I finally chose the music studio of Miss Irene Gogol at 4 West Eager Street. The exhibition opened on December 19, 1925. I waited impatiently for a review. It finally came out in the *Sun* and was signed A.D.E. It was favorable, and I wondered who A.D.E. was. It was, I learned, A. D. Emmart, a young staff writer who in time became the paper's most important art critic and one of its leading editorial writers. He was a man remarkable for his wide knowledge and was greatly honored.

Because of the publicity about "Modern Art" in 1925, many people came to my show, among them Dr. Claribel and Miss Etta Cone. Each bought a drawing, the first things I had ever sold. They also invited me to visit them and see their collection . . .

When I arrived at the large Marlboro [sic] apartments on Eutaw Place I went down the rather somber, silent building hall and as I waited for an answer to my bell I remembered how many times I had seen the sisters sweeping majestically down the aisle of the Lyric [Theater] for a concert. They always took four seats (two for their wraps) near the orchestra.[1] Eventually the door opened quietly. Dr. Claribel, her long hair hanging loose and a comb in her hand, said "Come in, my dear, I am just combing my hair."

I followed her through the narrow hall, made narrower by canvases hung on either side, almost touching each other, to her dressing room. She sat down in front of a large marble-topped table, her cameo-like features reflected in the mirror above. On one side was Marie Laurencin's painting *Self-Portrait, Picasso, Fernande Olivier and Apollinaire*, which now hangs in the Baltimore Museum of Art. She continued combing her hair while questioning me about myself, my work and whose work I liked.

She then asked: "Shall we see the paintings?" Miss Etta joined us and I was then shown the beginning of what was to be in time the world-renowned Cone Collection of the Baltimore Museum of Art.

I had been to small galleries in Paris, but never had I seen so much impressionist and post-impressionist art together. It was exhilarating. We talked then of when Baltimore would be ready for "Modern Art." It came sooner than we had hoped.

A young professor of philosophy, Dr. George Boas, had come to the Johns Hopkins University. His wife was French and a sculptor, Simone Brangier. They knew French contemporary work well and Dr. Boas, in an interview, said of modern work: "It is the art of our day, and people living in this day must know something about the new school, if only to decide whether to avoid it."

A "Friends of Modern Art" group was formed under the sponsorship of Dr. Boas and Miss Grace Turnbull, who became treasurer. One hundred adventurous souls, including the Cone sisters, each contributed $5. With such wealth, we went off to find a place suitable for exhibitions. Elinor and John Graham had an apartment at 15 Pleasant Street with a large front room they consented to have us use under their care. John Graham was already an advanced and well-known painter. Here, in January 1926, our small door was opened to the avant garde, and exhibitions were held regularly throughout that winter . . .

There had been a showing of French painting at the Baltimore Museum of Art in January 1925. Miss Etta Cone loaned Matisse's *Étretat,* and a Cézanne was loaned by the Reinhardt Gallery of New York. There was also work by Picasso, Derain, Vlaminck and others. In spite of a newspaper heading saying "Pictures of Monet, Cézanne and others seem to many but daubs of madmen" there seems to have been little attention paid to this impressive show. It took Schuler's later rejection to arouse the public.

In 1926 I married Dr. Richard T. Cox, a physicist, and moved to New York. When I returned to Baltimore in 1943, great changes had taken place. The Walters Art Gallery was open to the public, and uptown, next to the Johns Hopkins University, there was a handsome "new" Baltimore Museum of Art. Since then I have seen the opening of the famous Cone Collection and that of the Sadie May Wing, the installation of the Wurtzburger Collection of African and oceanic art, the beautiful Benesch Collection at the Baltimore Museum of Art, and I am looking forward to the opening of the Wurtzburger sculpture garden adjoining the Johns Hopkins University. Baltimore is fortunate in these institutions. What we need now are galleries showing both "outside" and local art, and to build up a clientele for buying art so that collectors will not always feel it necessary to go to New York.

One might say that the Maryland Institute flies high a banner: "Let Freedom Ring."

So the wheel turns.

Statement sent by Shelby Shackelford Cox in 1975 to Ellen Hirschland, with a letter giving permission to use these passages. Much of this essay was published in the Baltimore *Sun* magazine, January 25, 1976.

APPENDIX F

George Boas on the Cones

It is fitting to conclude this book with the eloquent observations of George Boas. The Cones met Boas when Claribel first took a serious interest in modern art. For a few years thereafter he was their teacher and for many more their friend. In 1967 Professor Boas wrote in his introduction to a new catalogue of the Cone Collection:

I confess to a certain uneasiness in writing about the Misses Cone and their brother Frederic. For I have never known human beings who so detested publicity. Though both Etta Cone and her sister, Dr. Claribel, had clear-cut personalities, traits which were far from nebulous, and talents which could easily have brought them before the public, they both preferred the peace of their homes and the small confidences of their friends. And Mr. Cone seemed so shy that usually he was but a presence, there, to make one comfortable, to draw one out, but never to obtrude his own thoughts into a conversation.

None of them was, however, a hermit. Dr. Cone was an active participant in civic affairs and a scientist. Mr. Cone was a helpful member of the Board of Trustees of the Baltimore Museum. Miss Etta Cone was member of the Board of the Union Memorial Hospital. Moreover, I suppose that there was no day which did not bring to their doors one or two—and sometimes many more— visitors asking to see their collections. And it was only in the last years of Miss Cone's life that she showed any reluctance to let them in.

Their correspondence was very large and usually the letters were answered, though Dr. Cone was more likely to keep hers unopened in a beautiful Spanish box, to comfort the people who vainly sought to challenge her. They dined out; they went to concerts assiduously; they attended lectures with the modesty of well-behaved schoolgirls. But few people ever knew them intimately and both kept their personal affairs to themselves. To most people they were names constantly being repeated on the labels and in the catalogues of exhibitions preceded by the words, *Lent by . . .* That was their identity as far as the general public knew and that was their desire.

But none of this was due to their dislike of the human race. On the contrary, they were gracious and generous hostesses, courteously seconded by their brother. They had something of the nineteenth century in their manner, a kind of breadth which never let them do things on a small scale. One had the feeling that they should have received in one of those large mansions of the brownstone era, instead of in a little apartment.

For there was nothing restricted in either their conversation or even their appearance. They swept the whole length of civilization in their tastes and one might at one moment be talking of French painting and at another of German politics, at one moment of Liszt's manner of teaching the piano and at another of [Sir William] Osler's manner of teaching medicine.

Similarly one entered a door whose glass panel was backed with a Japanese brocade, came into a hall to put one's coat on an old Italian chair, saw a Matisse over the Steinway piano, sat on Hepplewhite chairs in the dining room, and if one were young, sat entranced watching a pendant composed of three long Spanish earrings slowly rise and fall on Dr. Cone's bosom. One could continue sketching a picture both too amusing and too intimate of this interior and of its inhabitants—amusing as all survivals are amusing, too intimate because of their desire for privacy.

I shall not therefore indulge our national hunger for laughable anecdotes, for gossip, for what the newspapers call the human touch. The Cones were satisfied to embody themselves in their collection, as if it were sufficient expression of their personalities. And indeed it was. For just as it took a certain daring to enter Johns Hopkins Medical School in 1900,[1] so it took great daring to buy a Matisse in 1905. This collection, it should be remembered, was started well before the famous Armory Show in New York. It was started at a time when most Americans were buying Tarbells and Dewings and, if specially adventurous, Childe Hassams. It was a time when Whistler was still a subject of dispute and when artistic young ladies were framing prints of Alexander's "Pot of Basil" to hang in their bedrooms.[2]

Even Gertrude Stein, who writes with good-natured amusement of Miss Cone's typing *Three Lives* for her, lacked the stamina to finish her medical course. Does one need much imagination to see the courage it took for two young women to spend their allowances on such strange, repulsive and clearly insane pictures as those of Matisse and Picasso? I can well recall how on coming to Baltimore in 1921 I was warned that of course I might visit the Cone Collection if I wished, but that its owners were beyond doubt mental cases.

The Misses Cone, for I shall leave their brother out of this as he would have wished, had the bad fortune to express a taste ahead of their time. That is a very simple and naive way of stating it . . . The Misses Cone seem to have been able to dodge the steamroller. They were sensitive to that shudder of anticipation that was in the air at the turn of the century, that new way of thinking and feeling which one perceives in the work of the Curies, Proust, and even Ravel . . .

It has sometimes been said that the Misses Cone owed their taste for modern painting to Gertrude Stein and her brother Leo. What debt there was has always been gratefully acknowledged. But it should also be recalled that Claribel Cone was a doctor and Etta Cone an accomplished musician before either of them left for Paris. Moreover, they were frank to admit that they did not agree with Miss Stein in many of her opinions. I should be more inclined to attribute Dr. Cone's taste to that openness of mind that sent her to the

Medical School in the beginning of the twentieth century.[3]

It was the willingness to admit that points of view might change and were not decreed once and for all by supernatural powers at some early date in human history that distinguished the Misses Cone from most of their contemporaries . . . We [who had lived through the First World War] were trying to put together a world which both science and the arts had torn to pieces.

Those of us who were enamored of pictures saw as the most important problem that of *seeing* the world. When one could go for an evening to the home of the Cones, the picture frames were so many windows looking out at a universe which had been visualized through new eyes and those eyes—when they belonged to Matisse—never attempted to create solidity, to substitute physics for vision, but had skimmed off the visual surface so that the world turned into a spectacle. And what is more, the home of the Cones was the one place in Baltimore where such things could be found, for in that period our Museum was but an infant and refused to show pictures that it now welcomes with such enthusiasm.

Thus the apartments of the Misses Cone were a sort of refuge to those of us who came to Baltimore from distant places—distant culturally if not geographically—and one sat there contentedly, as if one were at home. This was one's world and the rather dull red brick and, to be sure, charmingly quaint nineteenth-century city outside was flatly put in its place . . . here were two middle-aged women who had grown up in this self-satisfied city and had not become either devitalized or submissive . . .

But perhaps the greatest and most moving trait of both of these women was their intellectual humility. There might have been—and indeed was—some doubt on the part of their friends that they did not really know what it was all about. But some of us can bear witness to their intense study of modern art and indeed of the whole history of art. This interest went to the point of actually attending courses in aesthetics at the Johns Hopkins University. There are of course plenty of people who attend courses and popular lectures, but few who really follow them studiously, reading the books assigned and discussing the issues involved. It was both a challenge to one's integrity and a stimulus to work to have them there before one, calmly looking one in the eyes, like a double conscience which one did not dare deceive . . .

It is very easy to slip into mawkish tributes to the dead. But [such tributes] both disfigure their characters and betray their privacy. A minimum of reticence at least is desirable. Moreover, in a few years there will be no one alive to recall their living bodies and this collection will have to speak for them.

But lest they become a name on a plaque too soon, it is just as well for a last time to declare one's gratitude not only for the material possessions which they brought together only to give away, but also for the less tangible gifts which they were always ready to dispense so lavishly, their hospitality, their encouragement, their appreciation, their friendship. These things can be only rhetoric to those who had no personal acquaintance of them, but they were typical of two very solicitous friends who never used their pictures as a background for themselves but submitted themselves entirely and persistently to their pictures. One went to see the Cone Collection; one came away with a vivid image of two beautiful people.

George Boas, "The Cones," in *The Cone Collection* (Baltimore: Baltimore Museum of Art, 1967), 9–15, an exhibition catalogue.

NOTES

Preface

1. Claribel Cone's will, dated April 25, 1929. In the Maryland State Archives, Annapolis.

2. Ellen B. Hirschland, "The Cone Sisters and the Stein Family," in *Four Americans in Paris: The Collections of Gertrude Stein and Her Family* (New York: Museum of Modern Art, 1970), 74–86.

3. Ellen B. Hirschland and Nancy H. Ramage, "Bucking the Tide: The Cone Sisters of Baltimore," *Journal of the History of Collections* 8 (1996): 103–16.

Chapter 1: Presenting Miss Etta and Dr. Claribel

1. Gertrude Stein's "Two Women" is a "word portrait" of the Cones, first published in Robert McAlmon, ed., *The Contact Collection of Contemporary Writers* (Paris: Three Mountains Press, Contact Editions, 1925). See excerpt on p. 43.

2. Alice B. Toklas quoted in James R. Mellow, *Charmed Circle: Gertrude Stein and Company* (New York: Henry Holt, 2003), 124.

3. Alice B. Toklas to Mark Lutz, 1950, quoted in Alice B. Toklas, *Staying On Alone: Letters of Alice B. Toklas*, ed. Edward Burns (New York: Liveright, 1973), 216–17.

4. Laura Cone, wife of Julius Cone, one of Claribel and Etta's brothers; oral communication with Ellen Hirschland. There were thirteen Cone children of whom one, Albert, died in infancy. They were, in order of birth: Moses, Ceasar, Carrie, Monroe, Claribel, Albert, Solomon, Sydney, Etta, Julius, Bernard, Clarence, and Frederick.

5. Claribel Cone from Baltimore to Etta Cone in Blowing Rock, North Carolina, May 22, 1910. All letters were in the Ellen B. Hirschland Archives unless otherwise noted. They have now been donated to the Baltimore Museum of Art.

6. Claribel Cone from Munich to Etta Cone in Blowing Rock, June 7, 1915.

7. Etta Cone to Gertrude Stein, May 9, 1908, Beinecke Rare Books and Manuscripts, Yale University Library.

8. Claribel's notes to herself, July 16, 1928, Baltimore Museum of Art Archives.

9. Laura Cone, oral communication with Ellen B. Hirschland.

10. Etta Cone to Gertrude Stein, July 23, 1912, Beinecke Rare Books and Manuscripts, Yale University Library.

Chapter 2: Impoverished Peddler to Prosperous Merchant

1. See Marcus Lee Hansen, *The Immigrant in American History* (Cambridge, Mass.: Harvard University Press, 1948), 77–78; and Marcus Lee Hansen, *The Atlantic Migration, 1607–1860* (Cambridge, Mass.: Harvard University Press, 1940), 146–71.

2. Philip Taylor, *The Distant Magnet: European Emigration to the U.S.A.* (London: Eyre and Spottiswoode, 1971), 37–42.

3. Myron Berman, *Richmond's Jewry, 1769–1976* (Charlottesville, Va.: Jewish Community Federation of Richmond, in association with University Press of Virginia, 1979), 136.

4. Sydney M. Cone Jr., ed., "The Cones from Bavaria" (typescript, 2 vols., Greensboro Public Library, Greensboro, N.C., 1973), 1:3, 20; and Philip T. Noblitt, *A Mansion in the Mountains* (Boone, N.C.: Parkway Publishers, 1996), 4. Sydney M. Cone Jr. also prepared an extensive Cone genealogy in 1972 that was updated in 1995.

5. Berman, *Richmond's Jewry*, 134–38.

6. Noblitt, *Mansion*, 4.

7. Noblitt, *Mansion*, 4–5; Paul M. Fink, *Jonesborough: The First Century of Tennessee's First Town, 1776–1876* (Johnson City, Tenn.: Overmountain Press, 1989), 51. The original spelling of *Jonesborough* has been retained, although the name was changed to *Jonesboro* in 1870 and then changed back again to the original spelling in 1983.

8. Recollections of Sam M. Adler (F-1030), sec. 1, p. 31, Leo Baeck Institute, New York (hereafter cited as Adler Recollections with section and page numbers).

9. Unhappily, this state of affairs did not last. When Herman's grandson, also named Herman, visited Jonesborough in 1916, the chief of police told him "there was not a Jew left in Jonesboro, [which he] attributed [to] the unprogressiveness of the town," as quoted in S. Cone, "Cones of Bavaria," 2:147.

10. Herman went back to Germany once more, taking Claribel with him. He had hoped to dissuade her from pursuing a career in medicine.

11. Helen from shipboard to the children, May 8, 1882.

12. Helen Guggenheimer Cone, diary entry, July 24, 1882, Leo Baeck Institute, New York City.

13. For "Clara," see Adler Recollections, 1:31; for "Lette," see Helen G. Cone to Herman Cone, January 28, 1872, Adler Recollections, 2:49.

14. Noblitt, *Mansion*, 7, based on records in the Washington County Chancery Court Minute Books for 1866–67.

15. Ibid., 6.

16. Samuel Guggenheim may have been a relative of Helen Guggenheimer Cone; simplifying names was common among immigrants.

17. Noblitt, *Mansion*, 7.

18. Fink, *Jonesborough*, 52.

19. Text of advertisement courtesy of the Jonesborough Civic Trust for Historic Restoration and Preservation.

20. Her birthplace has sometimes erroneously been claimed to have been Jonesborough; see, for example, B. Richardson, "What's in a Frame?" in *The Spotlight* (Baltimore Museum of Art, 1993), 47. The error almost certainly stems from Etta's obituary notice in the Baltimore *Sun*, September 1, 1949, which stated that Etta and Claribel were both born in Jonesborough. But the family had moved to Baltimore in May; and an old Cone family Bible, now owned by Herman Cone Jr., records Etta's birth in Baltimore on November 30, 1870.

21. *Jonesborough Herald and Tribune*, January 25, 1873.

22. Fink, *Jonesborough*, 52. See also "The community loses an estimable family," *Jonesborough Herald and Tribune*, April 10, 1873.

23. Fink, *Jonesborough*, 157.

24. *A Century of Excellence: The History of the Cone Mills, 1891–1991* (Greensboro, N.C.: Greensboro Mills Corp., 1991), 13. On Moses Cone in particular, see *Dictionary of American Biography*, s.v. "Cone, Moses."

25. Ethel Stephens Arnett, *Greensboro North Carolina: The County Seat of Guilford* (Chapel Hill: University of North Carolina Press, 1955), 170–74.

26. Noblitt, *Mansion*, 11.

27. The Cone involvement with the grocery business was not, however, completely at an end. Herman's grandson Ceasar Cone Jr. opened a shop on Summit Avenue in Greensboro, which—according to a 1916 price list—specialized in such small goods as chewing gum, soaps, baking powder, Arm & Hammer soda, Quaker Oats, grains, and biscuits.

28. The remains of this mill burned to the ground in 1995.

29. Andrews, *Man and Mills*, 68.

30. Noblitt, *Mansion*, 16.

31. All the while the Cones were expanding their industrial network, the United States as a whole was reeling from events that occurred in Pullman, Illinois, in 1894.

George Pullman, inventor of the Pullman sleeping car, had built an "ideal town" for his employees, complete with low-cost housing, schools, churches, and even a railroad station. But when a recession cut orders for the railroad cars, Pullman cut his workforce in half, dropped salaries by 25 percent, and refused to lower rents. In May 1894, many desperate Pullman workers joined the American Railway Union (ARU), and a group of strikers took possession of the factory. The strike's ramifications extended beyond Chicago when the ARU refused to move railroad cars made by the Pullman Company, an action which affected national mail service and attracted the attention of President Grover Cleveland. Violence erupted, and after it was all over, twenty Pullman strikers were dead as a result of their clash with the federal troops Cleveland sent in to restore order. The outcome of the Pullman strike was a clear demonstration of the government's ability to intervene in labor disputes that affected the public at large.

32. *The Half Century Book 1891–1941*, privately printed by the Cone Export and Commission Co.

33. Noblitt, *Mansion*, 18–20. For a study of the relationship of industrialists and mill workers, see Cathy L. McHugh, *Mill Family: The Labor System in the Southern Cotton Textile Industry, 1880–1915* (New York: Oxford University Press, 1988), 18–22.

34. Noblitt, *Mansion*, 20–21.

35. Melton A. McLaurin, *Paternalism and Protest: Southern Cotton Mill Workers and Organized Labor, 1875–1905* (Westport, Conn.: Greenwood Press, 1971), 154–55; C. Vann Woodward, *Origins of the New South 1877–1913* (Baton Rouge: Louisiana State University Press, 1971), 422.

36. McLaurin, *Paternalism and Protest*, 156.

37. The best account of the construction is by Noblitt, *Mansion*, 41–48.

38. Elizabeth Seymour, "A Conecopia: Etta and Claribel Cone," in *Triad* (local newspaper, Greensboro, N.C., 1980), 28–30. These lovely ways, which wind through Moses's model orchards, are today open to the public.

39. Noblitt, *Mansion*, 47–48.

40. Noblitt, *Mansion*, 88, and oral communication with the authors, 1993.

41. Noblitt, *Mansion*, 31.

42. Buncombe County Deeds, Asheville, North Carolina. We are grateful to Phil Noblitt for this information.

43. Claribel Cone from Asheville to Etta Cone, December 31, 1894.

Chapter 3: Etta Opens the Door

1. S. Cone, "Cones from Bavaria," 2:162.

2. See Brenda Wineapple, introduction to *Appreciation: Painting, Poetry, and Prose*, by Leo Stein (Lincoln: University of Nebraska Press, Bison Books, 1996), xii.

3. On the Stein family, see Brenda Wineapple, *Sister Brother: Gertrude and Leo Stein* (New York: Putnam, 1996), 7–46.

4. S. Cone, "Cones from Bavaria," 2:119–20.

5. Claribel Cone from Philadelphia to Etta Cone in Baltimore, January 5, 1891. Written on stationery of Blockley Almshouse, Philadelphia Hospital for the Insane, where she worked as a doctor.

6. For a perceptive study of Etta's contributions as opposed to Claribel's, see Jay M. Fisher, "Dr. Claribel and Miss Etta Cone: A Collection of Modern Art for Baltimore," in *Before Peggy Guggenheim: American Women Art Collectors*, ed. Rosella Mamoli Zorzi (Venice: Marsilio Editori, 2001), 107–29.

7. Bertha Cone from New York City to Etta Cone in Baltimore, March 27, 1898, Baltimore Museum of Art Archives.

8. Leo Stein, *Appreciation: Painting, Poetry and Prose* (Lincoln: University of Nebraska Press, Bison Books, 1996), 150.

9. As quoted in Irene Gordon, "A World Beyond the World: The Discovery of Leo Stein," in *Four Americans in Paris: The Collections of Gertrude Stein and Her Family* (New York: Museum of Modern Art, 1970), 21.

10. The fifth was given by Etta to her brother Bernard Cone, who bequeathed it to his son, Harold S. Cone, who in turn gave it to his daughter, Claribel Cone II.

11. See *Theodore Robinson: 1852–1896*, with introduction and commentary by Sona Johnston (Baltimore: Baltimore Museum of Art, 1973), an exhibition catalogue.

12. Harriet Clark from New York to Etta Cone, sent to London and forwarded c/o Thos. Cook, Venice.

13. Etta's journal, 1901, as quoted in Brenda Richardson, *Dr. Claribel and Miss Etta: The Cone Collection of the Baltimore Museum of Art* (Baltimore: Baltimore Museum of Art, 1985), 63.

14. Based on his conversations with Etta, Edward Cone wrote that "it was Leo, and not Gertrude, who had developed the real eye for modern art and hence had contributed to her own education," in Edward T. Cone, "The Miss Etta Cones, The Steins, and M'sieu Matisse: A Memoir," *American Scholar* 42, no. 3 (1973): 457.

15. Among others, by B. Richardson, *Dr. Claribel and Miss Etta*, 63–68.

16. Etta's journal, 1901, as quoted ibid., 63. The days of the week were incorrect in Richardson and have been amended here.

17. Etta's journal, 1901, as quoted ibid. Underlining in original text.

18. This word portrait, "Two Women," was first published in McAlmon, *Contact Collection*, published in 1925, but written in about 1912, according to Ulla E. Dydo, *A Stein Reader: Gertrude Stein* (Evanston, Ill.: Northwestern University Press, 1993), 104. The word portrait was reprinted in Barbara Pollack, *The Collectors: Dr. Claribel and Miss*

Etta Cone (New York: Bobbs-Merrill, 1962), 275–300; and Brenda Richardson, *Dr. Claribel and Miss Etta*, 23–43.

19. Mellow, *Charmed Circle*, 133.

20. Etta Cone's diary, as quoted in Hirschland, "Cone Sisters and Stein Family," 76.

21. A few months after Etta moved out, the Expressionist painter Gabriele Münter, lover of Wassily Kandinsky, moved into another apartment in the same building.

22. Etta's account book, 80–81, Baltimore Museum of Art Archives. The one gap in her piano playing occurred when she went on a world tour in 1906 and 1907, at which time she put her piano in storage in Paris until she could return to retrieve it.

23. Edward T. Cone reported having met a son of Mahonri Young. When he told him that Etta said Mahonri had asked her to marry him, the son replied, "Yes, that is well known in our family."

24. Laura Cone, oral communication with Ellen Hirschland.

25. Written for a freshman course at Wheaton College, Norton, Massachusetts.

26. Etta Cone from Greensboro to Gertrude Stein in Paris, January 7, 1908, Beinecke Rare Books and Manuscripts, Yale University Library.

27. From Claribel's notes for a lecture written on January 19, 1925; this is one of numerous almost identical versions of the same text, all preserved in Claribel's handwriting. A number of sources have mistakenly suggested that the comments were made by the Cone sisters, rather than by Claribel alone, and that the remarks were contemporaneous with the exhibit of 1905, whereas they were made two decades later. These errors appeared most recently in a passage by Marcel Nicolle in Arthur C. Danto, *After the End of Art* (Princeton, N.J.: Princeton University Press, 1995), 55; see also B. Richardson, *Dr. Claribel and Miss Etta*, 89. The several versions of Claribel's notes are in the Ellen B. Hirschland Archives.

28. Gordon, "A World Beyond the World: The Discovery of Leo Stein," *Four Americans in Paris*, 26.

29. In 1948, when Ellen Hirschland and her husband acquired an oil portrait of Clovis Sagot, a large Cézannesque painting by Picasso (1909), Etta told them that she remembered Sagot well from her early days in Paris. The portrait is now in the Kunsthalle in Hamburg. See John Richardson, *A Life of Picasso*, vol. 2, *1907–1917: The Painter of Modern Life* (New York: Random House, 1996), 108. For a modern spoof of Picasso, Einstein, and Sagot, see *Picasso at the Lapin Agile*, a play first produced in 1993: Steve Martin, *"Picasso at the Lapin Agile" and Other Plays* (New York: Grove Press, 1996).

30. L. Stein, *Appreciation*, 168.

31. Painted in 1905. Now in the Konstmuseum, Göteborg, Sweden. Leo Stein's recollection of this first visit to Sagot's shop was written more than forty years after the event.

32. L. Stein, *Appreciation*, 169.

33. Fernande Olivier, *Picasso and His Friends* (London: Heinemann, 1964), 144–45.

34. Picasso's abode in Montmartre had served as a piano factory and then a locksmith's shop and a place where laundresses plied their trade. In 1889 it was converted to studios where the rent was cheap and the amenities scarce. Quite a few Spaniards lived in these literally floating barracks. Picasso moved there in 1904 and remained until 1909. See John Richardson, *A Life of Picasso*, vol. 1, *The Early Years: 1881–1906* (New York: Random House, 1991), 296.

35. Ibid., 404.

36. The original expense book is in the Baltimore Museum of Art Archives.

37. Although many sources have claimed that "the sisters" picked up drawings from the floor, it was Etta who was in Picasso's studio at that time, not both sisters. Claribel was living in Frankfurt. See Jay M. Fisher, *Works on Paper* (Baltimore: Baltimore Museum of Art, 1995), 3.

38. Gertrude Stein, *The Autobiography of Alice B. Toklas* (New York: Vintage Books, 1933), 64.

39. J. Richardson, *Early Years*, 410.

40. G. Stein, *Autobiography of Toklas*, 62.

41. The brooch is in the Fitzwilliam Museum, Cambridge. See Vincent Giroud, "Picasso and Gertrude Stein," *The Metropolitan Museum of Art Bulletin* (Winter 2007), 23; and Bolaffi *Gioielli*, no. 9 (1980): 19. The brooch is mentioned in Gertrude Stein's description of the first time Toklas met her: "There I went to see Mrs. Stein who had in the meantime returned to Paris, and there at her house I met Gertrude Stein. I was impressed by the coral brooch she wore and by her voice" (G. Stein, *Autobiography of Toklas*, 5).

42. Mellow, *Charmed Circle*, 129.

43. G. Stein, *Autobiography of Toklas*, 62. Vallotton borrowed the picture back from the Steins and exhibited it in the 1907 Salon d'Automne, to which Gertrude refers here.

44. J. Richardson, *Early Years*, 410, referring to Gertrude's use of the term. The original letter is dated October 6, 1906, and is in Beinecke Rare Books and Manuscripts, Yale University Library.

45. Etta Cone from Frankfurt to Gertrude Stein in Paris, October 6, 1906, Beinecke Rare Books and Manuscripts, Yale University Library.

46. J. Richardson, *Early Years*, 404; *Painter of Modern Life*, 110.

47. J. Richardson, *Painter of Modern Life*, 110.

48. J. Richardson, *Early Years*, 404. The painting became the property of the Russian government at the time of the revolution, when the Communists confiscated Shchukin's collection.

49. Alfred H. Barr, *Matisse: His Art and His Public* (New York: Museum of Modern Art, 1951), 84.

50. Hirschland, "Cone Sisters and Stein Family," 76 n. 8, suggests that this painting may be the *Nature morte* [*Still Life*] exhibited in the 1905 Salon d'Automne as no. 716. There is no documentation about when *Yellow Pottery* was purchased, but Etta recalled it to have been in the fall of 1905. Brenda Richardson, however, states that the painting has been "definitively dated to 1906" (*Dr. Claribel and Miss Etta*, 158 n. 35), which, if true, would put the acquisition a few months later and eliminate the possibility that it appeared in the 1905 Salon d'Automne.

51. B. Richardson, *Dr. Claribel and Miss Etta*, 158 n. 35.

52. Etta Cone from Cairo to Gertrude Stein, February 6, 1907, Beinecke Rare Books and Manuscripts, Yale University Library.

53. Etta Cone from Baltimore to Gertrude Stein, January 7, 1908, Beinecke Rare Books and Manuscripts, Yale University Library.

54. Etta Cone from Baltimore to Gertrude Stein, January 7, 1908, Beinecke Rare Books and Manuscripts, Yale University Library. Quoted in B. Richardson, *Dr. Claribel and Miss Etta*, 66.

55. Etta Cone from Baltimore to Gertrude Stein, April 14, 1908, Beinecke Rare Books and Manuscripts, Yale University Library. Quoted in B. Richardson, *Dr. Claribel and Miss Etta*, 66.

56. Notebook D, circa 1908–11, Gertrude Stein papers, Beinecke Rare Books and Manuscripts, Yale University Library. We are grateful to Brenda Wineapple for this quotation.

57. Etta Cone from Asheville to Gertrude Stein in Paris, September 9, 1907, Beinecke Rare Books and Manuscripts, Yale University Library.

58. During that period the Blue Ridge Parkway was built and had to go around the Cone estate.

59. Etta Cone from Greensboro to Gertrude Stein in Paris, February 11, 1910, Beinecke Rare Books and Manuscripts, Yale University Library.

60. Claribel Cone from Frankfurt am Main to Etta in Blowing Rock, July 5, 1910.

61. Etta Cone from Blowing Rock to Claribel Cone in Frankfurt am Main, July 16, 1911. Another letter, written on June 18, had also signaled her depression.

62. Etta Cone to Claribel Cone, July 16, 1911.

63. Etta Cone from Blowing Rock to Gertrude Stein in Paris, July 25, 1909.

64. Etta Cone from Blowing Rock to Gertrude Stein in Paris, September 26, 1909, Beinecke Rare Books and Manuscripts, Yale University Library.

65. Etta Cone from Baltimore to Gertrude Stein in Paris, December 12, 1909, Beinecke Rare Books and Manuscripts, Yale University Library.

66. Etta Cone to Gertrude Stein, January 10, 1910.

67. Ibid.

68. Mellow, *Charmed Circle*, 147.

69. Gertrude Stein from Hôtel de Provence, Saint-Rémy, to Etta Cone in Baltimore, n.d. [November 2, 1922].

70. See, e.g., Etta Cone to Gertrude Stein, December 12, 1909, January 10, 1910, and June 12, 1910; all in the Beinecke Rare Books and Manuscripts, Yale University Library.

71. See Douglas Cooper, "Gertrude Stein and Juan Gris," *Four Americans*, 73 n. 4: ref. to a letter from Claribel to Etta, September 20, 1910.

72. Claribel Cone from Paris to Etta Cone in Blowing Rock, September 9, 1910.

73. Etta Cone to Gertrude Stein, January 14, 1911, Baltimore Museum of Art Archives.

74. Georges Duby and Michelle Perrot, eds., *A History of Women: Toward a Cultural Identity in the Twentieth Century*, vol. 4 (London: Belknap Press, 1994), 94.

75. Moses Cone from Greensboro to Etta Cone in Baltimore, 1890 (?), as quoted in S. Cone, "Cones from Bavaria," 2:119–20.

76. Gertrude Stein, *Selected Writings of Gertrude Stein*, ed. Carl Van Vechten (New York: Random House, 1946), 44.

77. Etta Cone to Gertrude Stein, August 8, 1922, Beinecke Rare Books and Manuscripts, Yale University Library.

78. E. Cone, "Miss Etta Cones," 458.

79. Max Nordau, *How Women Love and Other Tales* (New York and Chicago: F. Tennyson Neely, 1896), in the book collection of Nancy Hirschland Ramage.

80. Laura Cone, oral communication with Ellen Hirschland.

81. Claribel Cone from Munich to Etta Cone in Baltimore, December 10, 1919. Note the use of the term "Charmed Circle," the title of James Mellow's 1974 book on Gertrude Stein.

Chapter 4: The Decided Doctor Claribel

1. G. Stein, *Autobiography of Toklas*, 154.

2. A practice she recommended to her niece, Dorothy Long Berney—Ellen Berney Hirschland's mother.

3. Claribel Cone from Munich to Etta Cone in Blowing Rock, June 22, 1915.

4. Claribel Cone from Munich to Etta Cone in Greensboro, June 26, 1915.

5. Claribel Cone from Munich to Etta Cone in Lake Placid, New York, August 3, 1915.

6. Claribel Cone from Munich to Etta Cone in Baltimore, July 1, 1916.

7. Flora (1865–98), the daughter of Jacob Adler and Sofie Kahn Adler (sister of Herman Cone, father of Claribel), was about half a year younger than Claribel.

8. See, e.g., Claribel Cone from Atlantic City to Carrie Cone, August 3, 1883.

9. See the Archives of Woman's Medical College, Baltimore, 1892–1944. An exhibition, "Women Doctors in America: 1835–1920" (see Style page of *New York Times*, January 20, 1986) outlines the history of education and professional development of women in medicine during that period.

10. *Journal of the American Medical Women's Association* 7, no. 11 (November 1952): 431.

11. Claribel Cone from Philadelphia to Etta Cone in Baltimore, January 5, 1891. Written on stationery from her workplace with the following heading: Department of Charities and Correction, Philadelphia Hospital for the Insane, Blockley Almshouse, Philadelphia.

12. Ibid.

13. Claribel Cone from Baltimore to Etta Cone at Monmouth House in Spring Lake, New Jersey, August 4, 1895. This was the second letter of the day from Claribel to Etta.

14. Fourteenth Annual Announcement and Catalogue of the Woman's Medical College of Baltimore, 1895–96, Archives of Woman's Medical College, Baltimore.

15. William H. Welch, M.D. (1850–1934), was a pathologist, educator, and public health advocate. Sir William Osler, M.D. (1849–1919), a Canadian professor of medicine, taught at McGill, Pennsylvania, Johns Hopkins (1889–1905), and Oxford. He gave his outstanding medical library to McGill University. Simon Flexner, M.D. (1863–1946), was a microbiologist and medical administrator of great note. He became the director of laboratories at the Rockefeller Institute for Medical Research (1903–35) and was editor of the *Journal of Experimental Medicine*. *The Cambridge Dictionary of American Biography*, ed. John S. Bowman (Cambridge: Cambridge University Press, 1995).

16. "News Digest" (New York: Milbank Memorial Fund, 1930), 41–42.

17. William H. Welch from Baltimore to Claribel Cone, May 15, 1900, in the private collection of Edward C. Hirschland.

18. Karl Weigert (1845–1904), director of the Senckenberg Institute, is most remembered for his discoveries in bacteriology and his progress in combating smallpox.

19. Hermann Strauss, M.D. (1868–1944), is known especially for his work on how an increase in fat in the blood results from eating fatty foods.

20. Eugen Albrecht was director of the Senckenberg Institute. Paul Ehrlich (1854–1915), a German Jewish physician who was the inventor of modern chemotherapy, shared the 1908 Nobel Prize in Physiology or Medicine with Élie Metchnikoff (see next note). A movie about him and his discovery of Salvarsan was entitled *Dr. Ehrlich's Magic Bullet*. Claribel wrote of Ehrlich's discovery to Etta: Claribel Cone from Frankfurt am Main to Etta Cone in Blowing Rock, September 2, 1910. *Chambers Biographical Dictionary*, ed. Magnus Magnusson, 5th ed. (Edinburgh: Chambers, 1990).

21. Dr. Élie Metchnikoff (1845–1916), a Russian-born physician (originally Ilya Ilich

Metchnikov) who was a professor of zoology and comparative anatomy, shared with Dr. Albrecht the 1908 Nobel Prize in Physiology or Medicine for his discovery of phagocytosis. (Phagocytes are protective cells that fight against bacteria that cause infectious diseases.) *Chambers Biographical Dictionary*.

22. Claribel Cone from Frankfurt am Main to Etta in Blowing Rock, June 18, 1910.

23. Claribel Cone from Munich to Etta Cone, December 20, 1916, Baltimore Museum of Art Archives.

24. Claribel Cone from Frankfurt am Main to Etta Cone in Blowing Rock, August 22, 1910.

25. Beatrice S. Levin, *Women and Medicine* (Metuchen, N.J.: Scarecrow Press, 1980), 71, 96.

26. On the history of women in medicine, see: Enid M. Bell, *Storming the Citadel: The Rise of the Woman Doctor* (London: Constable, 1953); and Levin, *Women and Medicine*.

27. Baltimore *Sun*, January 17, 1910.

28. Typescript, Baltimore Museum of Art Archives.

29. Baltimore *Evening Sun*, April 8, 1911, quoted in *Journal of the American Medical Women's Association*, November 5, 1921, 432.

30. Written on a loose sheet of an undated letter to Etta.

31. Claribel Cone from aboard ship to Etta Cone in Blowing Rock, June 1, 1910.

32. Claribel Cone from aboard ship to Etta Cone in Blowing Rock, June 3, 1910.

33. Ibid.

34. Claribel Cone from Munich to Etta Cone in Baltimore, December 7, 1919, Baltimore Museum of Art Archives.

35. Claribel Cone from Frankfurt am Main to Etta Cone in Blowing Rock, June 30, 1910.

36. Claribel Cone from Frankfurt am Main to Etta Cone in Blowing Rock, June 22 and 30, 1910.

37. Claribel Cone from Munich to Etta Cone in Blowing Rock, July 8, 1910.

38. Claribel Cone from Weimar to Etta Cone in Blowing Rock, August 25, 1910.

39. Claribel Cone from Frankfurt am Main to Etta Cone in Blowing Rock, September 2, 1910.

40. Claribel Cone from Munich to Etta Cone in Blowing Rock, July 18, 1910.

41. Claribel Cone from Munich to Etta Cone in Blowing Rock, June 19, 1915.

42. Claribel Cone from Paris to Etta Cone in Venice, July 24, 1923 (an example of a long letter, 21 pages). Baltimore Museum of Art Archives.

43. Claribel Cone from Munich to Etta Cone in Baltimore, March 7, 1920.

44. Claribel Cone from Paris to Etta Cone in Cannes, September 4, 1924.

45. Claribel Cone from Munich to Etta Cone in Baltimore, December 7, 1919, Baltimore Museum of Art Archives.

46. Claribel Cone from Munich to Etta Cone in Blowing Rock, June 7, 1915.

47. Claribel Cone from Munich to Etta Cone in Baltimore, June 8, 1915.

48. Claribel Cone from Paris to Etta Cone in Venice, July 25, 1923, Baltimore Museum of Art Archives.

49. Claribel Cone to Etta Cone, September 2, 1910 (sent in an envelope with a letter dated August 31, 1910).

50. Claribel Cone from Paris to Etta Cone in Blowing Rock, September 20, 1910.

51. Claribel Cone from Baltimore to Gertrude Stein, January 25, 1914, Beinecke Rare Books and Manuscripts, Yale University Library.

52. Claribel Cone from Paris to Etta Cone in Venice, July 29, 1923.

53. Quoted in S. Cone, "Cones of Bavaria," 2:135. These comments were written in 1972.

54. Claribel Cone from Munich to Etta Cone in Greensboro, June 26, 1915.

55. Claribel Cone from Munich to Etta Cone in Baltimore, August 30, 1915.

56. Claribel Cone from Munich to Etta Cone in Baltimore, February 24, 1920.

57. Claribel Cone from Munich to Etta Cone in Baltimore, November 17, 1916, Baltimore Museum of Art Archives.

58. Claribel Cone from Munich to Etta Cone in Baltimore, September 2, 1919.

59. Claribel Cone to Etta Cone, June 26, 1915.

60. Claribel Cone from Munich to Etta Cone in Blowing Rock, June 22, 1915. This comment came on page 38. (She would sometimes divide a letter into several envelopes so as to get by the censors' rules limiting the size of letters.)

61. Claribel Cone from Munich to Etta Cone in Blowing Rock, June 19 and 22, 1915.

62. Claribel Cone to Etta Cone, June 22, 1915.

63. Claribel Cone to Etta Cone, November 17, 1916.

64. Claribel Cone from Munich to Etta Cone in Baltimore, December 1919. This letter was started on December 7, but Claribel was still adding pages on December 23; the whole letter is more than thirty pages long. Another letter on the subject was written on March 7, 1920, and mailed on April 3, 1920.

65. Claribel Cone from Munich to Etta Cone in Baltimore, October 1, 1916, Baltimore Museum of Art Archives.

66. Ibid.

67. Heinrich Rosengart, 1850–1921, father of Siegfried, who became Etta's most important art dealer after Claribel's death. Ellen B. Hirschland, "Siegfried Rosengart as I Knew Him—Siegfried Rosengart Mein Freund," in *Von Matisse Bis Picasso Hommage an*

Siegfried Rosengart, ed. Martin Kunz (Lucerne: Kunstmuseum Luzern, 1988), 46–51.

68. Claribel Cone from Munich to Etta Cone in Baltimore, December 22, 1916. Prinz Regent Luitpold's son became King Ludwig III, who reigned from 1913 until 1918, at which time he abdicated.

69. Claribel Cone from Munich to Etta Cone in Baltimore, August 9, 1916.

70. Claribel Cone from Lausanne to Etta Cone in Baltimore, February 21, 1918.

71. Claribel explains this in a letter written from Munich on August 22, 1919, to Etta in Baltimore and again in a letter dated August 27, 1919, written on the back of a letter dated July 31, 1917.

72. Claribel Cone to Etta Cone, August 22, 1919.

73. Claribel Cone from Munich to Etta Cone in Baltimore, March 7, 1920. She continued to work on this letter until it was twenty-four pages long, mailing it finally with another letter on April 3, 1920.

74. Claribel Cone to Etta Cone, September 2, 1919.

75. Claribel Cone from Munich to Etta Cone in Baltimore, November 19, 1919.

76. Claribel Cone from Munich to Etta Cone in Baltimore, December 4, 1919.

77. Claribel Cone to Etta Cone, April 10, 1920.

78. Claribel Cone to Etta Cone, December 4, 1919.

79. Etta Cone from Baltimore to Claribel Cone in Munich, February 9, 1920.

80. Claribel Cone from Munich to Etta Cone in Baltimore, February 21, 1920.

81. Claribel Cone from Munich to Etta Cone in Greensboro, March 16, 1920, Baltimore Museum of Art Archives.

82. Ibid.

83. Claribel Cone from Munich to Etta Cone in Baltimore, March 26, 1920.

84. Claribel Cone from Munich to Etta Cone in Baltimore, April 4, 1920.

85. Claribel Cone from Munich to Etta Cone in Baltimore, April 25, 1920.

86. Claribel Cone from The Hague to Etta Cone in Baltimore, May 2, 1920.

87. Claribel Cone from The Hague to Etta Cone in Baltimore, May 3, 1920.

Chapter 5: The Roaring Twenties

1. Etta Cone from Blowing Rock to Michael Stein in Paris, February 20, 1910, Beinecke Rare Books and Manuscripts, Yale University Library.

2. Etta Cone from Greensboro to Gertrude Stein in Paris, March 5, 1911, Beinecke Rare Books and Manuscripts, Yale University Library.

3. Fisher, "Dr. Claribel and Miss Etta Cone," 119.

4. Dorothy Schwartzmann, wife of the architect Duke Schwartzmann, remembered seeing them there, and she also remembered "the Guttmacher boys" who lived there too. Alan and Manfred were twins; Alan became the highly distinguished gynecologist and

obstetrician who was central to the founding of Planned Parenthood, and it is for him that the Guttmacher Institute is named. Oral communication to Ellen Hirschland.

5. Oral communication to Ellen Hirschland from Laura Cone. Brenda Richardson explains that many of Fred's purchases were actually paid for by Etta, but apparently not these, since she didn't know about them until after the fact. B. Richardson, *Dr. Claribel and Miss Etta*, 182.

6. Recollected by Dorothy Long Berney and told to Ellen Hirschland.

7. B. Richardson, *Dr. Claribel and Miss Etta*, 170–73; John Elderfield, *Henri Matisse: A Retrospective* (New York: Museum of Modern Art, 1992), 293.

8. Dated September 23, 1924. Both of these lists are in a small notebook written by Claribel and housed in the Baltimore Museum of Art Archives.

9. For a view of the painting hanging in Claribel's apartment, see a photo reproduced in the Baltimore *Sun Sunday Magazine*, December 14, 1924, 20.

10. Elderfield, *Henri Matisse*, 85. In an interview in the Baltimore *Sun*, December 14, 1924, Claribel described this picture as an interior with Madame Matisse sick in bed.

11. B. Richardson, *Dr. Claribel and Miss Etta*, 170.

12. In *Les tulipes*, painted by Matisse early in 1914, the pewter jug filled with tulips is the central and only subject. See Christie's catalogue for April 3, 1996, *Important Modern Paintings, Drawings, and Sculpture* (Part 1), item no. 52, pp. 134–37. See also *The Pewter Jug* (another version), belonging to Hans R. Hahnloser, Bern, in the exhibition catalogue *Henri Matisse*, texts by Jean Leymarie, Herbert Read, William S. Lieberman (Los Angeles: UCLA Art Council and UCLA Art Galleries, 1966), 77.

13. The museum has now introduced a more archivally sensitive storage arrangement. Regarding the color lavender, Ellen Hirschland treasured Claribel's luscious purple velvet throw rug.

14. B. Richardson, *Dr. Claribel and Miss Etta*, 170, says it isn't clear which of the sisters bought this painting, but it was almost certainly Claribel.

15. A less abstract and aggressive version of the same model in a turban was bought by Chester Dale and is now in the National Gallery of Art in Washington, D.C.

16. Oral communication to Ellen Hirschland.

17. Victor Carlson, *Matisse as a Draughtsman* (Baltimore: Baltimore Museum of Art, 1934), 88.

18. Barr, *Matisse*, 206. Compare the oil painting *The White Plumes* in the Minneapolis Institute of Art; see ibid., plate 427.

19. She owned a second drawing from the same series, *A Young Girl with Plumed Hat, in Profile,* probably made in the same year. See Carlson, *Matisse as Draughtsman*, catalog no. 35, p. 91.

20. Claribel Cone from Paris to Etta Cone in Milan, July 21, 1923.

21. For *L'Esclave blanche* (*The White Slave*), 1921–22, see *Collection Jean Walter-Paul Guillaume Orangerie des Tuileries* (Paris: Réunion des Musées Nationaux 1966), p. 123, no. 58. An exhibition catalogue. The painting is now in the Orangerie, Paris.

22. Velásquez, *Venus and Cupid*, 1651, National Gallery, London; Manet, *Bar at the Folies-Bergères*, 1881, Courtauld Institute of Art Gallery, London; Cassatt, *The Coiffeur*, 1891, drypoint and aquatint, in many collections including the National Gallery of Art, Washington; Picasso, *Girl Before a Mirror*, 1932, Museum of Modern Art, New York.

23. From an interview at the Baltimore Museum of Art; see B. Richardson, *Dr. Claribel and Miss Etta*, 140.

24. Edward T. Cone, "The Miss Etta Cones, The Steins, and M'sieu Matisse," *The American Scholar* (1973): 457.

25. B. Richardson, *Dr. Claribel and Miss Etta*, 175.

26. Jack Cowart, *Henri Matisse: The Early Years in Nice 1916–1930* (Washington, D.C.: National Gallery of Art, in association with Harry N. Abrams, 1986), 321. An exhibition catalogue.

27. See, for instance, Pieter de Hooch's *The Mother*, ca. 1659–60, Gemäldegalerie, Staatliche Museen zu Berlin.

28. Claribel Cone from Paris to Etta Cone in Milan, July 21, 1923.

29. Claribel Cone from Paris to Etta Cone in Cannes, September 5, 1924, Baltimore Museum of Art Archives.

30. Registration of May 22, 1919, Municipal Archives of Munich. We are grateful to Birgit Gast for finding and checking this for us.

31. Claribel Cone from Paris to Etta Cone in Avignon, August 27, 1924, Baltimore Museum of Art Archives.

32. Claribel Cone from Paris to Etta Cone in Cannes, September 5, 1924.

33. Claribel Cone from Paris to Etta Cone in Cannes, September 4, 1924.

34. Claribel Cone from Paris to Etta Cone at the Rue d'Antibes, Cannes, September 14, 1924, Baltimore Museum of Art Archives.

35. Claribel Cone from Paris to Etta Cone in Venice, July 29, 1923.

36. Gertrude Stein to Michael Stein, n.d., "Michael Stein—1920" file, Beinecke Rare Books and Manuscripts, Yale University Library.

37. Michael Stein to Alice B. Toklas, June 6, 1925, Beinecke Rare Books and Manuscripts, Yale University Library. Louis Favre (1892–1956), a Swiss artist, was much appreciated by both Cone sisters.

38. Gertrude Stein to Etta Cone, June 22, 1924, Beinecke Rare Books and Manuscripts, Yale University Library.

39. Etta Cone to Gertrude Stein, June 24, 1924, Beinecke Rare Books and Manuscripts, Yale University Library.

40. Michael Stein to Gertrude Stein, August 26, 1926, Beinecke Rare Books and Manuscripts, Yale University Library.

41. Dr. and Mrs. Boas, conversation with Ellen Hirschland, December 17, 1971.

42. Kahnweiler to Gertrude Stein, June 6, 1925, Beinecke Rare Books and Manuscripts, Yale University Library.

43. Irene Gordon, the editor of the Museum of Modern Art catalogue *Four Americans in Paris*, reversed the identity of the two women in Laurencin's *Group of Artists* (plate 26), although she had been advised in advance that the caption contained this error. This misidentification has been reinforced by repetition through the years.

44. Olivier, *Picasso and His Friends*, 92.

45. G. Stein, *Autobiography of Toklas*, 74.

46. Olivier, *Picasso and His Friends*, 86.

47. Alice B. Toklas, *What Is Remembered* (New York: Holt, Rinehart, and Winston, 1963), 35.

48. See also Henri Rousseau's *The Poet and His Muse*, 1909, Kunstmuseum, Basel; and Picasso's *Saltimbanques*, 1905, National Gallery, Washington, D.C. (Chester Dale Collection).

49. G. Stein, *Autobiography of Toklas*, 72.

50. Olivier, *Picasso and His Friends*, 36.

51. G. Stein, *Autobiography of Toklas*, 23–24.

52. Ibid., 17.

53. Ibid., 76–77; Olivier, *Picasso and His Friends*, 109.

54. Mellow, *Charmed Circle*, 62; B. Richardson, *Dr. Claribel and Miss Etta*, 176; Irene Gordon, "A World Beyond the World: The Discovery of Leo Stein," in *Four Americans*, 32 n. 45. Venturi dated the painting to about 1895, Rewald to 1898–1900; see Lionello Venturi, *Cézanne* (New York: Rizzoli, 1978); and John Rewald, *Cézanne, The Steins, and Their Circle* (London: Thames and Hudson, 1986).

55. G. Stein, *Autobiography of Toklas*, 38. The second small Cézanne of *Bathers* was sold by Leo to Dr. Albert C. Barnes in 1915 (Rewald, *Cézanne and Circle*, 50).

56. For a photo of Gertrude sitting near where it was hanging on the wall, see figure 5.14, p. 114.

57. Gertrude described the breakdown of the siblings' long collaboration succinctly: "In short in this spring and early summer of nineteen fourteen the old life was over" (G. Stein, *Autobiography of Toklas*, 175).

58. Michael Stein from Montigny-sur-Loing to Gertrude Stein, April 12, 1918, in D. Gallup, ed., *The Flowers of Friendship: Letters Written to Gertrude Stein* (New York: Alfred A. Knopf, 1953), 125.

59. It is to the upper left of the mantel, just above the head of Alice B. Toklas. See

also Leon Katz, "Matisse, Picasso, and Gertrude Stein," in *Four Americans in Paris*, 61.

60. Gertrude Stein, *Lectures in America* (Boston: Beacon Press, 1935), 76–77.

61. Etta Cone from Baltimore to Gertrude Stein, October 29, 1934, Beinecke Rare Books and Manuscripts, Yale University Library.

62. Leo Steinberg, "Resisting Cézanne: Picasso's 'Three Women,' " *Art in America*, November–December 1978. For an illustration of Picasso's *Three Women*, see William Rubin, *Picasso and Braque: Pioneering Cubism* (New York: Museum of Modern Art, 1989), 111.

63. Mellow, *Charmed Circle*, 111. For *Les Demoiselles*, see Rubin, *Picasso and Braque*, 73.

64. Written from Nice, November 10, 1936. See Barr, *Matisse*, 40.

65. The letter came from Adeline Cacan de Bissy, Conservateur en Chef du Musée du Petit Palais.

66. Michael Stein to Gertrude Stein, July 28 [1926], Beinecke Rare Books and Manuscripts, Yale University Library.

67. Rainer Maria Rilke, *Letters on Cézanne* (New York: Fromm, 1985), viii.

68. Sale price from *New York Times*, June 26, 1925, Foreign Exchange.

69. The dealer was Bernheim-Jeune, and Michael Stein acted as intermediary. Barr, *Matisse*, 199; Judith Zilczer, *The Noble Buyer: John Quinn, Patron of the Avant-Garde* (Washington, D.C.: Smithsonian Institution Press, 1978), 117.

70. John Russell, *The World of Matisse 1869–1954* (New York: Time-Life Books, 1969), 75. He writes that Quinn bought the small sketch *Music* from Leo and Gertrude Stein at the same time. Another scholar has said that Quinn paid $4,500 for *Blue Nude*; see Zilczer, *Noble Buyer*, 117.

71. Barr, *Matisse*, 201.

72. Ibid., 83.

73. L. Stein, *Appreciation*, 162. In 1905, Leo had broken ground by buying Matisse's *Woman with Hat* (now housed at the San Francisco Museum of Modern Art). This astonishing Fauvist painting was said to be Matisse's first sale. See Barr, *Matisse*, 58.

74. The friend was Mildred Aldrich; see Mellow, *Charmed Circle*, 99. Henry McBride recalled the incident: see his "Pictures for a Picture of Gertrude," *Art News* 49, no. 10 (February 1951): 18.

75. G. Stein, *Autobiography of Toklas*, 21.

76. E. Cone, "Miss Etta Cones," 446–47; see also Edward T. Cone, "Aunt Claribel's *Blue Nude* Wasn't So Easy to Like," *Art News*, September 1980, vol. 79, no. 7: 162–63.

77. Hans Purrmann to Alfred Barr, March 3, 1951, quoted in Barr, *Matisse*, 58, 533 n.

3. For a photograph of Michael and Sally Stein, Matisse, Allan Stein, and Hans Purrmann at Michael and Sally's apartment, see Rewald, *Cézanne and Circle*, fig. 22.

78. See Milton W. Brown, *The Story of the Armory Show* (Washington: Hirshhorn, 1963); and Walter Pach, *Queer Thing, Painting: Forty Years in the World of Art* (New York: Harper and Bros., 1938).

79. They had intended to burn in effigy Matisse, Brancusi, and Walter Pach, who helped organize the show, but in the end, they burned *Blue Nude* and *Le Luxe II* instead. See John Cauman, "Henri Matisse's Letters to Walter Pach," *Archives of American Art Journal* 31, no. 3 (1991): 3, 13 n. 12; Brown, *Armory Show*, 209–10; Hilary Spurling, *The Unknown Matisse: The Early Years, 1869–1908* (New York: Alfred A. Knopf, 1998), 374–76, 384–85, 404. All of these quotations come from an unsigned article in the Chicago *Reader*, March 10, 1989, 4.

80. Harriet Monroe, *Chicago Tribune* (Feb. 23, 1913). Quoted in Brown, *Armory Show*, 172.

81. L. Stein, *Appreciation*, 162.

82. Barr, *Matisse*, 94.

83. The large nude figure first appeared in the artist's work in *Luxe, Calme et Volupté, 1904–5* (first bought by the painter Paul Signac); Barr, *Matisse*, 316, and Russell, *World of Matisse*, 46–67; and then again as one of the two central figures in *Le Bonheur de Vivre*, better known as *The Joy of Life*, painted in 1906 and bought first by Leo Stein (now in the Barnes Foundation, Merion, Pennsylvania); see Barr, *Matisse*, 320, and the exhibition catalogue *Great French Paintings from the Barnes Foundation* (New York: Alfred A. Knopf, 1993), 227.

84. Renoir quoted in John House, *Renoir* (London: Arts Council of Great Britain, 1985), 253–54. An exhibition catalogue.

85. For portraits of Paul Vallotton painted by Félix Vallotton, see Sasha M. Newman, *Félix Vallotton* (New York: Yale Art Gallery and Abbeville, 1991), figs. 117–18.

86. Claribel Cone from Lausanne to Etta Cone in Venice, August 21, 1927, Baltimore Museum of Art Archives.

87. Claribel Cone from Lausanne to Etta Cone in Venice, August 18, 1927, Baltimore Museum of Art Archives.

88. Claribel Cone from Lausanne to Etta Cone in Venice, August 20, 1927, Baltimore Museum of Art Archives.

89. Claribel Cone to Etta Cone, August 21, 1927.

90. Claribel Cone to Etta Cone, August 18, 1927.

91. Ibid.

92. Etta Cone from Venice to Claribel Cone in Lausanne, August 21, 1927.

93. Newman, *Félix Vallotton*, 78 ff., 142 ff.

94. B. Richardson, *Dr. Claribel and Miss Etta*, 176.

95. G. Rosenthal, ed., *Paintings, Sculpture, and Drawings in the Cone Collection* (Baltimore: Baltimore Museum of Art, 1967), 18.

96. Paul Vallotton from Lausanne to Claribel Cone in Baltimore, February 19, 1927, Baltimore Museum of Art Archives.

97. Claribel Cone from Lausanne to Etta Cone in Zurich, August 22, 1927, Baltimore Museum of Art Archives.

98. Claribel Cone to Etta Cone, September 4, 1924.

99. Claribel Cone from Baltimore to Etta Cone in New York, January 12, 1927. The letter was written at 4:15 A.M.

100. The story was reported by Laura Cone to Ellen Hirschland in conversation.

101. Claribel Cone from Paris to Etta Cone in Venice, August 11, 1923.

102. B. Richardson, *Dr. Claribel and Miss Etta*, 176.

103. The invoice in the Baltimore Museum of Art says, "un chat égyptien, en bronze de la 18me dynastie provenant des fouilles de Mitrahina." The Eighteenth Dynasty was during the New Kingdom. The purchase price was 30,377.40 Swiss francs.

104. See, for example, Claribel Cone from Lausanne to Etta Cone at Lake Como, August 16, 1927, Baltimore Museum of Art Archives.

105. Claribel Cone to Etta Cone, August 18, 1927.

106. Claribel Cone from Lausanne to Etta Cone in Vienna, August 22, 1927, Baltimore Museum of Art Archives. This was the third long letter from Claribel to Etta on this date.

107. Not to be confused with the sculptor of the same name. The sculptor made a bust of the collector, a piece that is in the Cone Collection.

108. Claribel Cone from Lausanne to Etta Cone in Lausanne, July 20, 1929, Baltimore Museum of Art Archives. Another letter, written the same day and sent to Etta in Munich, is incredibly petty, talking about the manicurist and other trivia. Claribel Cone from Lausanne to Etta Cone in Munich, July 20, 1929.

Chapter 6: A Tribute to Claribel

1. Nora Kaufman, oral communication to Ellen Hirschland.

2. Hirschland, "Cone Sisters and Stein Family," 84 n. 24; Pollack, *Collectors*, 197. Probably written in October 1929.

3. Pollock, *Collectors*, 197.

4. Siegfried Rosengart to Etta Cone, June 20, 1931, Baltimore Museum of Art Archives.

5. Barr, *Matisse*, 220.

6. Dr. Albert C. Barnes (1872–1951) invented Argyrol, an antiseptic drug used in treating infections of the eye and throat. See William Schack, *Art and Argyrol: The Life*

and Career of Dr. Albert C. Barnes (New York: Sagamore Press, 1963). He was one of the foremost art collectors of the day and was a great patron of Matisse. He established the Barnes Foundation in 1922 "to promote the advancement of education and the appreciation of the fine arts" (Barnes Foundation official Web site, "About the Barnes Foundation," http://www.barnesfoundation.org).

7. Laura Cone, oral communication with Ellen Hirschland.

8. The Steins to Etta Cone, January 2, 1931, Baltimore Museum of Art Archives; Margot Duthuit to Etta Cone, February 21, 1931, in Carlson, *Matisse as Draughtsman,* 128.

9. On the Barnes mural, see Pierre Cabanne, *The Great Collectors* (London: Cassell, 1963), 196–97.

10. Carlson, *Matisse as Draughtsman,* 128.

11. We are indebted to Victor Carlson for drawing our attention to this passage. The translation is by Esther Hecq. The letter is quoted in Schneider, *Matisse,* 416 n. 52.

12. B. Richardson, *Dr. Claribel and Miss Etta,* 188.

13. Both Edward Hirschland and Alice Hoffberger have copies still retaining the cover sheets.

14. In *News Record of the Baltimore Museum of Art* 6, no. 8 (December 1935), signed by G.K.L., the author states, "Miss Cone has very generously presented a copy to the Museum Library and all who are interested in this superb collection will welcome the opportunity of studying the catalogue, of which only 250 copies were privately printed. The edition is typical of the finest work in typography being done today."

15. Alfred H. Barr Jr. to Etta Cone, November 22, 1935, Baltimore Museum of Art Archives.

16. Lionello Venturi to Etta Cone, December 16, 1935, Baltimore Museum of Art Archives.

17. Curt Valentin to Etta Cone in Baltimore, December 7, 1940, Baltimore Museum of Art Archives.

18. E. Cone, "Miss Etta Cones," 455.

19. *The Cone Collection of Baltimore-Maryland Catalogue of Paintings-Drawings-Sculpture of the Nineteenth and Twentieth Centuries,* with foreword by George Boas (Baltimore: privately printed, 1934), 11.

20. E. Cone, "Miss Etta Cones," 455–56.

Chapter 7: Etta's Acquisitions of the 1930s and 1940s

1. Etta Cone from Paris to Ellen Hirschland on the Cunard Line, Cherbourg, July 12, 1937. Needless to say, Ellen loved cheese. Ellen also recalled that Etta sent Edam spheres and boxes of "patisseries" from Fiske, a Baltimore baker, to her at college.

2. Patrick Skene Catling, Baltimore *Sun*, January 13, 1950. The Cone piece is cast number 7/10. Madame Duthuit told Ellen Hirschland (in Paris, March 3, 1971) that there are ten numbers, but only nine were executed. In *A Century of Modern Sculpture* (April 5 to May 31, 1987), *Large Seated Nude*, marked "9/10," is dated 1925–29.

3. See Charles de Tolnay, *The Medici Chapel*, vol. 3, *Michelangelo* (Princeton, N.J.: Princeton University Press, 1970), plate 8 for the statue of *Day*; and vol. 2, *The Sistine Chapel*, fig. 107 for the *Ignudi*.

4. See Herbert Read, *Modern Sculpture* (New York: Thames and Hudson, 1985), fig. 83.

5. Barr, *Matisse*, 218.

6. As cited in B. Richardson, *Dr. Claribel and Miss Etta*, 129.

7. *Pink Nude* and the twenty-two photographs are illustrated, ibid., 135–37.

8. Ibid., 183; Rosenthal, *Cone Collection*, 21–23.

9. Michael Stein from his home Les Terrasses in Garches, outside of Paris, to Gertrude Stein, probably in Bilignin, n.d. [before September 1929], Beinecke Rare Books and Manuscripts, Yale University Library. Irene Gordon, together with Ellen Hirschland, figured out by process of elimination that the Picasso he was discussing was *Woman with Bangs*.

10. Mellow, *Charmed Circle*, 99. Fernande Olivier recalled that she and Picasso were delighted with the purchase and quite happy with the price.

11. See J. Richardson, *Early Years*, 180 ff., 194 ff; Robert J. Boardingham, "Gustave Coquiot and the Critical Origins of Picasso's 'Blue' and 'Rose' Periods," in *Picasso: The Early Years, 1892–1906*, ed. Marilyn McCully (Washington, D.C.: National Gallery of Art, 1997), 143–46, an exhibition catalogue.

12. B. Richardson, *Dr. Claribel and Miss Etta*, 183.

13. Ibid., 186.

14. Wineapple, *Sister Brother*, 339 ff., 357 ff.

15. Toklas, *Staying On Alone*, 315–16.

16. Etta Cone from Baltimore to Gertrude Stein, January 9, 1932, Beinecke Rare Books and Manuscripts, Yale University Library.

17. Etta Cone from Paris to Gertrude Stein, September 14, 1932, Beinecke Rare Books and Manuscripts, Yale University Library. Etta thanked Gertrude for the "manuscript," but the gift was actually a "typescript." Laura Cone gave it to Yale after Etta died.

18. L. Stein, *Appreciation*, 196.

19. Alice B. Toklas to Donald Gallup, July 31, 1950, quoted in Toklas, *Staying On Alone*, 199.

20. Toklas, *Staying On Alone*, 316.

21. Barr, *Matisse*, 56–57.

22. J. Richardson, *Painter of Modern Life*, 37; B. Richardson, *Dr. Claribel and Miss Etta*, 189. *Nude with Drapery* is now at the Hermitage in St. Petersburg, Russia. Christian Zervos, in his *Pablo Picasso*, vol. 3, *Oeuvres de 1912 à 1917* (Paris: Editions Cahiers d'Art, 1932), reproduces six versions of the same figure (numbers 671–76, pp. 300–301), none of which is the Cone version.

23. Victor Carlson, *Picasso Drawings and Watercolors 1899–1907 in the Collection of the Baltimore Museum of Art* (Baltimore: Baltimore Museum of Art, 1976), 88–89. *Demoiselles d'Avignon* is at the Museum of Modern Art in New York.

24. B. Richardson, *Dr. Claribel and Miss Etta*, 189.

25. John Richardson, ed., G. *Braque 1882–1963: An American Tribute* (New York: Public Education Association, 1964), figs. 38, 39.

26. See Gary Tinterow, Michael Pantazzi, and Vincent Pomarède, *Corot* (New York: Metropolitan Museum of Art, distributed by Harry N. Abrams, 1996), 316–27; and Polly Sartori, "Corot's Private World: An Invitation to His Studio," *Christie's International Magazine*, September–October 1994, 17–19. The only one of the six still in private hands, belonging to the estate of William S. Paley, was sold in the Christie's sale to Spencer and Marlene Hays (Tinterow, Pantazzi, and Pomarède, *Corot*, 326).

27. Etta Cone from the Savoy Plaza, New York, to Alfred Stieglitz in New York, September 18, 1944.

28. For Lisette Clarnet's reminiscences of the time she spent with Matisse, see C. de Pesbuan, "Matisse photographe," *Jours de France Madame*, November 27, 1989, 39–41.

29. E. Cone, "Miss Etta Cones," 454.

30. Henri Matisse from Nice to Etta Cone in Baltimore, April 1, 1937, Baltimore Museum of Art Archives. He had also sent her a telegram two days before, on March 30: "Envoyer seulement *Jeune Fils Assise Robe Jaune* lettre suit Matisse" ("Send only *The Yellow Dress* letter to follow Matisse"). The painting had been exhibited in 1933 at the International Art Show held at Radio City Music Hall in New York City.

31. Baltimore *Sun*, June 16, 1986, sec. B, p. 1.

32. See Carlson, *Matisse as Draughtsman*, 138: "Erasures were used to suggest motion, as if Matisse had just turned towards the viewer."

33. Hélène Roth Galitzine died November 29, 1966; see her obituary in the Baltimore *Sun*, December 2, 1966.

34. Emily Genauer, "Perpetual Modernity," *New York Herald Tribune*, April 19, 1953, reproduced a comparison of this sort that was made in the exhibit, 4000 Years of Modern Art, at the Walters Art Gallery in Baltimore.

35. Oral communication from Laura Cone to Ellen Hirschland.

36. C. F. Stuckey, *Gauguin: The Art of Paul Gauguin* (Washington, D.C.: National Gallery of Art; Chicago: The Art Institute of Chicago, 1988), 259.

37. John Rewald, *Gauguin* (London: Walter Heinemann, 1943), 22.

38. Stuckey, *Gauguin*, 261. Etta's Gauguin is illustrated in color on the cover of Stuckey's book, as well as on page 259.

39. Bengt Danielsson, "Gauguin's Tahitian Titles," *Burlington Magazine* 9, no. 760 (April 1967): 233 n. 82.

40. No. 2 in the catalogue for 450 francs, at the Vente Gauguin in Paris. For this sale, see Rewald, *Gauguin*, 25–26.

41. *Von Matisse bis Picasso: Hommage à Siegfried Rosengart* (Lucerne: Kunstmuseum Luzern, Verlag Gerd Hatje, 1988), 21.

42. Oral communication from Siegfried Rosengart to Ellen Hirschland.

43. William Rubin, "Who Was Picasso's Woman in White?" *Art News* 93, no. 5 (May 1994): 138–47. This theory was explored further by Michael C. Fitzgerald in the catalogue *Picasso and Portraiture: Representation and Transformation* (New York: Museum of Modern Art, 1996), 312–22. The painting is actually dated "'22," but as Rubin suggests, the date might have been added later, either by accident or on purpose.

44. Laura Cone, oral communication with Ellen Hirschland.

45. Ibid.

46. Ibid.

47. Ibid.

48. Notebook in the Baltimore Museum of Art Archives.

49. In the exhibition catalogue *Four Americans in Paris* (New York: Museum of Modern Art, 1970), 168.

50. Toklas, *What Is Remembered*, 30.

51. A few weeks earlier, Sally had offered the painting to Mrs. Elise Haas. After it was sold to Etta, it was in fact Sally who sent the painting to Baltimore from Palo Alto.

52. Oral communication from Laura Cone to Ellen Hirschland.

Chapter 8: Etta and Ellen

1. Etta was enormously knowledgeable about laces, their history, and their quality.

2. Mary Nice was a nurse in Union Memorial Hospital. As it so happened, her brother, Harry W. Nice, was governor of Maryland at the time.

3. Grace Glueck, who wrote the accompanying article in the *Times*, described the Picasso acquisition as follows: "*Boy Leading a Horse* was also originally owned by [Gertrude and Leo] Stein . . . Mr. [William S.] Rubin [director emeritus of the museum's department of painting and sculpture] said Mr. Paley bought it in the 1930's while on a skiing trip in Switzerland, where it was brought to his attention by the publisher Albert Skira. 'He bought it so fast he never even had a moment to ask about it,' Mr. Rubin recalled." In fact, he bought it in late summer of 1936—not while on a skiing trip.

4. This comment added after Ellen Hirschland's death. She would have been too modest to allow it.

5. June 30, 1936, at 132 rue Montparnasse.

6. At the big Matisse retrospective show at New York's Museum of Modern Art in 1992 and 1993, the daring painting *Harmony in Yellow* had the same type of silver frame as the one for the drawing Matisse gave to Ellen. The painting was taken out of the show and was sold for $14.5 million at Christie's. We wonder if the buyer knows that Matisse's daughter designed this frame herself.

7. The drawing is now in the private collection of Edward C. Hirschland.

8. Etta Cone from Paris to Dorothy Berney in Baltimore, July 2, 1936.

9. Pierre Matisse to Ellen Hirschland, April 26, 1986.

10. Dr. Margrit Hahnloser-Ingold to Ellen Hirschland, April 9, 1986.

11. See Robert Sage and E. Tériade, "Henri Matisse's Aviary in His Paris Studio," in *Verve: An Artistic and Literary Quarterly* (Paris: Éditions de la Revue Verve, 1937).

12. The typewritten bill is in the Baltimore Museum of Art Archives.

13. Paul S. Wingert, *The Sculpture of William Zorach* (New York: Pitman, 1938), plate 32.

14. Etta acquired the yellow marble head *Hilda* in New York on May 12, 1934, from the artist for $1,200. See ibid., plate 27; the *Magazine of Art*, April 1941, 166; and William Zorach, *William Zorach* (New York: American Artists Group, 1945), n.p.

15. Ellen Hirschland recalled visiting the foundry with Bill Zorach in Long Island (L. I. City Bronze Foundry, 51–25 Thirty-fifth Street) and how he pointed out certain uneven bumps in the bronze that he wanted smoothed down.

16. William Zorach, *Zorach Explains Sculpture* (New York: Tudor, 1960), 79, 80, 83.

17. William Zorach, *Art Is My Life: The Autobiography of William Zorach* (Cleveland: World, 1967), 129.

Chapter 9: Legacy

1. Morris S. Lazaron from Baltimore to Dorothy and Sidney Berney in Baltimore, April 6, 1942.

2. Oral communication from Laura Cone to Ellen Hirschland.

3. Claribel Cone's will. Original in the Maryland State Archives.

4. Stephen C. Clark to Etta Cone, December 1, 1929, Baltimore Museum of Art Archives. Written on stationery of 46 East Seventieth Street (now the Explorers Club), although sent from Pinehurst, North Carolina.

5. Etta Cone to Gertrude Stein, April 17, 1934, Beinecke Rare Books and Manuscripts, Yale University Library.

6. Arnold Lehman, foreword to B. Richardson, *Dr. Claribel and Miss Etta*, 15.

7. Toklas, *Staying On Alone*, 80.

8. Baltimore *Sun*, March 30, 1980, D2.

9. Actually, Mrs. Breeskin never knew Claribel, but as she said herself, she felt she knew her through Etta. "To most of us, Dr. Claribel Cone remains vivid through the stories told about her by her devoted sister." Adelyn Breeskin, foreword to *Painting, Sculpture and Drawings in the Cone Collection*, edited by Gertrude Rosenthal (Baltimore: Baltimore Museum of Art, 1967), 7.

10. Baltimore *Sun*, October 30, 1977. Philip Perlman was Etta's friend and attorney and also a trustee of the Baltimore Museum of Art and the Walters Art Gallery.

11. Lehman, foreword, 14.

12. Grace Glueck, "Adelyn Dohme Breeskin, 90, Curator at National Museum," July 25, 1986.

13. Typescript of eulogy in Ellen B. Hirschland Archives.

14. The story of Etta Cone's death and the problems with the shipment containing Allan Stein's portrait was told to Ellen Hirschland by Laura Cone.

15. Ellen Hirschland recalled: "I met the grandson Danny when I visited Mrs. Michael Stein in Palo Alto in 1939 and 1940. Sally Stein had sold their paintings, largely to Elise Haas, as they needed money. In the forties most of these were on display in the Leland Stanford Jr. Museum in Palo Alto."

16. Ruth Moose, "Moses H. Cone Memorial Park," in *National Parks and Conservation Magazine*, October 1971, 18–19. The hospital trustees transferred the manor to the State of North Carolina, which in turn passed it on to the U.S. Department of the Interior. Today it houses the Parkway Crafts Center operated by the Southern Highlands Handicraft Guild.

17. Bernard M. Cone, speech at cornerstone laying, Moses H. Cone Memorial Hospital, May 2, 1951, Moses H. Cone Memorial Hospital Archives, Greensboro, N.C.

18. Quoted from Etta's will. "Piper prints" refers to the Piper Druck printing company, one of the finest art print publishers of the day. Copy of will in Ellen B. Hirschland Archives. Original, dated May 18, 1949, in the Maryland State Archives.

19. Etta's will; Baltimore *Sun*, January 15, 1950.

20. B. Richardson, "What's in a Frame?" 4; italics added.

Appendix B

1. Ann Moore practiced obstetrics in New England in the seventeenth century. See Kate Campbell Hurd-Mead, *A History of Women in Medicine* (Haddam, Conn.: Haddam Press, 1938), 409. On the sisters Elizabeth and Emily Blackwell, see Esther Pohl Lovejoy, *Women Doctors of the World* (New York: Macmillan, 1957); Joyce Leeson and Judith Gray, *Women and Medicine* (London: Tavistock, 1978), 24–25, 27; and Levin, *Women and Medicine*, 58–97. See also Elizabeth Blackwell's own account, *Pioneer Work in Opening the*

Medical Profession to Women (London: Longmans, Green, 1895).

2. Charles Frederick Worth (1825–95) was a successful and influential Anglo-French dress designer, whose firm later made clothes for both Etta and Claribel Cone.

3. See Virginia G. Drachman, "Women Doctors and the Quest for Professional Power: 1881–1926" in *Women Physicians in Leadership Roles*, ed. Leah J. Dickstein and Carol C. Nadelson (Washington, D.C: American Psychiatric Press, 1986), 4–5; and Glen O. Gabbard and Roy W. Menninger, eds., *Medical Marriages* (Washington, D.C.: American Psychiatric Press, 1988), esp. 79–88, the essay "The Woman Physician's Marriage," by Carol C. Nadelson and Malkah T. Notman.

Appendix C

1. On the uphill battle that women have faced in the medical profession, see Mary Roth Walsh, *Doctors Wanted: No Women Need Apply* (New Haven, Conn.: Yale University Press, 1977).

Appendix E

1. Etta usually sat at the back, but apparently she sometimes joined Claribel in the front of the theater.

Appendix F

1. Actually, she entered in 1887 and received her medical diploma in 1890.

2. The reference is to *Isabella and the Pot of Basil* (1897) by American painter John White Alexander (1856–1915), now in the Museum of Fine Arts, Boston.

3. Actually toward the end of the nineteenth century, in 1887.

SELECT BIBLIOGRAPHY

Primary Sources and Archives

Archives of Woman's Medical College, 1892–1944, Baltimore, Maryland.

Baltimore Museum of Art Archives.

Baltimore *Sun* archives.

Beinecke Rare Books and Manuscripts. Yale University Library.

Buncombe County Deeds. Asheville, North Carolina.

Cone, Sydney M. Jr., ed. "The Cones from Bavaria," typescript, 4 vols. Greensboro Public Library, Greensboro, North Carolina. 1973.

Ellen B. Hirschland Archives, private collection. The letters have now been given to the Baltimore Museum of Art.

Jonesborough Civic Trust for Historic Restoration and Preservation, Jonesborough, Tennessee.

"The Community Loses an Estimable Family," *Jonesborough Herald and Tribune*, April 10, 1873. Archives, Jonesborough Public Library, Jonesborough, Tennessee.

Municipal Archives of Munich.

Moses H. Cone Memorial Hospital Archives, Greensboro, North Carolina.

Recollections of Sam M. Adler. Leo Baeck Institute, New York.

Books, Periodicals, and Exhibition Catalogues

Andrews, Mildred Gwin. *The Men and the Mills: A History of the Southern Textile Industry*. Macon, Ga.: Mercer University Press, 1987.

Arnett, Ethel Stephens. *Greensboro North Carolina: The County Seat of Guilford*. Chapel Hill: University of North Carolina Press, 1955.

Barr, Alfred H. Jr. *Matisse: His Art and His Public*. New York: Museum of Modern Art, 1951.

Bell, Enid M. *Storming the Citadel: The Rise of the Woman Doctor*. London: Constable, 1953.

Berman, Myron. *Richmond's Jewry, 1769–1976: Shabbat in Shockoe*. Charlottesville, Va.: Jewish Community Federation of Richmond, in association with the University Press of Virginia, 1979.

Billings, Dwight B. Jr. *Planters and the Making of a "New South": Class, Politics, and Development in North Carolina, 1865–1900*. Chapel Hill: University of North Carolina Press, 1979.

Blackwell, Elizabeth. *Pioneer Work in Opening the Medical Profession to Women*. London: Longmans, Green, 1895.

Boardingham, Robert J. "Gustave Coquiot and the Critical Origins of Picasso's 'Blue' and 'Rose' Periods." In *Picasso: The Early Years, 1892–1906*. Edited by Marilyn McCully. Washington: National Gallery of Art, 1997. An exhibition catalogue.

Breeskin, Adelyn. Foreword to *Painting, Sculpture and Drawings in the Cone Collection*, by Gertrude Rosenthal. Baltimore: Baltimore Museum of Art, 1967. An exhibition catalogue.

Brown, Milton W. *The Story of the Armory Show*. Washington, D.C.: Hirshhorn, 1963.

Buder, Stanley. *Pullman: An Experiment in Industrial Order and Community Planning 1880–1930*. New York: Oxford University Press, 1967.

Burke, Carolyn. "Gertrude Stein, The Cone Sisters, and the Puzzle of Female Friendship." *Critical Inquiry* (Spring 1982) Vol. 8.3: 543–64.

Cabanne, Pierre. *The Great Collectors*. London: Cassell, 1963.

Carlson, Victor I. *Matisse as a Draughtsman*. Baltimore: Baltimore Museum of Art, 1971. An exhibition catalogue.

———. *Picasso Drawings and Watercolors 1899–1907 in the Collection of the Baltimore Museum of Art*. Baltimore: Baltimore Museum of Art, 1976.

Cauman, John. "Henri Matisse's Letters to Walter Pach." *Archives of American Art Journal* 31, no. 3 (1991): 3, 13.

A Century of Excellence: The History of the Cone Mills, 1891–1991. Greensboro, N.C.: Cone Mills Corp., 1991.

Cone, Claribel. "Introductory Address to the Medical Class of the Woman's Medical College." *Bulletin of the Medical Society of Woman's Medical College of Baltimore* 11, no. 1 (February 1, 1896): 1–3.

The Cone Collection of Baltimore-Maryland: Catalogue of Paintings, Drawings, Sculpture of the Nineteenth and Twentieth Centuries. Introduction by George Boas. Baltimore: privately printed, 1934.

Cone, Edward T. "Aunt Claribel's Blue Nude Wasn't So Easy to Like." *Art News* 79, no.7 (September 1980): 162–63.

———. "The Miss Etta Cones, The Steins, and M'sieu Matisse: A Memoir." *American Scholar* 42, no. 3 (1973): 441–60.

Cooper, Douglas. "Gertrude Stein and Juan Gris," in *Four Americans in Paris*, 65–73.

Cowart, Jack, and Dominique Fourcade. *Henri Matisse: The Early Years in Nice 1916–1930*. Washington, D.C.: National Gallery of Art, in association with Harry N. Abrams, 1986. An exhibition catalogue.

Danielsson, Bengt. "Gauguin's Tahitian Titles." *Burlington Magazine* 9, no. 760 (April 1967): 233.

Danto, Arthur C. *After the End of Art*. Princeton, N.J.: Princeton University Press, 1995.

Drachman, Virginia G. "Women Doctors and the Quest for Professional Power: 1881–1926." In *Women Physicians in Leadership Roles*, edited by Leah J. Dickstein and Carol C. Nadelson. Washington, D.C.: American Psychiatric Press, 1986.

Duby, Georges, and Michelle Perrot, eds. *A History of Women: Toward a Cultural Identity in the Twentieth Century*, vol. 4. London: Belknap Press, 1994.

Dumas, Ann, et al. *Matisse, His Art and His Textiles: The Fabric of Dreams*. London: Royal Academy of Arts, 2004.

Dydo, Ulla E., ed. *A Stein Reader: Gertrude Stein*. Evanston, Ill.: Northwestern University Press, 1993.

The Eightieth Birthday of William Henry Welch. New York: Milbank Memorial Fund, 1930.

Elderfield, John. *Henri Matisse: A Retrospective*. New York: Museum of Modern Art, 1992. An exhibition catalogue.

Fink, Paul M. *Jonesborough: The First Century of Tennessee's First Town, 1776–1876*. Johnson City, Tenn.: Overmountain Press, 1989.

Fisher, Jay M. "Dr. Claribel and Miss Etta Cone: A Collection of Modern Art for Baltimore." In *Before Peggy Guggenheim: American Women Art Collectors*, edited by Rosella Mamoli Zorzi. Venice: Marsilio Editori, 2001.

———. *Works on Paper*. Baltimore: Baltimore Museum of Art, 1995.

Flam, Jack D. *Matisse and Picasso: The Story of Their Rivalry and Friendship*. Cambridge, Mass: Westview Press, Icon Edition, 2003.

———, ed. *Matisse: A Retrospective*. New York: Macmillan, 1988.

———. *Matisse in The Cone Collection: The Poetics of Vision*. Baltimore: Baltimore Museum of Art, 2001.

———. *Matisse: The Man and His Art*. Ithaca, N.Y.: Cornell University Press, 1986.

Four Americans in Paris: The Collections of Gertrude Stein and Her Family. New York: Museum of Modern Art, 1970. An exhibition catalogue.

Gabriel, Mary. *The Art of Acquiring: A Portrait of Etta and Claribel Cone*. Baltimore: Bancroft Press, 2002.

Galenson, Alice. *The Migration of the Cotton Textile Industry from New England to the South: 1880–1930.* New York: Garland, 1985.

Gallup, Donald, ed. *The Flowers of Friendship: Letters Written to Gertrude Stein.* New York: Alfred A. Knopf, 1953.

Giroud, Vincent. "Picasso and Gertrude Stein," *The Metropolitan Museum of Art Bulletin* vol. 64 no. 3 (Winter 2007): 7–55.

Gordon, Irene. "A World Beyond the World: The Discovery of Leo Stein." In *Four Americans in Paris*, 13–33.

Hahnloser, Margrit. *Matisse: The Graphic Work.* New York: Rizzoli, 1988.

The Half Century Book 1891–1941, privately printed by the Cone Export and Commission Co., 1941.

Hansen, Marcus Lee. *The Atlantic Migration, 1607–1860.* Cambridge, Mass.: Harvard University Press, 1940.

———. *The Immigrant in American History.* Cambridge, Mass.: Harvard University Press, 1948.

Hirschland, Ellen B. "Cone, Etta and Claribel Cone." In *Dictionary of American Biography*, Supplement 4, 1946–1950, 174–75. New York: Scribner's, 1974.

———. "The Cone Sisters and the Stein Family." In *Four Americans in Paris*, 74–86.

———. "Siegfried Rosengart as I Knew Him; Siegfried Rosengart—Mein Freund." In *Von Matisse Bis Picasso: Hommage an Siegfried Rosengart*, ed. Martin Kunz, 46–51. Lucerne: Kunstmuseum Luzern, 1988.

Hirschland, Ellen B., and Nancy H. Ramage. "Bucking the Tide: The Cone Sisters of Baltimore." *Journal of the History of Collections* 8 (1996): 103–16.

House, John. *Renoir.* London: Arts Council of Great Britain, in association with Harry N. Abrams, 1985. An exhibition catalogue.

Hurd-Mead, Kate Campbell. *A History of Women in Medicine.* Haddam, Conn.: Haddam Press, 1938.

Journal of the American Medical Women's Association 7, no. 11 (November 1952): 431.

Katz, Leon. "Matisse, Picasso, and Gertrude Stein," in *Four Americans in Paris*, 51–63.

Leeson, Joyce, and Judith Gray. *Women and Medicine.* London: Tavistock, 1978.

Levin, Beatrice S. *Women and Medicine.* Metuchen, N.J.: Scarecrow Press, 1980.

Lovejoy, Esther Pohl. *Women Doctors of the World.* New York: Macmillan, 1957.

Malcolm, Janet. "The Mystery of Gertrude Stein: How Did She and Alice B. Toklas Survive the Second World War in France?" *New Yorker*, June 2, 2003, 57–81.

Marcus, Jacob Rader. *This I Believe: Documents of American Jewish Life.* Northvale, N.J.: Jason Aronson, 1990.

McAlmon, Robert, ed. *The Contact Collection of Contemporary Writers.* Paris: Three Mountains Press, Contact Editions, 1925.

McBride, Henry. "Pictures for a Picture of Gertrude." *Art News* 49, no. 10 (February 1951): 81.

McHugh, Cathy L. *Mill Family: The Labor System in the Southern Cotton Textile Industry, 1880–1915.* New York: Oxford University Press, 1988.

McLaurin, Melton A. *Paternalism and Protest: Southern Cotton Mill Workers and Organized Labor, 1875–1905.* Westport, Conn.: Greenwood Press, 1971.

Mellow, James R. *Charmed Circle: Gertrude Stein and Company.* New York: Praeger, 1974.

Mitchell, Broadus. *The Rise of Cotton Mills in the South.* New York: Da Capo Press, 1968. First published 1921 by Johns Hopkins.

Moose, Ruth. "Moses H. Cone Memorial Park." *National Parks and Conservation Magazine,* October 1971, 18–19.

Newman, Sasha M. *Félix Vallotton.* New York: Yale Art Gallery and Abbeville, 1991.

Noblitt, Philip T. *A Mansion in the Mountains.* Boone, N.C.: Parkway Publishers, 1996.

Olivier, Fernande. *Picasso and His Friends.* London: Heinemann, 1964.

Pach, Walter. *Queer Thing, Painting: Forty Years in the World of Art.* New York: Harper and Bros., 1938.

Pollack, Barbara. *The Collectors: Dr. Claribel and Miss Etta Cone.* New York: Bobbs-Merrill, 1962.

Rewald, John. *Cézanne, The Steins and Their Circle.* London: Thames and Hudson, 1986.

———. *Gauguin.* London: Walter Heinemann, 1943.

Richardson, Brenda. *Dr. Claribel and Miss Etta: The Cone Collection of the Baltimore Museum of Art.* Baltimore: Baltimore Museum of Art, 1985.

———. "What's in a Frame?" In *The Spotlight* (Baltimore Museum of Art, 1993).

Richardson, John, ed. *Georges Braque, 1882–1963: An American Tribute.* New York: Public Education Association, 1964.

———. *A Life of Picasso.* Vol. 1, *The Early Years: 1881–1906.* New York: Random House, 1991.

———. *A Life of Picasso.* Vol. 2, *1907–1917: The Painter of Modern Life.* New York: Random House, 1996.

Rilke, Rainer Maria. *Letters on Cézanne.* New York: Fromm, 1985.

Rosenthal, Gertrude, ed. *Paintings, Sculpture and Drawings in the Cone Collection.* Baltimore: Baltimore Museum of Art, 1967. An exhibition catalogue.

Rubin, William. *Picasso and Braque: Pioneering Cubism.* New York: Museum of Modern Art, 1989. An exhibition catalogue.

———, ed. *Picasso and Portraiture: Representation and Transformation.* New York: Museum of Modern Art, 1996. An exhibition catalogue.

———. "Who Was Picasso's Woman in White?" *Art News* 93, no. 5 (May 1994): 138–47.

Russell, John. *Matisse: Father and Son.* New York: Harry N. Abrams, 1999.

———. *The World of Matisse 1869–1954*. New York: Time-Life Books, 1969.

Sage, Robert, and E. Tériade. "Henri Matisse's Aviary in His Paris Studio." In *Verve : An Artistic and Literary Quarterly*. Paris: Éditions de la Revue Verve, 1937.

Sartori, Polly. "Corot's Private World: An Invitation to His Studio." *Christie's International Magazine*, September–October 1994.

Schack, William. *Art and Argyrol: The Life and Career of Dr. Albert C. Barnes*. New York: Sagamore Press, 1963.

Schneider, Pierre. *Matisse*. New York: Rizzoli, 1984.

Seymour, Elizabeth. "A Conecopia: Etta and Claribel Cone." In *Triad* (local paper, Greensboro, N.C., 1980).

Spurling, Hilary. *Matisse the Master: A Life of Henri Matisse; The Conquest of Colour, 1909–1954*. New York: Alfred A. Knopf, 2005.

———. *The Unknown Matisse: The Early Years, 1869–1908*. New York: Alfred A. Knopf, 1998.

Stein, Gertrude. *The Autobiography of Alice B. Toklas*. New York: Vintage Books, 1933.

———. *Lectures in America*. Boston: Beacon Press, 1935.

———. *Selected Writings of Gertrude Stein*. Edited by Carl Van Vechten. New York: Random House, 1946.

Stein, Leo. *Appreciation: Painting, Poetry and Prose*. Lincoln: University of Nebraska Press, Bison Books, 1996.

Steinberg, Leo. "Resisting Cézanne: Picasso's 'Three Women.'" *Art in America* 66, November–December 1978, 114–33.

Stuckey, C. F. *Gauguin: The Art of Paul Gauguin*. Washington, D.C.: National Gallery of Art; Chicago: Art Institute of Chicago, 1988.

Taylor, Philip. *The Distant Magnet: European Emigration to the U.S.A.* London: Eyre and Spottiswoode, 1971.

Tinterow, Gary, Michael Pantazzi, and Vincent Pomarède. *Corot*. New York: Metropolitan Museum of Art, 1996. Distributed by Harry N. Abrams.

Toklas, Alice B. *Staying On Alone: Letters of Alice B. Toklas*. Edited by Edward Burns. New York: Liveright, 1973.

———. *What Is Remembered*. New York: Holt, Rinehart and Winston, 1963.

Theodore Robinson, 1852–1896. Introduction and commentary by Sona Johnston. Baltimore: Baltimore Museum of Art, 1973. An exhibition catalogue.

Walsh, Mary Roth. *Doctors Wanted: No Women Need Apply*. New Haven, Conn.: Yale University Press, 1977.

Warne, Colston E., ed. *The Pullman Boycott of 1894: The Problem of Federal Intervention*. Boston: D. C. Heath, 1955.

Wineapple, Brenda. Introduction to *Appreciation: Painting, Poetry and Prose*, by Leo Stein. Lincoln: University of Nebraska Press, Bison Books, 1996.

———. *Sister Brother: Gertrude and Leo Stein*. New York: Putnam, 1996.

Wingert, Paul S. *The Sculpture of William Zorach*. New York: Pitman, 1938.

Woodward, C. Vann. *Origins of the New South 1877–1913*. Baton Rouge: Louisiana State University Press, 1971.

Zervos, Christian. *Pablo Picasso*. Vol. 3, *Oeuvres de 1912 à 1917*. Paris: Éditions Cahiers d'Art, 1932.

Zilczer, Judith. *The Noble Buyer: John Quinn, Patron of the Avant-Garde*. Washington, D.C.: Smithsonian Institution Press, 1978.

Zorach, William. *Art Is My Life: The Autobiography of William Zorach*. Cleveland: World, 1967.

———. *William Zorach*. New York: American Artists Group, 1945.

———. *Zorach Explains Sculpture: What It Means and How It Is Made*. New York: Tudor, 1960.

INDEX

ABOUT THE AUTHORS

Ellen B. Hirschland (1918–99) was an art history teacher, a collector of nineteenth- and twentieth-century art, and a frequent lecturer on the Cone sisters and on modern art. As the great-niece of the sisters, in 1936 she traveled with Etta Cone to Switzerland and Paris, where she met artists, dealers, and collectors and developed a friendship with Henri Matisse.

Nancy Hirschland Ramage is the Charles A. Dana Professor of the Humanities and Arts Emerita at Ithaca College. She too is an art historian and has written and lectured widely in her fields of Greek and Roman art, eighteenth-century neoclassicism, and the history of collecting.